PROVINCIAL BATTLES, NATIONAL PRIZE?

Provincial Battles, National Prize?

Elections in a Federal State

LAURA B. STEPHENSON, ANDREA LAWLOR,
WILLIAM P. CROSS, ANDRÉ BLAIS,
AND ELISABETH GIDENGIL

McGill-Queen's University Press
Montreal & Kingston • London • Chicago

© McGill-Queen's University Press 2019

ISBN 978-0-7735-5738-3 (cloth)
ISBN 978-0-7735-5739-0 (paper)
ISBN 978-0-7735-5840-3 (ePDF)
ISBN 978-0-7735-5841-0 (ePUB)

Legal deposit third quarter 2019
Bibliothèque nationale du Québec

Printed in Canada on acid-free paper that is 100% ancient forest free
(100% post-consumer recycled), processed chlorine free

This book has been published with the help of a grant from the Canadian
Federation for the Humanities and Social Sciences, through the Awards to
Scholarly Publications Program, using funds provided by the Social Sciences
and Humanities Research Council of Canada. Funding was also received
from the J.B. Smallman Publication Fund, and the Faculty of Social Science,
the University of Western Ontario.

Funded by the Government of Canada   Financé par le gouvernement du Canada   Canada   Canada Council for the Arts   Conseil des arts du Canada

We acknowledge the support of the Canada Council for the Arts.

Nous remercions le Conseil des arts du Canada de son soutien.

Library and Archives Canada Cataloguing in Publication

Title: Provincial battles, national prize?: elections in a federal state /
   Laura B. Stephenson, Andrea Lawlor, William P. Cross, André Blais,
   and Elisabeth Gidengil.

Names: Stephenson, Laura Beth, 1976– author. | Lawlor, Andrea, 1982–
   author. | Cross, William P. (William Paul), 1962– author. | Blais, André,
   1947– author. | Gidengil, Elisabeth, 1947– author.

Description: Includes bibliographical references and index.

Identifiers: Canadiana (print) 20190110783 | Canadiana (ebook) 20190110848 |
   ISBN 9780773557390 (softcover) | ISBN 9780773557383 (hardcover) |
   ISBN 9780773558403 (ePDF) | ISBN 9780773558410 (ePUB)

Subjects: LCSH: Canada. Parliament—Elections, 2015. | LCSH: Regionalism—
   Political aspects—Canada. | LCSH: Political participation—Canada. |
   LCSH: Voting—Canada. | LCSH: Mass media—Political aspects—Canada. |
   LCSH: Political campaigns—Canada.

Classification: LCC JL193 .S74 2019 | DDC 324.97107/4—dc23

This book was typeset by Marquis Interscript in 10.5/13 Sabon.

Contents

Figures and Tables

FIGURES

TABLES

Acknowledgments

We would like to thank Scott Pruysers and Mark Bencze (Carleton University), Jean-Michel Lavoie, Eric Guntermann, and Jean-François Daoust (Université de Montréal), Jennifer June Schmidt (University of Western Ontario) and Tyler Paget (King's University College) for assistance with data collection and analysis. We would also like to acknowledge the generous support of the Social Science and Humanities Research Council of Canada, which enabled us to collect much of the data analyzed in this book, and the assistance of the J.B. Smallman Publication Fund, and the Faculty of Social Science, The University of Western Ontario.

Abbreviations

BQ	Bloc Québécois
CCF	Cooperative Commonwealth Federation
CPC	Conservative Party of Canada
FPTP	First-past-the-post
LPC	Liberal Party of Canada
MP	Member of Parliament
NDP	New Democratic Party
PCO	Privy Council Office
PCS	Progressive Conservatives
PLQ	Parti libéral du Québec
PMO	Prime Minister's Office
PQ	Parti Québécois
ROC	Rest of Canada
TPP	Trans-Pacific Partnership

PART ONE

The Regionalization of Elections

1

Addressing a Regionalized Outcome

When the dust settled after the Canadian federal election on 19 October 2015, many were surprised that the country was left with a majority Liberal Party of Canada (LPC) government. In a dramatic swing, the Conservative Party of Canada (CPC) was voted out of office and into opposition, and the New Democratic Party (NDP) was reduced to its traditional third-party standing in vote shares. While the outcome of the election had national significance, the results were met with varying amounts of surprise depending on where one lived in the country. The Liberals dominated in the Eastern provinces and continued all the way west until Manitoba. In Saskatchewan and Alberta, the Conservatives maintained strong support. An interesting pattern appears for the Liberals and Conservatives – each has a base of support in a different part of the country (see figure 1.1).

Is the 2015 election outcome unique in this regard? As any observer of Canadian politics knows, not by a long shot. Large discrepancies in party support across provinces is a fact of modern Canadian political life. Conservative parties have consistently done well in the Western provinces (whether the Reform, Canadian Alliance, or Conservative parties), while the Liberals typically do well (often over 50 per cent vote support) in the Maritimes. In 2006, for example, the Conservatives received 65 per cent support in Alberta, while the Liberals got 53 per cent in PEI. In 2004, the Conservatives got 62 per cent support in Alberta, but only 9 per cent in Quebec.

Provincial vote share differences were particularly dramatic in the 1997 election, when the election included two parties that did not even compete nationally. The Reform Party focused its efforts and

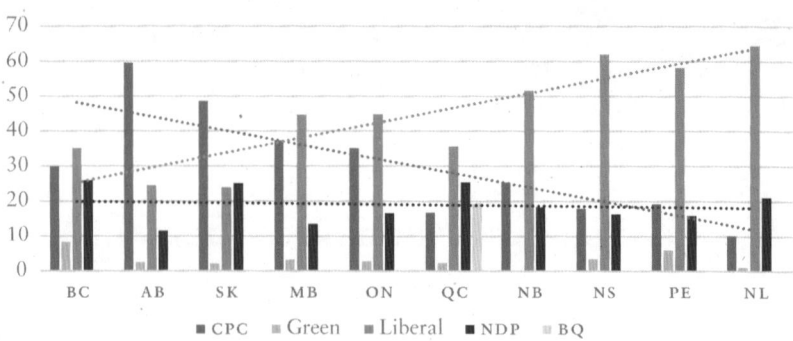

Figure 1.1 2015 Canadian election results

drew its support from the Western provinces and Ontario, while the
Bloc Québécois competed only in Quebec. When the dust settled after
that election, the electoral map was very colourful – green in the West
(for the Reform Party); light blue in Quebec (for the Bloc Québécois);
red in Manitoba, Ontario, Newfoundland, PEI, and the Northwest
Territories (for the Liberals); small pockets of orange (for the NDP);
and darker blue (for the Progressive Conservatives).

In some ways, that the parties are not equally popular across the
country should not be surprising. The nature of the Canadian electoral
system is such that voters only contribute directly to the election
outcome in their own riding. Voters can be motivated by local and
community issues. These issues, which can vary dramatically, can
affect which party is seen as best able to deliver a region's or city's
preferred policies. However, the majority of campaign materials,
especially advertising, often emphasize the national leader rather than
the local candidate and national polls rather than regional ones.

The prominence of a national focus in campaigns might lead one to
think that elections in Canada are truly national affairs, and that
issues raised in the campaign speak to a national interest. But is
that assumption legitimate? Is there a single national campaign? If
that were the case, would voting patterns across the country not be
more similar? To decide whether the assumption is warranted, we
need to investigate to what extent geography influences election campaigns. It is certainly possible that Canadians across the country feel
very differently about the political parties depending on where they
live. If so, then the variation in voting may simply reflect different
preferences across the provinces. Yet, it is also possible that those

evaluations could be shaped by party and media strategies that tailor campaign information to address local issues. We tend to assume that there is a national focus in campaigns, but do parties differentiate by region? Without a careful analysis of the campaign in each province, it is difficult to know.

What we do know is that there are electoral incentives for parties to adopt different strategies in different parts of the country. Cairns (1968) argued that the first-past-the-post (FPTP) electoral system used in Canada creates incentives for parties to concentrate their campaign efforts in specific parts of the country. FPTP elections tend to provide a seat bonus to winning parties, such that a bare plurality of votes can become a strong majority of seats. Only three times since 1921 has a majority government had the support of a majority of the voters, and the last such occurrence was the victory of the Mulroney Conservative Party in 1984. Furthermore, the distribution of seats across the provinces is uneven. Of the 338 seats in today's parliament, 121 come from Ontario, 78 from Quebec, and 42 from British Columbia. Theoretically, if a party sweeps Ontario and Quebec, it could govern with a majority without support from any other province. In recent elections, both provinces have, on occasion, given a large majority of their seats to a single party. Thus, it is possible that parties contribute to the uneven distribution of voter support by concentrating their campaign efforts in certain parts of the country.

This possibility is not unrealistic. Cross (2002b) notes that the parties engaged in just such regional strategies in the 1997 election. In that election, only the Liberals truly competed in all parts of the country. Examining the constellation of competitive parties in each province in that election, he found eight different groupings, with only Newfoundland, Nova Scotia, and New Brunswick sharing the same pool of competitive parties. In the West, the Reform Party was strong, and it sought a breakthrough in Ontario. In Quebec, the Bloc Québécois was a major force, and the NDP and PCs concentrated their efforts in specific ridings in order to regain official party status after their disastrous results in the 1993 election. The result of these differences, Cross argues, is that the parties, facing different competitors in each region, often talked about different issues and highlighted divergent positions in the different provinces: "The national election was really a patchwork of distinct regional contests" (126). This was not the first time this had happened, but it marked an interesting step (backward, as we explain below) in campaign communication.

According to Carty, Cross, and Young (2000), there are three major periods of campaign communication in Canada. The first, lasting until the development of radio (first used widely in the 1930 election), was fully local. Because there was little national media, candidates and leaders relied on personal communication (speeches, visits, etc.) to get their messages to voters, and these could be tailored to each location. There was little attention to the contradictions that arose. In the next period of campaign communication, radio broadcasts enabled candidates to reach a wider audience with a single speech. This innovation also meant that regional and national issues were emphasized more than local ones. The widespread use of television marked the next period of communication. Leaders, images, and national issues took on even greater importance. At the same time, public opinion polling provided crucial information about the issues that were important to voters and allowed the parties to tailor their messages to their own supporters.

That the 1997 election marked a step backward is evident in how the parties chose to campaign. Since the 1960s, the party system had been pan-Canadian. All three major parties (the Liberals, PCs, and NDP) sought support from voters across the country. The success of the Reform Party and Bloc Québécois in the 1993 election, however, changed the party system dramatically. Both had strong early success, winning the second and third largest shares of parliamentary seats in both 1993 and 1997. And, both parties had strong regional bases – Reform in the four Western-most provinces and the Bloc in Quebec. Each party won virtually no seats in the remainder of the country (for the Bloc, this was by design, as it did not run candidates outside of Quebec). Largely as a result of the influence of these two parties, federal election campaigns became highly regionalized (Carty et al. 2000).

The new regionalized nature of party competition meant that the incentives for parties to launch national campaigns were lost. It was more cost effective, in electoral terms, to focus on areas of strength and potential growth. Thus, the parties regressed to a time of more regionalized communication behaviour. The emergence of the Reform Party's successor, the Canadian Alliance, as a strong contender in the 2000 election was a positive development for the Liberals, as it gave them "the opportunity to run one strong national campaign, rather than dilute the effect by running five or more regional campaigns as in the previous election. This would allow for consistency of communications, and more effective and better understood messaging." (Marzolini 2001, 265)

The electoral landscape evolved once again when the Canadian Alliance merged with the PCs in 2003 to create the current Conservative Party of Canada and when the Bloc lost ground in Quebec. At present, it is unclear whether elections have once again become pan-Canadian affairs. As noted above, the 2015 election suggests that there are still substantial regional differences in party support. The parties' role in those differences is one of the key elements we examine in this book.

Of course, parties are not the only factor to consider. Another major player in elections is the mass media. Although parties create platforms and develop strategies for reaching voters, most voters – particularly those who are not party members – get their election information in a mediated form. Even if parties campaign similarly across the entire country, the extent to which messages are filtered through the regional media could mean that the information reaching voters is very different. The issues that are salient in different provinces can vary, just as their economic bases do. Energy policy may be far more relevant to voters in Alberta; unemployment insurance might be salient in the Atlantic Provinces, where seasonal employment is more prominent. Certainly, this was the logic followed in the campaign strategies of the parties in 1997, and it makes sense that media outlets, concerned about appealing to their readers or viewers, might emphasize what is salient and newsworthy for a particular location.[1]

Of course, the final consideration when assessing the nature of elections in Canada must be the voters themselves. Research has demonstrated that there are different political cultures across the country (McGrane and Berdahl 2013), and the variation in vote shares could simply reflect that voters in different parts of the country have different political preferences. If that is the case, then even without the parties and media, voters themselves may be the key to the story.

This book addresses each of these topics in turn. We analyze how the 2015 federal election unfolded in three different provinces – British Columbia, Ontario, and Quebec – and focus on three different sets of actors – the parties, the media, and the voters. Our research agenda is to evaluate whether we should understand elections in Canada as national wars or individual provincial battles. Given the election results, and experiences from previous elections, the latter is a distinct possibility. The analyses in this book can help us understand whether

Canadians in different provinces really have such different political preferences, and whether parties and the media play a role by framing the options differently across provinces. As such, they also contribute to the literature on regionalism in Canada by helping to parse out the source of regionalized election outcomes.

In this book, we document how political parties and candidates structured their messages and strategies across the three provinces, how the media communicated and framed those messages, and how voters ultimately responded with their choices. We draw upon a wide variety of data sources to do so, including voter and candidate surveys,[2] party campaign behaviour, and media coverage of the election. Our analyses combine the best available data with the most appropriate methods to provide the best evidence available to address our research questions.

This approach to studying the 2015 Canadian election is both novel and important. It is the first and only thorough treatment of the party, media, and voter aspects of a federal election campaign through a subnational lens. National elections, including Canadian elections, tend to be studied either with data from across the country, or by separating Quebec from the rest of Canada (ROC). Furthermore, the majority of election studies use a single data source (such as voter surveys). This book addresses the lack of attention to the subnational arenas of federal election campaigns, triangulating campaign efforts and effects through a variety of data sources.

The framework we use for our analysis follows the one used by Cross et al. (2015). In that volume, the 2011 Ontario election is studied through the lenses of parties, the media, and voters. Explicit in that framework is the recognition that understanding the outcome of an election requires an understanding of what the parties did to appeal to voters, how the media interpreted party messages and shaped (or did not shape) how they were conveyed to voters, and ultimately how the voters responded. Our findings shed light on the ultimate outcomes of the 2015 contest in British Columbia, Ontario, and Quebec, but they have relevance for understanding elections in federal political systems more generally.

In this introduction, we set the stage for later analyses by considering two elements that may provide some insight into the variation observed at the national level. First, we consider the obvious question of whether the variation is based upon socio-demographic differences between the provinces. One might suspect, for example, that if a party supports policies that favour immigrants, then provinces with greater proportions of immigrants may lend their support to that party in greater numbers. Second, we provide some background about the federal and provincial party systems as well as consider the degree to which they are linked. The provincial context is important to our understanding of why political competition may vary, as replicating provincial support patterns could be a potential explanation for the observed patterns. In both cases, we show that there is no easy answer and that considering the strategies of parties and the media is warranted. We then review the chapters to come and indicate how they contribute to our overall analysis.

ARE THE REGIONAL DIFFERENCES AUTHENTIC?

Differences in vote outcomes can arise in two different ways. First, vote shares can differ because of differences between provinces in terms of residents' social background characteristics, ideological orientations, partisan ties, issue attitudes, and leader evaluations. These are compositional differences. Second, vote shares can differ because of differences in the effects of these factors. In other words, provinces may differ in the weight that voters attach to various considerations when deciding how to vote. If we want to understand the variation in the parties' vote shares across the three provinces, we need to take account of both compositional differences and differences in effects.

Most importantly, identifying the effect of compositional differences on vote shares can tell us whether or not the observed differences in vote shares constitute true regional differences. The "region-as-artifact" thesis raises the possibility that the variation in parties' electoral fortunes from one part of the country to another simply reflects differences in the socio-demographic makeup of the population (Gidengil et al. 1999; McAllister and Studlar 1992). According to this thesis, regional differences should only be considered true regional differences if we cannot account for them in terms of differences in the composition of the population. If the region-as-artifact thesis is valid, people sharing the same social background characteristics should distribute their vote similarly, whichever region of Canada they live in.

For example, Catholics' support has been one of the keys to Liberal dominance (Blais 2005; Gidengil et al. 2012). Even when the Liberals lost, Catholic voters were more likely to vote for the party than non-Catholics. If regional variation in vote shares is a mere artifact of compositional differences, the gap in Liberal voting between British Columbia and Ontario might be explained by the fact that Catholics make up a larger share of the Ontario electorate. On the other hand, if Catholics distribute their vote differently depending on where they live, we would have more confidence that the vote share gap between the two provinces reflects a true regional difference. This would be reflected in a difference in effects.

It is difficult to disentangle compositional differences and differences in effects. To the average observer, they appear as one and the same, but there are quantitative analysis tools that can be applied to survey data to separate the two. Here we use a method that was developed in labour economics to understand the sources of wage differentials based on factors like gender and race to quantify the contribution of differences in the provinces' social composition. Known as the Blinder-Oaxaca decomposition (Blinder 1973; Oaxaca 1973) and originally restricted to linear models, this method has since been adapted for use with nonlinear models such as logit. Based on the output from binary logistic regression models for two groups, the method partitions a group difference into two components, one attributable to compositional differences and one attributable to differences in effects (including differences in the intercepts). Thus, it allows us to understand how much of the observed differences in vote choice can be attributed to different provincial demographics.

The particular method of analysis used here, a multivariate decomposition model (mvdcmp), has two key advantages (Powers, Yoshioka, and Yun 2011).[3] First, it allows for the use of weights. This enables us to reproduce the actual differences in reported vote shares between the provinces. Second, it provides detailed results, making it possible to estimate the contributions of individual explanatory factors. However, like any method based on logistic regression, it is vulnerable to problems caused by sparse or empty cells. This causes problems, for example, if first language is included in the models given the small number of francophone voters in Ontario and British Columbia. For this reason, language is not included among the explanatory factors, and our Quebec analyses in this instance are restricted to Francophones. Since the results of decompositions differ depending on which group is taken as the reference category, we present the average contributions taking first one province and then the other as the reference.

Table 1.1
Decomposing the vote share gaps

	Gap	Contribution	Per cent contribution
CONSERVATIVE			
Quebec–Ontario	18.5	-1.4	-7.6
Quebec–British Columbia	13.3	-3.4	-25.6
Ontario–British Columbia	5.2	0.2	4.0
LIBERAL			
Quebec–Ontario	12.8	-0.2	-1.6
Ontario–British Columbia	9.7	-0.3	-3.2
NDP			
Quebec–Ontario	11.6	0.8	0.7
Ontario–British Columbia	9.4	-1.2	-12.3

Note: The column entries indicate how much the gap would decrease or increase if the composition of the provinces was the same in each pair of provinces. Note that the figures for Quebec exclude respondents whose first language is not French.

The differences in vote shares are clearly not an artifact of differences in the social makeup of the provinces (see table 1.1).[4] They represent true regional differences. Compositional differences are no help at all in explaining the gap in NDP voting between Quebec and Ontario, and they are virtually no help in explaining the gaps in Liberal voting. Compositional differences do contribute to the gap in NDP voting between Ontario and British Columbia. The key factor is professing no religion, a traditional correlate of NDP voting. If secular voters made up similar shares of the population of the two provinces, the gap would have been one point smaller. Differences in other relevant characteristics, such as union membership and income, contributed little or nothing to the gap because the two provinces are very similar in these respects.

Differences in the social composition of the provinces account for by far the largest proportion of the gap (25 per cent) when it comes to the Conservative vote in Quebec and British Columbia. The key factors are income and religious affiliation. The gap in Conservative voting between the two provinces would have been smaller had Francophone Quebeckers been more affluent and if the province had had fewer Catholics. Compositional differences account for a much smaller proportion of the gap in Conservative voting between Quebec and Ontario but the same factors are at play. Overall, though, it is clear that differences in the social composition of the provinces are little help in explaining the differences in vote shares. We need to look elsewhere, then, to understand the patterns of voting across the country. In the next section, we evaluate whether differences in party systems at the federal and provincial levels are a viable explanation.

PARTY SYSTEMS ACROSS CANADA

Canadians are sometimes said to inhabit two political worlds at the same time. The federal structure of the country means that there are two levels of government that bear constitutionally designated authority for specific policies. However, those two levels of government can differ substantially.

Until the 1930s, Canadian politics at the federal level was essentially a two-party affair. The Liberals and Conservatives battled for control and took turns forming the government. The entry of the Cooperative Commonwealth Federation (CCF) and Social Credit parties, and later the NDP, changed the status quo but only slightly. None of these smaller parties were able to control the government, and both the CCF and Social Credit had a highly regionalized support base.

In what is often known as the third-party system (Carty, Cross, and Young 2000), electoral politics took on a more national tenor. All three of the main parties that competed from the 1960s until the 1990s sought support from across the country. The success of the PCS under Brian Mulroney, for example, is largely credited to the coalition of support that was brokered between Quebec and the Western provinces. However, as mentioned above, the party system experienced change with the success of Reform and the Bloc, and again when the new Conservative Party formed.

The current party system in Canada consists of three major national parties, one provincial party, and one minor party. As has been the case since Confederation, the Liberals and Conservatives are the two main competitors for government. The NDP, the other major party, has threatened this dominance at times, most notably in 2011 when it displaced the Liberals to become the Official Opposition party to the governing Conservatives. Nonetheless, the national vote share outcome of 2015 is more in keeping with the outcome of previous contests – the Conservatives and Liberals were close competitors and the NDP had less, although still significant, support. The Bloc Québécois, another party that served as Official Opposition (from 1993 to 1997), contests seats only in the province of Quebec. Its raison d'être is representing the interests of Quebec (nationalism and sovereignty) at the federal level. Finally, the Green Party has become a minor – but national – factor over the past decade.

While subnational party systems in other countries often mirror those at the federal level, there is little connection between federal success and provincial success in Canada (Stewart, Sayers, and Carty 2015). Indeed, whereas federally, Canada poses a challenge to the coordination logic inherent in Duverger's Law about two-party competition in first-past-the-post elections, the provincial level is far more acquiescent (Johnston 2017). Although multi-party competition has been a reality for many years at the national level, competition in the provinces tends to be between two main actors. Johnston (2017) suggests that the substantial dissimilarity between federal and provincial electoral outcomes can be traced to the presence of the NDP, minor parties (which he calls insurgents), and provincial-level party responses to NDP strength. The precise nature of political competition varies by province, in some cases involving provincial parties that have no federal counterparts.

Furthermore, there are varying ties between provincial and federal parties, even of the same name, across the country (Esselment 2010). Esselment (2010) theorizes that policy is unlikely to be influenced by a counterpart at another level, given the need to respect provincial priorities, but that party organization can be. Thus, while in other countries voters may have the same party loyalty across levels of government, it is far more difficult in Canada, especially in certain provinces, as both the party system and the nature of competition can vary. Many Canadians have different party identifications at the federal and provincial levels (Blake 1982; Clarke and Stewart 1987; Stewart and Clarke 1998).

Along with being the largest provinces in Canada, the three provinces we analyze in this book are notable for having very different provincial party systems. Table 1.2 shows the results of the most recent election in each province before the federal 2015 contest. The differences would not be immediately obvious from looking at the governing parties, as a Liberal government emerged in each one. Those provincial parties, however, are neither officially linked to each other nor to the federal Liberals. There is variation in which parties compete and are most competitive. For example, the PC Party was the runner-up in the 2014 Ontario election, but the Conservatives in British Columbia were one of the "other" parties that received about 5 per cent of the provincial vote. Similarly, an NDP party has existed at the provincial level in Quebec since 2014, but it did not field candidates in a provincial election until 2018 (despite the federal NDP's strong performance in the 2011 federal election); however, the NDP was the runner-up in British Columbia in 2013 and has formed a government in Ontario in the past.

Only Ontario's provincial parties can boast strong congruence with the federal party system, with the presence of Liberals, PCs, and New Democrats. The parties generally fill the same places on the ideological spectrum as their federal counterparts, despite the name variation on the right-wing, so it is not surprising that we observe the strongest ties between federal and provincial politics in this province (see Pruysers 2015; Koop 2011). Although the Liberals have controlled the government after four of the past five elections, and the NDP did form the government in the early 1990s, historically, Ontario was known as being very "blue" (Progressive Conservative).

The politics of British Columbia and Quebec, however, are quite different. In British Columbia, provincial politics are dominated by the Liberals and New Democrats. Here, the Liberals are a centre-right party attracting support – electorally and organizationally – from many federal Conservatives, while federal Liberal supporters are divided between the two parties. There is no formal relationship between the provincial and federal Liberal parties, but the New Democrats are organizationally connected at the two levels. There is no meaningful conservative party at the provincial level, though the party has performed well in recent federal elections in the province. The Social Credit Party dominated British Columbia politics from the 1953 election until 1991, with the NDP as its main competitor. However, the Liberal Party held power from 2001 to 2017.

Quebec's system is the most distinct. For four decades, provincial politics has been defined along the federalist/sovereigntist cleavage, with competition mostly dominated by the Parti libéral du Québec (PLQ) and Parti Québécois (PQ). The PQ does not exist at the federal level. The party does have a supportive relationship with the federal Bloc Québécois, but this has waned as the federal party has seen little success in recent elections. The provincial Liberal Party has no formal ties to the federal Liberals and is supported electorally by federalists

Table 1.2
Provincial vote shares for elections prior to 2015 federal vote

British Columbia 2013		Ontario 2014		Quebec 2014	
Party	*%*	*Party*	*%*	*Party*	*%*
BC Liberal Party	44.1	Ontario Liberal Party	38.7	Quebec Liberal Party	41.5
BC Conservative Party	4.8	Progressive Conservative Party of Ontario	31.3	Parti québécois	25.4
BC NDP	39.7	New Democratic Party of Ontario	23.7	Coalition avenir Québec	23.1
Green Party of BC	8.2	Green Party of Ontario	4.8	Québec solidaire	7.6

Note: Not all parties that received votes are reported.

from across the political spectrum. The Quebec New Democratic Party is not affiliated with the federal New Democrats, who finished first in the province federally in 2011 and second in 2015, and ran candidates for only the first time in the 2018 provincial election. Left-of-centre provincial voters tend to support either the PQ or the fledgling Québec Solidaire (which also has no federal counterpart), though left-of-centre federalists may support the provincial Liberals. The other principal provincial party, Coalition Avenir Québec, also does not compete in federal politics, though its roots lie in the former provincial Action démocratique du Québec, which was influenced by the now-defunct federal PC Party.

Does this provincial variation impact the federal level? One might expect that support for the federal parties would reflect the strength of the corresponding parties at the provincial level. Using data from the 1993 and 2000 elections, Clough (2007) finds that there is some influence of provincial partisanship on federal vote choice, although it is not enough to explain the non-Duvergerian persistence of more than two competitive parties at the federal level. In table 1.3 we consider whether there is evidence of voting links between the two levels in the 2015 election using survey data. The values show how voters in each province reported voting in their previous provincial election (BC, 2013; Ontario, 2014; Quebec, 2014) according to their federal vote. For ease of interpretation, the modal response for each federal vote choice is bolded.

Even ignoring cases in which there is no corresponding party to vote for, it is clear that the link between federal and provincial preferences among voters is not consistently strong. In Ontario, there is substantial overlap between federal and provincial vote choice, but it is not overwhelming other than for the conservative parties (over 80 per cent). Less than 71 per cent of federal NDP and Liberal voters in Ontario indicate support of the corresponding provincial party, and the proportion is far lower (less than 50 per cent) for the Greens. In British Columbia, more federal Conservative voters than federal Liberal voters indicate that they vote Liberal provincially. In this province, the most consistent vote choices are among NDP supporters, but no value reaches 75 per cent. Finally, in Quebec, where completely different parties compete, provincial Liberal supporters were drawn from the Conservatives, NDP, and federal Liberals (the latter most strongly). Not surprisingly, given their similar policy stances, almost 79 per cent of BQ supporters had voted PQ provincially.

Clearly, the variation in loyalty to a party name among voters is significant and differs by province. Support in Ontario matches fairly well, although the levels are somewhat low. In the other provinces, support for the Liberal Party comes from voters of different provincial stripes. We do see some evidence of consistent cross-level party support, most intensely for conservatives in Ontario and sovereigntists in Quebec, but it is not strong enough to explain the differences in federal election outcomes by province.

The variation observed in table 1.3 also indicates that we cannot understand the federal vote outcome by simply observing provincial outcomes. In British Columbia, for example, the Liberals received the most votes in both cases (35 per cent federally and 44 per cent provincially) but the CPC came in second federally (30 per cent), compared to the NDP provincially (40 per cent). In Ontario, the ranking of the parties is the same, but in Quebec, the absence of the NDP and Conservative parties from the provincial scene at the time of the 2015 federal election makes comparisons difficult. The NDP received the second-most votes in the federal election (25 per cent), and the BQ received 19 per cent; however, there was no provincial NDP presence, and the PQ vote outstripped BQ support by earning 25 per cent. The differences in provincial party systems are clearly not the easy answer to the regionalized pattern of federal party support across the country.

Table 1.3
Distribution of previous provincial vote choice by 2015 federal vote choice (percentages)

Previous provincial vote choice	2015 Federal vote choice					
	CPC	NDP	LPC	BQ	Green	Other
BRITISH COLUMBIA						
Liberal	**52.9**	12.6	**49.6**		12.4	9.0
NDP	13.0	**73.2**	34.7		21.2	**48.6**
Green	2.2	9.7	5.4		**61.8**	7.8
Conservative	31.8	4.3	9.0		1.2	0.0
Other	0.2	0.3	1.2		3.4	34.6
ONTARIO						
Liberal	10.3	11.7	**66.9**		13.1	15.6
Progressive Conservative	**81.4**	13.9	11.0		18.2	**41.1**
NDP	5.6	**70.4**	16.0		11.7	24.9
Green	1.2	2.9	5.9		**47.4**	0.0
Other	1.5	1.2	0.2		9.6	18.4
QUEBEC						
Parti libéral du Québec	**48.2**	24.9	**68.6**	3.5	18.0	**41.2**
Coalition Avenir Québec	19.5	22.0	9.1	6.3	12.3	0.0
Parti Québécois	15.4	**28.3**	15.9	**78.9**	22.7	0.0
Parti vert	0.8	2.1	0.8	1.3	**34.7**	0.0
Québec Solidaire	3.1	14.9	3.3	5.3	6.9	32.7
Option nationale	2.3	1.2	0.3	2.1	3.8	0.0
Other	10.7	6.6	2.1	2.6	1.7	26.2

Note: Bolded values are the modal response for each federal vote choice.

CHAPTER OVERVIEW

In the following eight chapters, we seek to understand the factors that explain federal vote differences across Canada. To really understand the situation, however, a clear sense of context is needed. Chapter 2 sets the stage for our analysis by looking at the role of regionalism in various aspects of Canadian politics. As has surely become clear, all provinces are not the same, but the extent to which this is a defining feature of Canadian life can only be understood by considering the full extent of regionalism's impact. In chapter 3, we provide specific background about the 2015 election in order to contextualize the analyses to come. The chapter provides an overview of polls, party competitiveness, and expectations in the 2011–2015 period in our three provinces. It also tracks public opinion during the 2015 campaign in response to various events. Campaign events are national, but reactions need not be. This analysis provides some initial information about the similarities and differences in the election campaign across the provinces.

With the context established, we move on to consider the campaign from the perspective of the parties and candidates. In chapter 4 we focus on local candidates and their campaigns. National and provincial campaigns are important, but elections are actually fought in local constituencies, where the personalities of candidates and issues relevant to specific areas can be critical. This chapter focuses on understanding how the local candidates did or did not individualize their campaigns. While the party organization can develop policy, strategize, and plan, it is individual candidates and their supporters that must take the messages to the voters, therefore we might expect differences in messaging and personality to produce differences here. If there are divergent regional or provincial messages being delivered to voters, it may well be through these local campaigns. We shift the focus to consider the actions of the national campaigns in chapter 5. We present evidence about leader visits, press releases, and social media. Each of these campaign elements are directly managed by the parties themselves, and our analysis is aimed at evaluating whether specific regions were targeted.

The next chapter considers the role of the media and the mediated information that voters received during the campaign. We focus on two types of media – newspapers and television. For newspapers, we look at national and regional sources, and for television we provide a careful study of campaign coverage on one network (CTV) across three major cities (Vancouver, Toronto, and Montreal). We concentrate on what was covered during the 2015 campaign, how it varied by province or region, how much coverage focused on the leaders compared to the candidates, and how the information from the media compared to what the parties themselves were putting forward. As variation may be subtle, we also consider whether the media emphasized the horserace, or competition between frontrunners, and whether the tone of coverage differed across the provinces. Again, our goal is to understand how the messages put forth by the parties were transmitted to (and translated for) the voters and whether this varies across provinces.

The next two chapters consider voters. First, we assess how much media coverage was consumed by voters: who paid attention to what kinds of media, did it vary by province, and how may it have affected voters? We analyze whether differences in the nature and extent of newspaper and televised election coverage across the provinces are reflected in the attitudes, perceptions, evaluations, and expectations of residents.

The final consideration for understanding the 2015 elections in British Columbia, Ontario, and Quebec is vote choice. Chapter 8 analyses how attitudes, perceptions, and evaluations of parties, candidates, and issues affected vote choice. We evaluate vote choice using a standard vote model that considers social background characteristics, partisanship and ideology, issues, party leaders, and strategic considerations.

Chapter 9 summarizes our findings and reflects upon their implications for how we understand elections in federal countries. While our focus is on the 2015 Canadian election, federal elections take place in countries around the world. Thus, our results are important for the study of federal states more broadly. Although we are agnostic about which part of our title is true, provincial battles or national war, we expect to find that the differences in provincial vote shares in federal elections were, at least partially, the product of party strategy, media focus, and voters' priorities.

2

Regionalization and Canadian Elections

Regionalism has been described as "one of the pre-eminent facts of Canadian life" (Simeon and Elkins 1980, 31) and it has been central to the understanding of elections and electoral behaviour in Canada. Indeed, the very first book based on Canadian election study data focused on the persistence of regionalism (Schwartz 1974). Yet the phenomenon has been undertheorized and surprisingly understudied. "'Everybody knows' that regionalism is important in Canada" (Cheal 1978, 337), but there have been few attempts to formulate a theoretical framework to interpret the observed differences in voting behaviour and electoral outcomes among Canada's regions. Too often the analysis of regionalism in Canadian voting patterns does not go much beyond an empirical demonstration of political differences among regions, leaving the concept largely devoid of explanatory content. As one of the classic studies of regionalism in Canada acknowledges, the term regionalism is used "simply as a descriptive statement about the way provinces or other areas differ. It is not an explanation" (Simeon and Elkins 1980, 33). An empirical demonstration of regional differences has little meaning without a theoretical framework to interpret them, and as we noted in the previous chapter, the goal of this book is to understand better the variation that emerges in elections. Thus, we aim to contribute to the literature on regionalism by better understanding one of its most-observed manifestations. Regionalism, even though it is a common explanation for the differences in party support across the country, has tended to remain a largely residual concept. As Simeon and Elkins (1980) observed, "regions are containers, and other factors are necessary to account for variation in their contents" (33). In this chapter, we consider the literature on regionalism and its effects on Canadian elections.

DEFINING REGIONS

Despite the centrality of regionalism to explanations of electoral outcomes and vote choice in Canada, studies of voting behaviour have
given surprisingly little systematic consideration to how regions should
be defined in Canada. Typically, studies of voting behaviour have treated
regions as synonymous with provincial groupings such as Atlantic
Canada, the Prairies, or the West. To the extent that a rationale is
provided, these definitions are justified on the grounds of "political
relevance" or "historical importance" or the observed variation in
voting patterns and political attitudes. Often, the justification for group-
ing provinces is pragmatic: it is "perhaps as much to build up respect-
able sample numbers as anything else" (Elkins and Simeon 1980, xi).

Recent years have witnessed several attempts to reconceptualize
region. Henderson (2004, 601) argues for "the existence of regions
that occur within and across jurisdictional boundaries." Drawing on
Statistics Canada data for all federal constituencies, she used cluster
analysis to identify nine regions. Some regions lay within provinces
(such as "cosmopolitan Quebec" and "metropolitan Toronto") but
others transcended provincial and territorial boundaries (such as
"urban Canada" and "rural and mid-Northern").

For their part, Cochrane and Perrella (2012, 831) conceptualize
region as "the physical space that surrounds an individual." According
to this conception, regions can be defined at different levels of aggre-
gation from the household to the neighbourhood to the constituency
to the town or city to the province. In other words, people can belong
to multiple regions at the same time. Given this conception, it follows
that a search for a single explanation for regional differences is futile
since the causes of these differences are likely to vary from region to
region, from one level of analysis to another, and from one issue to
another. Cochrane and Perrella (2012, 831) conceptualize regionalism
in social-psychological terms as "an affective attachment to the people,
places and institutions within a geographic area." Their core assumption is that people care about those who live around them. They test
this argument by looking at attitudes toward government intervention
and show that the provincial and especially the constituency unemployment rate has a significant effect on respondents' attitudes, even
controlling for different measures of their own economic prospects.
It is not clear, though, how well the argument would work when it
comes to explaining spatial variation in opinion on non-economic
issues, such as crime, abortion, and same-sex marriage.

Silver and Miller (2014, 447), meanwhile, argue that regions "are not only large, geographically contiguous jurisdictions in the traditional sense but the style of life, the aesthetic, the imagery, the symbolic meaning accruing to distinct localities." However, this does not negate the relevance of regions in the traditional sense for understanding vote choice. When the authors explore the impact of "cultural scenes" on voting patterns, they find that region – as more conventionally defined (British Columbia, the Prairies, Ontario, Quebec, and Atlantic Canada) – continues to have a significant and frequently substantial effect on party vote shares, even controlling for a variety of scene dimensions.

Interesting as these reconceptualizations are, a strong case can be made for treating provinces as regions. Provinces have aptly been called "the small worlds of Canadian politics" (Elkins and Simeon 1980) and with good reason. Provincial boundaries are politically consequential and encompass important socio-historical realities (Henderson 2010). As Schwartz (1974, 310) observes, "For the most part, regions are political units, and where they are not, they are combinations of such units, with some independence as political actors. This in itself ensures that regionalism will continue to be a political phenomenon." Defining regions on the basis of provincial boundaries has been criticized, and certainly the heterogeneity *within* provinces in terms of social and economic characteristics and political behaviour cannot be overlooked. Intraprovincial differences can also have implications for understanding voting behaviour (Gidengil 1989a, b). In particular, there can be differences in political preferences and vote choice depending upon the type of community in which voters reside, and these differences may well cut across provinces (see, for example, Cutler and Jenkins 2000; Turcotte 2001; Walks 2004, 2005, 2006).

When it comes to defining regions, there is little agreement on the appropriate containers, much less on the content of those containers. Nonetheless, the persistence of references to "region" by political scientists to account for differences in party fortunes is remarkable. We next turn to consider some of the ways in which the role of region has been conceptualized.

REGION AND VOTE CHOICE

The regionalization of the vote, as demonstrated in the previous chapter, is not a peculiarly Canadian phenomenon. Party preference in Britain is also highly regionalized, with Labour faring well in areas with strong manufacturing sectors and cosmopolitan city centres, the Conservatives doing best among rural voters, and the Scottish National Party garnering an increasing number of seats in its eponymous home (Johnston and Pattie 1998; Detterbeck and Hepburn 2010). In contrast to Canada, however, regional patterns of voting in Britain have sparked a lively and ongoing debate about their meaning. It is instructive, then, to review the extant literature in both countries. There are two major streams of inquiry, one related to class and the other to the region-as-artifact thesis.

Region versus Class

Initially the debate focused on the role of social class. Johnston (1987, 15) lit the fuse by claiming that the geography of England's class structure was "insufficient to account for the geography of voting." Using a variety of indicators, he showed that working class voters were much more likely to vote Labour in some regions than their counterparts living elsewhere in the country. McAllister (1987, 353) rejected Johnston's conclusion, arguing that it only applied to the Labour vote and likely reflected factors such as "the significance of regional political traditions and patterns of party competition." However, later research found regional differences in Conservative voting that also could not be explained by the "geography of social class" (Fisher 2000, 347).

In Canada, too, region and social class have been viewed as "antithetical, for one emphasizes the geography of residence, while the other stresses stratification distinctions for which residence is irrelevant" (Cairns 1968, 74). However, unlike Britain, a classic study of class voting in the Anglo-American democracies declared Canada to be a case of "pure non-class politics," with regional and religious cleavages superseding class "almost entirely as factors differentiating support for national parties" (Alford 1963, x–xi). However, Alford predicted that regional (and religious) voting would diminish as Canada experienced increasing urbanization and industrialization. This came to be known as the evolutionary model. It sought to explain regional differences in Canadian voting patterns in terms of differences in levels of economic development from one part of the country to another.

Lipset and Rokkan's (1967) classic study of cleavage structures, party systems, and voter alignments was a stimulus to this line of

research. Their study identified territorial-cultural cleavages and functional cleavages as the two crucial cleavages that structure vote choice:
"In the one case the decisive criterion of alignment is *commitment to
the locality and its dominant culture:* you vote with your community
and its leaders irrespective of your economic position. In the other
the criterion is *commitment to a class and its collective interests:* you
vote with others in the same position as yourself whatever their localities..." (Lipset and Rokkan 1967, 13; emphases in the original). Lipset
and Rokkan (1967, 10) assumed that territorial-cultural conflicts are
the norm in the early phases of nation building, but tend to be superseded by functional conflicts with the advent of the Industrial
Revolution. Functional cleavages "*cut across* the territorial units of
the nation. They produce alliances of similarly situated or similarly
oriented subjects and households over wide ranges of localities and
tend to undermine the inherited solidarity of the established territorial
communities" (emphasis in the original).

In a similar vein, the regionalization of the Canadian party system
has been attributed to differences in the stage of development reached
by different provinces. According to Wilson (1974), as a society evolves
from the pre-industrial or beginning industrial stage through the
industrializing stage to the advanced industrial stage, there are corresponding changes in terms of the cleavages that structure the party
system and the kinds of interests that are served. However, this evolutionary model proves to be a poor empirical fit. Ontario is Canada's
most industrialized province, and yet its party system only qualifies
as transitional, as it has retained three-party competition. Worse,
Saskatchewan – one of Canada's least industrialized provinces –
emerges as the sole example of a modern party system. A similar
assumption that the development of modern industrial society will
result in a modernization of the party system motivated Jenson's
(1976) study of provincial party systems with equally anomalous
results. There is little evidence to suggest that the regionalization of
Canada's party system or the regionalization of the vote reflects differences in levels of industrialization and urbanization among the
provinces. Moreover, Blake (1972) found no evidence that the impact
of region on major-party support patterns had declined between 1908
and 1965.

Gidengil (1989a) sought to resolve the puzzle: Why have urbanization and industrialization failed to diminish regionalized patterns of
voting and to make social class a major determinant of vote choice?

Her study drew on dependency theory to develop a theoretical rationale for regional differences in electoral behaviour that focused on
the interplay between class and region in influencing voting behaviour
in Canada. Her central argument was that regional disparities and
the relationships of economic dependency that underlay them meant
that class voting took different forms from one region of Canada to
another. As a result of structural relationships of inequality between
the centre and periphery in Canada, voters sharing the same social
class membership perceive their position differently and respond to
it differently depending upon the structural context in which they are
located (Gidengil 1989a, 1989b).

The Region-as-Artifact Thesis

The second stream of research questions the authenticity of regional
variation. The inquiry into whether regionalized voting patterns in
Britain could be explained by the geographical distribution of working class voters gave rise to a more general question about whether
the differences across Britain's regions represented true regional voting.
An important catalyst was an article by McAllister and Studlar (1992).
According to the region-as-artifact thesis, regional variations in political preferences should only be considered true regional differences if
they cannot be explained by variations in the social composition of
the regions. If voters sharing the same social characteristics vote
similarly, regardless of where they live, regional differences are simply
an artifact of variations across the country in the proportion of residents sharing the relevant characteristics. McAllister and Studlar
(1992) conclude that compositional differences account for most of
the regional variation in voting in Britain in the 1980s.

Subsequent research produced contradictory results. In stark contrast to McAllister and Studlar, Johnston and Pattie (1998, 328) found
that "there are significant and substantial differences in voting behaviour between similar people living in different British regions." They
attributed the disparities to deeply rooted differences in political
culture from one part of the country to another. Subsequent studies
reaffirmed their conclusion that regional voting patterns could not
be explained in terms of differences in the social makeup of regions
(see, for example, Johnston et al. 2005, 2006). Further research,
however, led Johnston and his colleagues (2007, 640) to revisit their
conclusion about the authenticity of regional differences. They came

to share the view that regional variations in support for the three main political parties in England are "simply statistical artifacts." However, they attributed the observed regional variation to the aggregated effects of decision-making processes operating at more local levels, as opposed to simple compositional differences among regions. They concluded that regional patterns indicate that "different types of voters, living in different types of households and neighbourhoods and subjected to party campaigns of differing intensity, are concentrated in different regions" (2007, 653).[1]

More recently, the conclusion has changed yet again. When Pattie and his colleagues (2015, 1561) examined the impact of the local climate of economic opinion on three different spatial scales, they found, to their surprise, that "some contextual effects, at least, really are more powerful at the regional than at more local scales." They suggest that this finding – which runs counter to much of the research on contextual effects in Britain – reflects coverage of the state of the economy in the regional media. They make an important point: "Regions remain important reference points for voters when it comes to large issues such as the state of the economy; after all, so much media attention is paid to regional variation" (2015, 1572).

In Canada, too, questions have been raised about the authenticity of regional variation in voting patterns. The 1974 Canadian Election Study (Clarke et al. 1974) set out to discover whether regions were more than analytical categories and whether they had real meaning for their residents. Finding that there was no province where a majority of the population agreed on the boundaries of their own region, Clarke and his colleagues (1979) concluded that regions were indeed serving as little more than data containers.

A less stringent requirement for deciding whether regional variations in vote choices are real is to ask, as McAllister and Studlar (1992) did, whether they exist over and above differences in the composition of the population. If the region-as-artifact thesis were valid, people sharing the same social background characteristics would vote similarly, regardless of where they live in Canada. It turns out that people sharing the *same* social background characteristics often vote *differently* from one region of the country to another (Gidengil et al. 1999). The net effect of compositional differences proved to be small and explained little of the regional variation in Liberal and Reform support in the 1997 federal election. Most of the regional variation in support for the two parties was real. As we have seen in the previous chapter, a similar conclusion applies to all three of our provinces in the 2015 election.

Gidengil and her colleagues (1999) went on to develop an explanation of the regional differences. The regional partisan climate proved to be a key factor in explaining the regional variation in vote shares. The partisan climate refers to regional differences in the distribution of party identification over and above those that would be expected based on differences in social composition and political culture. The authors characterize the differences in partisan climate as a reflection of the historical legacy of party politics and Canada's political history more generally. The importance of partisan climate as an explanatory factor is consistent with Blake's (1972, 59) observation that "the historical association of particular parties with certain regions" is one of the "principal manifestations of regionalism in Canadian voting behaviour." As noted in the introduction to this book, regional variation in federal vote shares and provincial party systems is substantial. However, the most striking finding to emerge from the 1999 study related to differences in political priorities. In the 1997 election, voters in Ontario were preoccupied with job creation, whereas voters in Western Canada were concerned about taxes, the deficit, crime, and gun control. Resistance to accommodating Quebec was a major factor in Reform voting in the West, but registered only minimally in Ontario. These regional differences in the issue agenda highlight the strategic challenges for any political party that mounts a Canadawide campaign.

The third key factor identified by Gidengil and her colleagues (1999) was variation in regional political cultures, by which they meant regional differences in the distribution of cultural values over and above those that would be expected based on differences in the regions' social makeup. However, research into the existence of regional political cultures in Canada has led to conflicting results. The work of Matthews and Davis (1986), Wiseman (2007), Anderson (2010), Wesley (2011), Cochrane and Perrella (2012), and McGrane and Berdahl (2013) falls into one camp, where province or region of residence is an important predictor of attitudes and values. On the other hand, Ornstein and Stevenson (1999) and Ornstein, Stevenson, and Williams (1980) find that province of residence has limited impact on general value orientations. Addressing the variation, Matthews and Davis (1986) argue that what matters is the nature of the attitudes, whether they are general or about specific territorial identities, while

Héroux-Legault (2016), using factor analysis to avoid biasing the results through question choice, finds that socio-demographic variables account more variation in attitudes about moral traditionalism, pluralism, immigration, and personal responsibility than provincial or regional variables.

Of course, partisan climate, issue priorities, and political culture are only three elements that could explain regionalized voting patterns. Two other possible sources are examined in this book: variations in party campaigns and media coverage. We need to explore how regional political priorities are influenced by the campaign activities of parties and the media if we are to fully understand regionalism in elections. To complete our coverage of the relevant literature, then, we next turn to consider the research on the interplay between region and party campaigns and media coverage.

REGION AND PARTY STRATEGIES

There are good reasons to expect that "spatial criteria" (Mintz 1985) will influence federal parties' campaign strategies, given the nature of Canadian federalism, the regionalization of Canadian society, and the strategic incentives created by Canada's electoral system. Yet, there has been little in the way of thorough efforts to theorize party strategies in Canada. This lack of theorizing on the implications of regional cleavages for party strategies has been typical of the larger party literature. Nevertheless, there has been a significant amount of research conducted on how parties distribute their resources during election campaigns.

Theorizing Party Strategies in Regionalized Systems

As Hepburn and Detterbeck (2013, 76) observe, party scholars came "late to the territorial politics table." While this might be attributable to the fact that the devolution of powers to the substate level has been a relatively recent phenomenon in many countries, they think the more likely explanation lies in a normative bias in favour of "the nation-state as the only meaningful unit of political science … Indeed, scholarly understandings of parties are overwhelmingly state-centric" (2013, 76). Recently, though, there has been a flurry of interest in how both state-wide and regionalist parties approach the strategic challenges of competing in a policy space characterized by both a left-right dimension and a salient territorial dimension, where the latter is understood as "a conflict over the structuring of political authority within the state" (Elias, Szöcsik, and Zuber 2015, 843).

Drawing on this literature, Elias et al. (2015) have theorized about the possible strategic responses that parties might adopt. They assume that while political parties typically have a "core dimension," they cannot risk ignoring other dimensions. What interests them is how both types of parties, those with a state-wide orientation and those with a regional focus, deal with these secondary dimensions. Drawing on the notion that political parties can use positioning, selective issue emphasis, and framing to devise a strategy, they identify four strategic options for political parties competing in systems characterized by both left-right and territorial cleavages.[2]

The first option expands on Rovny's (2013) notion of position avoidance. Political parties that adopt the unidimensional strategy ignore the secondary dimension, instead emphasizing their core dimension and positioning themselves on their core issues. In the case of regionalist parties, this would entail only taking positions on the territorial dimension; in the case of state-wide parties, this would mean only taking positions on the left-right dimension. Elias et al. suggest that small ethnic minority parties are the most likely to adopt this strategy. Larger regionalist parties and state-wide parties, though, are much more likely to opt for one of the other three strategies, given the potential costs of dismissing a salient dimension.

Instead of ignoring their secondary dimension, Elias et al. (2015) suggest, parties can adopt a blurring strategy by assuming "vague, contradictory or ambiguous positions" (Rovny 2013, 5) on that dimension. This strategy enables them to emphasize their positions on their core issues without seeming to neglect the other dimension. Parties following this strategy address issues relating to the latter dimension but without articulating clear positions. The objective is to obscure the party's "spatial distance from voters in order to either attract broader support, or at least not deter voters on these issues" (Rovny 2013, 5–6). Surprisingly, when they have pursued a blurring strategy, both regionalist and state-wide parties in Spain and the United Kingdom have tended to blur their economic position (Alonso, Cabeza, and Gómez 2015). More predictably, state-wide parties in Italy opted to blur their position on territorial issues when faced with a challenge from the Lega Nord (Basile 2015).

Rather than blurring their positions, parties may opt for a subsuming strategy (Basile 2015; Elias et al. 2015; Massetti and Schakel 2015). The key to this strategy is framing: issues relating to the secondary dimension are reframed in terms of the party's core dimension (Basile 2015). This is also what the Italian parties did when responding to the Lega Nord challenge (Basile 2015). As Elias et al. (2015) emphasize, this is very much a "rhetorical strategy." A regionalist party could subsume the left-right dimension by calling for the national government to intervene less in the regional economy. Conversely, a state-wide party might subsume the territorial dimension by promising to remove barriers to interregional trade. As Elias et al. (2015, 842) point out, the subsuming strategy can be seen as an attempt to "alter the dimensional structure of the political space itself."

Finally, parties may adopt a two-dimensional strategy. As its name suggests, using this strategy entails taking clear stances on issues relating to both the core dimension and the secondary dimension (Alonso 2012). State-wide parties may have little choice but to articulate positions on both the left-right and territorial dimensions if there is a viable regionalist party or "territorially differentiated electoral preferences" (Elias et al. 2015, 845). A regionalist party, meanwhile, could risk a loss of support if it fails to take positions on the issues that define the left-right dimension. Indeed, most ethno-regionalist parties in Western Europe do take positions on issues relating to both their core territorial dimension and the left-right dimension that structures state-wide electoral competition. For example, a study of regions in Spain and the United Kingdom found that state-wide parties pursued a two-dimensional strategy when challenged by regional competitors (Alonso, Cabeza, and Gómez 2015).

Political parties, of course, face a variety of constraints when formulating their strategies. There are "structural limits to strategic behaviour" (Rovny 2015, 913). Moreover, "though party campaign strategies are broadly defined at the national level, they are implemented at the state, regional, provincial and local scales of analysis and are likely to be a response to the immediate settings, conditions and circumstances in which political parties operate" (Shin 2001).

Allocating Campaign Resources

While political party scholars have only recently focused attention on the strategic challenges posed by regionalized systems, there is a longer tradition of analyzing how political parties allocate their campaign efforts. Typically, campaign spending is used as a surrogate for campaign effort. Of course, this measure cannot take account of voluntary activity, but research suggests that it is an adequate proxy for overall effort (Fieldhouse and Cutts 2009; Pattie, Johnston, and Fieldhouse 1994).[3] The focus of this line of research has been whether political parties allocate their campaign funds in a rational manner.

One of the first studies suggested that this was the case in Britain. Pattie and his colleagues (1994) found that local party campaigners focused their campaign spending on winnable seats, aiming to defend seats that they already held and increase their chances of winning marginal seats. Subsequent studies have confirmed that British parties behave rationally, concentrating their campaign effort where it is most likely to make a difference. This is the case whether studies rely on campaign spending, the self-reports of local party agents, or a combination of these and other measures (see, for example, Denver et al. 2003; Fieldhouse and Cutts 2009; Pattie and Johnston 2003). Given that Britain and Canada are among the very few Western democracies that use the first-past-the-post plurality electoral system, we should expect the strategic incentives created by the electoral system to result in similarly rational behaviour on the part of Canada's federal political parties. However, the British research has also highlighted "forces of inertia" that constrain party rationality, including how well the party has performed previously (which influences the availability of resources), legal limits on spending, and the reluctance of local party workers to travel to marginal constituencies (Fieldhouse and Cutts 2009).

One of the first studies to examine how Canada's federal parties allocate their resources was Mintz's (1985) examination of the party leaders' campaign tours. He focused on leaders' tours because they garner a large amount of media attention, with journalists accompanying leaders on their travels across the country. He also pointed out that the tours enable leaders to highlight parts of their party's program that are particularly salient regionally or locally. Even absent such appeals, the very fact of paying a visit implies that the party cares about local concerns. Mintz expected that campaign strategists would target marginal constituencies, where the investment of scarce resources would be most likely to reap electoral returns. Accordingly, he predicted that party leaders would spend a disproportionate amount of their time visiting provinces where the proportion of marginal constituencies was high.

Mintz examined the distribution of the leaders' tours for the Liberals, PCs, and CCF-NDP in every federal election held between

1949 and 1980. Although there was a tendency for party leaders to spend more time in provinces with a higher proportion of marginal seats, this tendency was only consistently strong in the case of the CCF-NDP. Mintz attributed the pattern for the CCF-NDP visits to the fact that its support base at the time was more regionalized than the two major parties. He predicted that the incentives for the major parties "to pursue provincially defined campaign resource allocation strategies" (1985, 53) would increase as their bases of support became more regionalized. At the same time, he pointed to factors that decrease the incentives to pursue a regionalized strategy including internal party politics, the costs in terms of time and money, and the need to project an image of national appeal.

Carty and Eagles (2005, 100) revisited the geographical distribution of leaders' visits. They set out to assess whether these visits "are strategically planned to link the national and constituency-level campaigns." Their analyses were based on the leaders' itineraries in the federal election in 2000. They found little evidence of parties targeting marginal constituencies when it came to leader visits. All four of the Canada-wide parties focused disproportionate attention on Ontario, with more than half of all the leaders' visits targeting the province. Drilling down to the constituency level, the authors found that the Liberals, PCs, and NDP all focused their leaders' visits on constituencies where they had done well in the previous election. Carty and Eagles characterize this as a defensive strategy designed mostly to mobilize existing support rather than attract new supporters. The Bloc and the Canadian Alliance adopted the very opposite strategy, sending their leaders to constituencies where the party (or its predecessor, in the case of the Canadian Alliance) had done less well in the previous election, presumably in the hopes of attracting converts.

Carty and Eagles, like Mintz, concluded that the visits had a positive effect on the local vote, at least for the three long-established parties. They suggest that this is because a leader's visit helps to energize and mobilize the local campaign as well as garnering media attention and enhancing the visibility of the local candidate. This was apparently not the case for the Bloc or the Canadian Alliance, though. Indeed, a visit by Bloc leader Gilles Duceppe actually seemed to depress the local candidate's vote. We provide an analysis of leaders' tours in 2015 in chapter 4.

The Canadian findings with respect to the geographical distribution of leader visits are at odds with those from Britain where political parties do respond to the strategic incentives created by the first-past-the-post plurality system by focusing their leaders' visits on marginal constituencies (Middleton 2015). The story has been very different in the case of local campaign spending: Carty and Eagles (2005) found that, as in Britain, financial resources were targeted at marginal constituencies, at least in the case of the three competitive parties. However, the PCS and the NDP – who were fighting for electoral survival in 2000 – pursued a defensive strategy directed at their few safe seats.

Predictably, there was also evidence of an association between competitiveness and total local fundraising: the more competitive the race, the greater the amount of money raised by the candidates. As Carty and Eagles note, local party associations and candidates have an incentive to raise as much money as they can in order to boost local party finances, whether or not the constituency is marginal. Nonetheless, the incentives are stronger when more is at stake. Carty and Eagles also found a clear and unsurprising pattern: there was a close association between the amount of money raised in a region's constituencies and a party's regional strongholds.

The strategic incentives changed with the introduction of a per-vote subsidy for the national parties in 2003. In the 2006 federal election, the competitiveness of the constituency only appeared to influence national party transfers for the NDP and the Conservatives and, in the case of the latter, the effect was only modest (Coletto and Eagles 2011). Coletto and Eagles argue that, strategically, it made sense for the Liberals and Conservatives (given their financial resources) to ensure that local campaigns were adequately financed even in lost-cause constituencies since every vote generated a subsidy (see also Eagles and Hagley 2010). However, the elimination of the per-vote subsidy meant that the strategic incentives changed yet again in the 2015 election.

Intimately tied to the role of region in party strategies is understanding the balance between national and local considerations in constituency campaigns. Sayers (1999) has provided the most thorough attempt to theorize the nature of local constituency campaigns in Canada. The availability of resources, the campaign organization and activity, and the extent to which the local campaign is integrated with the national campaign vary systematically, depending on which of four types of candidates is running.[4] High-profile candidates typically get recruited in very competitive constituencies, and their campaigns are professional and integrated into the party's national campaign.

Indeed, national strategists may be involved in local decision making. Desirable constituencies are apt to see the selection of "local notable" candidates. Their campaigns tend to be very personalized and are largely independent of their party's national campaign. At the other extreme, undesirable constituencies typically recruit stop-gap candidates who go through the motions of campaigning. Their campaigns tend to parallel the national campaign. All three of these candidate types are typical of cadre-style parties like the Liberals. Mass-style parties, like the NDP, meanwhile, tend to nominate the fourth type of candidate, party insiders, whose campaigns are integral components of their party's national campaign.

Sayers based his theory on a study of contests in seven constituencies in the 1988 federal election. Carty and his colleagues (2005) provide a systematic test of the theory based on local party association data from the same election. Their analyses confirm that party insiders' campaigns tend to be the most party dominated, whereas the campaigns of high-profile and local notable candidates are the most candidate centred. Based on Sayers' typology, Carty and Eagles expected that high-profile, stop-gap, and party-insider candidates would receive the most outside party assistance from the regional or national levels. However, no clear patterns emerged. For example, party-insider candidates were actually the least likely to report having outside strategists or managers involved in their campaigns, though they were the most likely to report receiving extra-local resources. Nonetheless, the authors found support for Sayers' ideal types, especially in the case of local notables and party insiders. They conclude that his model "provides us with a framework for systematically studying the local dimensions of national election campaigns" (Carty and Eagles 2005, 81).

Overall, Carty and Eagles concluded that national and local campaigns are relatively autonomous. This reflects what Carty, in other work, has characterized as the stratarchical relationship between national and local party organizations in Canada (Carty 2002; Carty 2004; Carty and Cross 2006). According to Carty and Eagles (2005, 86), the decentralized nature of party organization in Canada and the candidate-driven nature of campaigns resulted in "a pattern of relatively weakly integrated and unevenly articulated national party election activity in the constituencies." This was evident when they looked at the use of national party funds. They argued that, "Following the trail of election spending can tell us much about how Canadian parties try to integrate their discrete riding campaigns into a coherent national contest" (Carty and Eagles 2005, 83). They found no evidence of parties' funnelling a disproportionate amount of party money into local campaigns in either their provincial strongholds or provinces where they were weak. Moreover, there was little evidence that national party money was directed to candidates in competitive constituencies where the money was most likely to make a difference to the outcome.[5] They concluded that the national parties were not investing substantial amounts in local campaigns, and that the modest amounts that were invested were not allocated in a strategic manner: "parties are not as rational as they might be, given the opportunities that the single-member electoral system creates for them" (Carty and Eagles 2005, 37).

These findings are at odds with those reported in Britain. Examining a similar time period, Denver and his colleagues (2003) found that election campaigns in Britain were becoming increasingly centralized as national party headquarters came to exert greater control over constituency campaigns in marginal seats. As a result, local campaigns were being integrated into the parties' national campaigns. The increased role of national party organizers in managing constituency campaigns has been attributed to the growing professionalization of British parties at the national level (Fieldhouse and Cutts 2009).

During the time period covered by Carty and Eagles, local party associations benefited from a much higher level of reimbursement of their candidates' election expenses than did the national party organizations. As a result, it was common for more money to be spent on the local campaigns than the national campaign (Carty and Eagles 2005). However, 2003 brought significant changes to the regulatory framework governing election financing, and these changes affected the balance between the local and national party organizations. Looking at internal party financial flows between 2004 and 2007, Coletto and his colleagues (2011) argue that the new regulatory regime was eroding the stratarchical relationship between the national and local party organizations: mutual autonomy was giving way to a growing centralization of power in the national organizations, especially in the case of the Bloc, the NDP, and the Conservatives in Quebec. The authors attribute the new pattern to two features of the new financing regime. First, it put a premium on soliciting small contributions from a large number of individuals, which the national organizations were much better placed to do. Second, political parties now qualified for a per-vote subsidy as well as a much higher level of reimbursement for elections expenses (though still lower than the level enjoyed by local constituency organizations).

However, even in Britain where political parties are more closely linked across levels, the national party is constrained by the "tension between the imperatives faced by the national party, and those faced by local parties and candidates" (Pattie and Johnston 2003, 389). The national party wants to maximize its share of seats, even if that means fewer votes in safe constituencies and lost deposits in lost-cause constituencies. Local parties and candidates, meanwhile, want to maximize their vote share, even in safe seats, and may well be unwilling or unable to transfer resources to marginal seats.

The per-vote subsidy was eliminated by the Conservatives in 2015, so it remains to be seen what effect this had on the national–local balance in the 2015 election. Knowing the answer matters. As Coletto and his colleagues (2011) argue, the extent to which party organizations are centralized is a particularly salient concern in regionalized countries like Canada because it can influence parties' ability to accommodate geographical diversity and manage regional tensions.

Our analyses in chapters 4 and 5 consider whether the Canadian parties adopted any identifiable strategy in the 2015 election. Instead of focusing on spending, we utilize data about leader visits, press releases, and a unique survey of candidates to build a picture of party activities. If the parties did have a strategy of targeting different provinces with different messages, then the parties could be partially responsible for the regionalized outcome. If not, we need to consider other sources of regional party preferences, such as the media's coverage of campaign activity.

REGION AND MEDIA COVERAGE

There has been surprisingly little study of the extent to which media coverage of elections is regionalized. One of the few studies to do so compared campaign coverage in Wales, Scotland, and the East Midlands (Deacon, Wring, and Golding 2006). The authors found that the parties' actions, strategies, and electoral prospects dominated coverage in all three regions of Great Britain, as they did in the UK-wide media. Moreover, even in Scotland and Wales (where there are competitive nationalist parties), the Labour Party received the most coverage, just as it did in UK-wide reporting. On the other hand, there was evidence of regionalization when it came to the issue agenda in both the print and broadcast media. Not surprisingly, there was more coverage of constitutional issues in the Welsh and Scottish media, but there were also regional differences in the amount of attention given to issues like crime and the National Health Service. The authors also found that coverage was less partisan in the Welsh and East Midlands reporting.

The conventional wisdom used to be that press coverage in Canada is regionalized. According to a 1980 study, "It is rather widely held in Canada that there is no 'national agenda'; and that the rank ordering of salient events by the press differs by region and/or language" (Soderlund et al. 1980, 349). Early work on the regionalization of media coverage in Canada focused on the implications for Canadian identity and national unity (see, for example, Elkin 1975; Gordon 1966; Siegel 1979; Soderlund et al. 1980). The consensus was that differences between the French and English press generally trumped regional differences but that issue emphases varied regionally as well.

Soroka's (2002) study of agenda-setting dynamics in Canada challenged the conventional wisdom. Using measures of internewspaper consistency, he concluded that "there is considerably more similarity in newspaper agendas in Canada than is generally assumed" (2002, 44). Despite regional differences in the relevance of stories, there was strong evidence of consistency in the amount of coverage given to tax issues, the environment, and inflation in the period from 1990 to 1995. There was less consistency when it came to the debt/deficit and unemployment, but there was no issue on which regional subgroups of newspapers could be identified. Moreover, even though the level of coverage might differ across provinces, the dynamics of issue salience tended to be similar across time, regardless of province.

Soroka's study did not focus on election coverage. However, he found that there was more evidence of a common newspaper agenda during times when issue salience is heightened. This suggests that coverage of election campaigns is more likely to be characterized by a Canada-wide issue agenda. Certainly, to the extent that press releases and party leaders' pronouncements help to drive coverage, it seems reasonable to assume that there is a common Canadian newspaper agenda when it comes to election coverage. A study of agenda setting during the 2006 federal election campaign confirms that this is the case (Gidengil 2014; see also Frizzell and Westell 1989). Using the same methods as Soroka (2002), Gidengil found that the extent to which it was possible to speak of a common issue agenda in coverage of the election varied from issue to issue. Evidence was strongest in the case of foreign affairs and defence, civil rights, ethics, crime and justice, finance and commerce, taxes, and health, and weakest in the case of the economy, the environment, social welfare, and trade. In some cases, weaker evidence of internewspaper similarity may have reflected differences in the relevance of the issue. Agriculture, forestry, and fishing, for example, are not likely to be of much interest to Toronto readers, whereas immigration could be very salient. Existing research supports this and has shown that variation exists between the content of national and local news outlets (Doyle 2002; Soderlund et al. 2012), and that local news tends to be more event-driven and sensationalized, lacking the detail that national news outlets provide (Graber 2009).

The extent to which the mediated messages in the 2015 election campaign differed by province or region is thus an open question. Research in Canada and the UK suggests that there may be a mix of national and regional messaging. Chapter 6 looks at newspaper and television coverage of the election in each province. It is possible that some of the differences in party fortunes reflect the way that the parties were portrayed to voters by the media, which may or may not have magnified the activities of the parties themselves.

CONCLUSION

Regionalism may be a fact of Canadian life, but its effects are not fully understood when it comes to electoral politics. It is easy to look at the outcome of elections like the one in 2015 and argue that the variation in parties' strength reflects the historical and contemporary preferences of voters in different provinces. But this argument can be nothing more than an assumption without an investigation into the way the election campaign unfolded in provinces that had very different outcomes. Our study of British Columbia, Ontario, and Quebec provides just such an investigation, thus making an important contribution to the study of regionalism and electoral politics.

We suspect that part of the explanation for regionalized election outcomes lies with the actions of the parties, and part lies with the media's messaging. These expectations are supported by the literature, although to varying degrees, and are ultimately logical. We simply expect that voters respond to the information context in which they are making decisions. As such, we have three related hypotheses:

1 Parties present different information to voters in different provinces.
2 The media presents campaign messages from the parties differently across the country.
3 There is some variation in media consumption, political culture, and priorities and preferences that is tied to geography.

The null hypothesis in each case is that there is no provincial variation. After presenting information about the context of the 2015 election, the remaining chapters address these hypotheses in turn.

PART TWO

Polls, Parties, and Media:
The 2015 Election

3

Contextualizing the Outcome:
The Lead-Up to 2015

To best understand the factors that contributed to regional variation in the 2015 election outcome, it is useful to first take a step back into the past to understand the political context. The 2015 contest was not a tabula rasa – the issues and preferences of voters reflect previous election results, the events that occurred in the inter-election period, and the campaign itself. In this chapter we review the outcome of the 2011 election and, using public opinion data, we examine how the popularity of the various parties evolved from 2011 to August 2015. We also review the events of the campaign period and consider public opinion about the parties both at the start of the election campaign and during the campaign itself.

THE PREVIOUS CONTEST

The 2011 contest was a unique election in many ways. First, it was the first time a Conservative majority government had emerged from an election since 1988 and the first majority government since the merger between the Progressive Conservatives and Canadian Alliance in late 2003. The Conservatives won the 2011 election with 40 per cent of the vote and 166 seats (54 per cent). Second, it was the first time in federal electoral history that the NDP had formed the Official Opposition, with 31 per cent of the vote and 33 per cent (103) of the seats. It was also the very first time that the NDP had obtained a plurality of the votes and a majority of the seats in Quebec – in fact, it was the first time that the NDP had received more than 12 per cent of the vote in that province. The outcome is also notable because of how poorly the Liberals fared, securing only 19 per cent of the votes and 11 per cent (34) of the seats in Parliament. Although the Greens' share of the vote was just 4 per cent, they managed to win one seat. Finally, the Bloc Québécois received 23 per cent of the votes in the province of Quebec, but that translated into only four seats, the party's weakest ever result.

Table 3.1 presents the vote shares and seats obtained in 2011 by the main parties in each of our three provinces. Much like the 2015 election outcome, there was substantial variation. In Quebec, the NDP won 43 per cent of the votes and 79 per cent (59) of the seats. The Conservatives won in the other two provinces, obtaining 44 per cent of the votes and 69 per cent (73) of the seats in Ontario and 46 per cent of the votes and 58 per cent (21) of the seats in British Columbia. The Conservatives were particularly weak in Quebec, whereas the Greens were particularly strong in British Columbia. There was also substantial local variation within each province. In Ontario, for instance, the Conservative vote went from a minimum of 14 per cent (in Davenport) to 64 per cent (in Wellington–Halton Hills). The equivalent figures were from 12 per cent (Eglinton–Lawrence) to 57 per cent (Hamilton Centre) for the NDP and from 7 per cent (in Oshawa) to 47 per cent (in York West) for the Liberals.

The uniqueness of the 2011 election outcome created several big questions going into the 2015 contest. Would the Conservatives be able to stay in power? Would the NDP be able to repeat its unprecedented success, especially in Quebec? Would the Liberals be able to re-establish themselves as one of the two major parties in Canada? Would the anti-Conservative vote split between the Liberals and the NDP, or would voters converge on one party? And, finally, would any party manage to win a majority of the seats? To address these questions it is useful to look at the competition between parties at the constituency level.

Going into the 2015 election, most constituencies were considered safe, that is, the 2011 winning candidate had a margin of more than 10 percentage points over the second-place candidate. If all else held, the results would not change substantially. However, the electoral boundaries changed between the two elections, creating thirty more constituencies with no incumbent. To understand how this could impact expectations for the 2015 vote, we need to consider the likely competitiveness of the new constituencies and add that to our safe-seat projections. According to an analysis available on Andrew Heard's

Table 3.1
Votes and number of seats in the 2011 election

	BRITISH COLUMBIA		ONTARIO		QUEBEC	
	% Votes	Seats	% Votes	Seats	% Votes	Seats
Conservative	45.6	21	44.4	73	16.5	5
NDP	32.5	12	25.6	22	42.9	59
Liberal	13.4	2	25.3	11	14.2	7
Bloc Québécois					23.4	4
Green Party	7.7	1	3.8	0	2.1	0
Others	0.6	0	0.9	0	0.8	0

elections website (https://www.sfu.ca/~aheard/elections/marginal-seats.html), across the whole country 93 seats out of 338, or 27 per cent, could be considered marginal (that is, the winning candidate's margin was less than 10 percentage points).[1] Interestingly, the proportion of marginal seats does not vary much across provinces. The percentage is 28–29 per cent in both Ontario and Quebec, and 38 per cent in British Columbia.

Which party was expected to benefit most from marginal seats? If a party often finished second in constituencies in 2011 and was thus not far behind the leading party, the party may have been encouraged to dedicate additional resources to the riding to improve their performance in 2015. On the other hand, a party that often finished first but had only a small winning margin could be considered to be in a more precarious position. From that perspective, the Conservatives could be seen to have an advantage in Quebec since they had finished second in four marginal constituencies, and they had won in only one. The Liberals, however, had reason to be nervous, since they had won in seven closely contested constituencies and had finished second in three. The situation was exactly the opposite in Ontario. Twenty of the thirty-five marginal constituencies had been won by the Conservatives, who were the runner-up in only eleven. The Liberals, for their part, had finished second in twenty-one constituencies and had won only nine. There is no such pattern in British Columbia. Going into the election, then, the Liberals probably hoped to make some gains in Ontario and feared losing a few seats in Quebec.

THE EVOLUTION OF PARTY SUPPORT, 2011–2015

Beyond the election results, many things changed between 2011 and 2015 that could have had an impact on the competitiveness of the parties. One way to identify any events that might account for shifts in party popularity between the two elections is to look at public opinion data.[2] Figure 3.1 presents the monthly evolution of vote intentions across Canada from the month after the 2011 election until the beginning of the campaign in August 2015.[3] Figures 3.2 to 3.4 show the evolution in each of the three provinces under study.

The first observation relates to the absence of an expected event: there seems to have been no honeymoon effect for the Conservatives. The party obtained 40 per cent of the vote in the May 2011 election and its support more or less stayed at that level for the following six months. From there, Conservative support progressively declined to about 35 per cent by early 2012.

Two potentially consequential events involved leadership changes. The first was the election of Thomas Mulcair as the leader of the NDP in late March 2012. This produced a gain of about 5 points for the NDP, whose support went from 30 per cent to 35 per cent. That boost quickly subsided, however, as NDP support was back to 30 per cent by the end of the year. This was followed by the election of Justin Trudeau as leader of the Liberal Party in April 2013, which led to a 10-point increase in Liberal vote intentions, from about 25 per cent to about 35 per cent. Unlike the boost the NDP received from electing Mulcair, the Trudeau boost proved to be more durable, lasting about eighteen months.

As a consequence of these two events, by September 2014, one year before the upcoming election, the Liberals seemed to be poised to win the election, though unlikely to have a majority. Their popularity rested at about 35 per cent, followed by the Conservatives, with slightly more than 30 per cent support, and the NDP trailing at around 22–23 per cent. Then came the terrorist attacks in Saint-Jean and Ottawa in late October 2014. These events seem to have boosted the governing Conservatives by 3 points, mostly to the detriment of the Liberals (probably owing to the public safety and crime dimensions that the Conservatives are typically strong on). By the beginning of 2015, then, the complexion of competition had changed to a close race between the Liberals and the Conservatives, both with slightly under 35 per cent support, and the NDP trailing by more than 10 points.

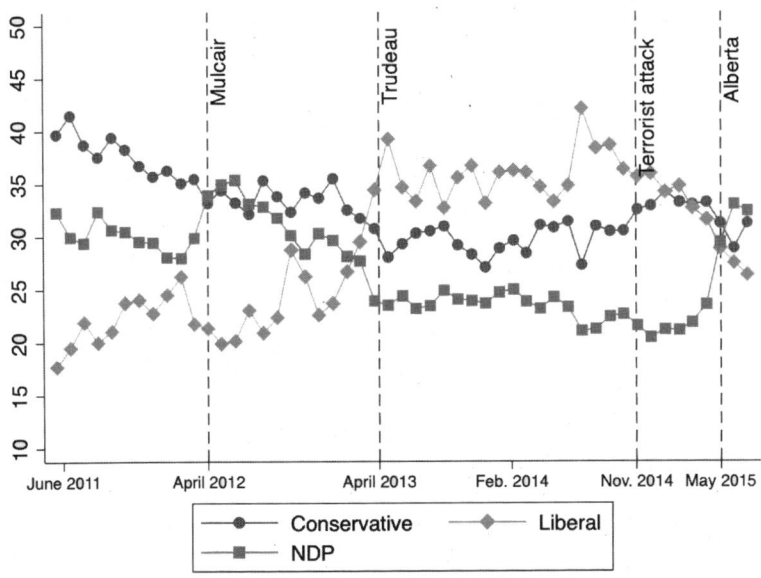

Figure 3.1 The evolution of vote intentions: Canada (2011–2015)

Once again, this new equilibrium proved to be short-lived. The stunning NDP provincial victory in Alberta in May 2015 was followed by a spectacular growth in NDP support at both the provincial and federal levels. NDP vote intentions increased by about 10 points, mostly at the expense of the Liberals. All of a sudden, the NDP took the lead in vote intentions, rising to about 33 per cent in a close contest with the Conservatives at about 30 per cent, while the Liberals moved to third place, trailing with around 27–28 per cent support.

For voters, pundits, and close observers, it was not clear what to expect at the beginning of the seventy-eight-day campaign, which started on 2 August 2015. At that point, the polls were showing a three-way contest, with the NDP having a slight edge over the Conservatives, and the Liberals trailing but not far behind. The Conservatives appeared very likely to have at least 30 per cent support. Their most serious competitor seemed to be the NDP, but the NDP had been ahead of the Liberals for only a couple of months. Given the novelty of the NDP lead and its association with the recent NDP victory in Alberta, pundits wondered whether the effect could endure or was bound to dissipate. The only thing that appeared almost certain was that no party would win a majority of the seats in the House since none had more than 35 per cent support. These dynamics raised the question of whether those who wanted to defeat the Conservatives would converge on whichever party appeared to be the strongest between the NDP or the Liberals, or whether the anti-Conservative vote would split between the two parties, possibly allowing the governing party to remain in power (but in a minority position).

Provincial party competition varied considerably from the national picture, but the dynamics of party support between 2011 and 2015 were remarkably similar in British Columbia, Ontario, and Quebec. With one exception, the four consequential events (the elections of Mulcair and Trudeau, the terrorist attacks, and the NDP victory in Alberta) moved the vote in the same direction in all three provinces. The exception was the terrorist attacks in Ottawa and Quebec, which did not seem to help the Conservatives in British Columbia. There were of course small differences in the magnitude of the effects: the NDP gains following the election of Mulcair were stronger in Quebec, and the impact of the NDP victory in Alberta was more substantial in neighbouring British Columbia. The big picture, however, is one of similar movement in opinion across the three provinces. This suggests that the dynamics of vote support were national, rather than provincial, in nature.

However, and most importantly, the fact that vote support moved the same way in the three provinces does nothing to eliminate the big differences across the provinces. Competition looked particularly fierce in Ontario. The Conservatives appeared to have a small edge, at around 35 per cent, over the Liberals and the NDP, both at around 30 per cent. Compared to the 2011 election, the Conservatives had lost about 10 points to the benefit of their two competitors, and they seemed destined to lose seats in Ontario, although they may have had some hope of keeping seats due to the splintering of support between the Liberals and the NDP on their left. The latter two parties were involved in a huge fight to secure the anti-Conservative vote. The NDP had momentum and hoped to capitalize on it, while the Liberals may have reasoned that the NDP surge following the Alberta victory was temporary and that they might be able to recover the strong support that they had enjoyed until the beginning of the year. Ontario was thus a crucial battlefield for the parties, making it difficult to predict the 2015 outcome in that province.

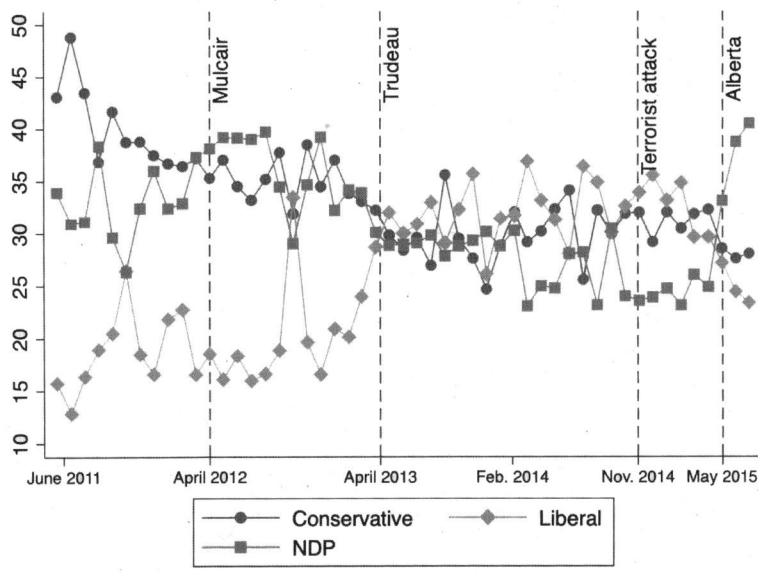

Figure 3.2 The evolution of vote intentions: British Columbia (2011–2015)

Things looked very different in Quebec. The NDP was clearly leading, with about 35 per cent in the polls – less than the 43 per cent the party had obtained in the 2011 election. The fact that it had a strong lead over all the other parties suggested that it would keep most of its seats. The Liberals had made some gains, from 14 per cent to 24 per cent, which made them the second-most popular party in the province, but since their vote was so concentrated in anglophone constituencies, the party's seat gains were likely to be modest. As for the Conservatives and the Bloc, in terms of vote intentions, they were more or less where they landed in 2011 and they looked destined to keep the few seats that they had. While this may have been the electoral picture leading up the start of the campaign in summer 2015, it masks the fact that from the election of Trudeau in May 2013 to the very end of 2014, the Liberals had been in the lead, with support hovering around 35 per cent. In other words, there was a strong undercurrent of support for the Liberals in the province owing, at least in part, to the popularity of its new leader. By August 2015, though, the idea of the Liberals doing well in the province seemed to be in the distant past.

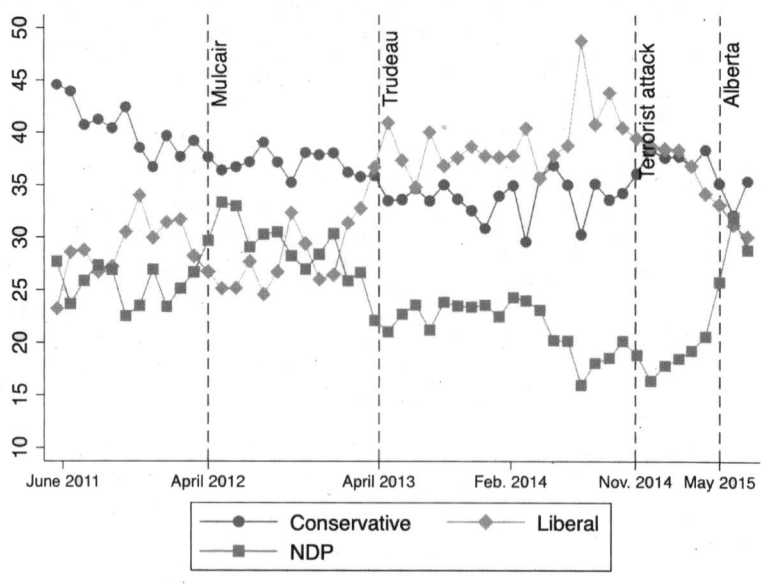

Figure 3.3 The evolution of vote intentions: Ontario (2011–2015)

What about British Columbia? As in Quebec, the NDP was clearly leading in that province. Support for the NDP had surged to about 40 per cent in the aftermath of the party's stunning win in Alberta. The Conservatives were trailing, at less than 30 per cent, a more than 15-point drop compared to 2011. These standings made it seem like the NDP would make substantial gains in that province, to the detriment of the Conservatives. The Liberals were in third place, with 23–24 per cent, but this was still a 10-point increase relative to 2011. It is likely that the party hoped to make some gains, although probably limited ones. But, just as in Quebec, the situation in the summer of 2015 was a departure from strong Liberal polling up until that point. In the eighteen months that followed the election of Trudeau as the leader of the Liberal Party, Liberal vote intentions hovered around 30 per cent and there was an intense three-party contest in the province. The big question as the campaign started in British Columbia, as elsewhere, was whether or not voters would converge on the two leading parties at the time, the NDP and the Conservatives.

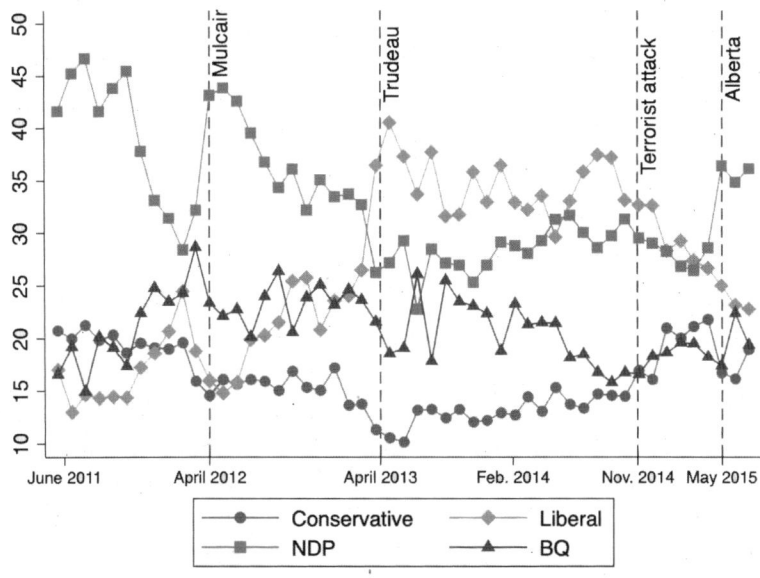

Figure 3.4 The evolution of vote intentions: Quebec (2011–2015)

THE CAMPAIGN: WHAT HAPPENED?

The 2015 campaign officially began when Prime Minister Harper asked Governor General David Johnston to dissolve Parliament on 2 August 2015. All three major party leaders launched their campaigns that day – Harper in Montreal, Mulcair in Gatineau, and Trudeau in Vancouver. The parties had already begun their advertising campaigns in attempts to shape the narrative, most memorably the "Just Not Ready" ads launched by the Conservatives in May that targeted Justin Trudeau's fitness for the office of prime minister. Trudeau had made a key election promise in June – that 2015 would be the last first-past-the-post federal election held in Canada. With a fixed election date, the parties were able to plan their appeals to Canadians very carefully to take advantage of timing.

The election campaign itself was called earlier than usual. The official requirement is for campaigns to last at least thirty-six days, and by calling the election when he did Prime Minister Harper set in motion the longest campaign since 1872 (seventy-eight days). This length of time meant that, in reality, many voters did not even start paying attention until after Labour Day. Nonetheless, it also meant that there was considerable time for events to occur that could shape (and reshape) public opinion. Moreover, it set in motion limits as to what could be spent by candidates, parties, and third parties.[4] The parties put forward their platforms and campaigned, as usual, on a combination of issues, including standard issues such as taxes, social services, and the economy, as well as issues specific to the political context at the time.

Throughout this volume, we refer to these two types of issues as core issues (common across most election campaigns) and campaign issues (driven by events that occur close to the election). Core issues include crime, the economy, public safety, social policy, and taxes, whereas campaign issues, in 2015, included perspectives on climate change; environmental protection; the building of pipelines such as Energy East, Northern Gateway, and Keystone XL; and women wearing the niqab while receiving public services. One issue of particular salience in the 2015 campaign was the protection and welcoming of refugees from the Syrian civil crisis, which galvanized certain segments of the voting public along the lines of how much should be done for refugees and how many Canada should welcome before the end of the 2015 calendar year.

Issues that are more proximate to the election itself often shape the narrative of the campaign in a unique way. The 2015 election was no different. Because of the fixed election date, some unique issues arose early, such as the Liberal promise to instigate electoral reform and promises from the NDP and Liberals to improve relations with Indigenous Peoples. Others simmered due to partisan disagreement over existing political issues, such as the Keystone XL, Northern Gateway, Energy East, and Trans Mountain pipeline projects. In the narrative that follows, we discuss how the official campaign unfolded and note several issues that became important considerations for voters.

August saw three main events. First, there was a leaders' debate on 6 August 2015. With the low expectations that the Conservatives had set for him, Justin Trudeau did well simply by holding his own. Second, the second phase of the fraud trial of Conservative Senator Mike Duffy took place from 12–25 August. The main issue of the Duffy trial was whether Senator Duffy had committed fraud by designating himself a resident of PEI and claiming his living expenses in Ottawa, although he had lived in the capital for decades. Duffy was charged with fraud, breach of trust, and bribery. The Harper government was implicated when it was revealed that Harper's former chief of staff Nigel Wright had personally repaid Duffy's expenses, and questions were raised about the awareness and involvement of the prime minister. Finally, the Liberals shocked many by promising to run small deficits. Contrary to the expectation that parties promise balanced budgets as a sign of good economic management, the Liberals promised modest deficits to be able to fund infrastructure spending. The Conservatives were quick to ridicule Trudeau over the idea that small deficits would be possible with the Liberal election promises.

In September, Canada entered a technical recession, although the boost it should have been for the NDP and Liberals was countered by news that the economy was strong. On 16 September 2015, the NDP promised balanced budgets for four years, an interesting move in light of Trudeau's deficit promise, and one that seemed to indicate a switch in ideological ordering among the parties. Three leaders' debates also took place that month – one on the economy on 17 September, a French-language debate on 24 September (where Duceppe accused Mulcair of having different messages in French and English), and a foreign policy debate on 28 September. Trudeau also announced his government's plan to legalize marijuana, a stance supported by the NDP.

More importantly, two other events occurred in September that affected the campaign. First, on 3 September 2015, the world was shocked when a photo of the body of three-year-old Alan Kurdi, a Syrian refugee who died trying to travel from Turkey to Greece, was published. The photo made the refugee crisis headline news and prompted calls for action from Canadians. It eventually led to election promises about the number of refugees that each leader would bring into Canada by the end of the year – 25,000 for Trudeau, 10,000 for Mulcair, and an increase to existing plans for Harper. It also brought attention to Canada's commitments abroad and the fight against ISIS. Second, on 16 September 2015, the Conservatives promised to appeal a decision released by the Federal Court of Appeal the day before that upheld a decision that an earlier ban on face coverings during citizenship ceremonies was unlawful. The Liberals and NDP both opposed the ban while the Bloc supported the Conservatives' position.

October opened with another French-language debate and a Conservative promise to develop a "barbaric cultural practices" hotline. This promise, combined with the niqab issue raised the previous month, increased the role of identity politics in the election. On 5 October 2015, the Trans-Pacific Partnership (TPP) between Canada and eleven other nations became reality, an achievement for the Conservatives that the NDP opposed. Although trade has dominated election campaigns in the past, and despite the conflict over the TPP and CETA (Comprehensive Economic and Trade Agreement between Canada and the EU), trade was not a major issue for most Canadians.

In addition to the events discussed above, some third parties also made their opinions known throughout the campaign period. By far, unions and interest groups outspent individuals, but all third parties were limited by strict regulations and low spending limits. In total, nine individuals spent a combined total of $19,576 across Canada. More than half of that spending was concentrated in British Columbia (six people); none of the individual spending occurred in Quebec. Across Canada, unions outspent interest groups, but that comparison largely rests on the ratio and volume of spending in Ontario. Twenty unions spent almost $3 million in that province, compared to twenty-nine interest groups that spent a little over $1.6 million. Interest groups were more active than unions in British Columbia and Quebec, although with far less spending (less than $650,000 in British Columbia and slightly over $160,000 in Quebec).

THE DYNAMICS OF VOTE INTENTIONS DURING THE LONG CAMPAIGN[5]

With the backdrop of specific campaign events in mind, we now consider trends in vote intentions to get an overall picture of what mattered to voters (or at least what appears to have affected public opinion) and where. Figures 3.5 to 3.8 present the evolution of vote intentions during the campaign, starting 2 August 2015, and ending 18 October, the day before the election.[6]

Throughout the campaign, support for the Conservatives at the national level remained remarkably stable, hovering between 28 per cent and 33 per cent. The Conservatives reached their lowest point in late August, which could be related to the Mike Duffy trial. However, the drop in Conservative support seems to have been driven by opinion in Ontario, where Conservative vote intentions decreased from about 35 per cent before the appearance of Nigel Wright, former chief of staff to Prime Minister Harper, on 12 August 2015, to about

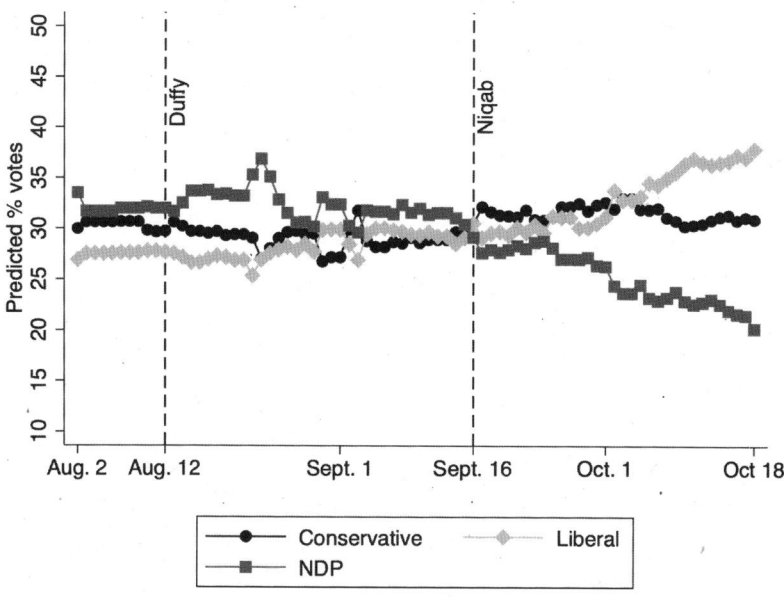

Figure 3.5 Campaign dynamics in Canada

30 per cent within a period of ten days. By mid-September, the Conservatives were back to about 33 per cent nationally, suggesting that the impact of the Duffy trial had gradually evaporated. For the rest of the campaign the Conservatives remained at slightly above 30 per cent support, with only minimal movement in Quebec as Conservative support increased slightly in the second half of September and modest gains in British Columbia throughout the campaign.

The picture was quite different for the Liberals. The party began the campaign with a support level around 27 per cent, but ended at 38 per cent, an increase of more than 10 points. There was a small increase in Liberal support in late August, which is most apparent in Ontario, where Liberal vote intentions increased from about 30 per cent to around 35 per cent. The explanation for this increase is not readily apparent, since it happened after the Duffy trial and before the Liberals promised to run deficits if elected (27 August). Nevertheless, Liberal support at the national level stayed at about 30 per cent for the whole month of September, before increasing more or less constantly throughout October. NDP support, for its part, stayed around 32 per cent from the start of the campaign to mid-September. This

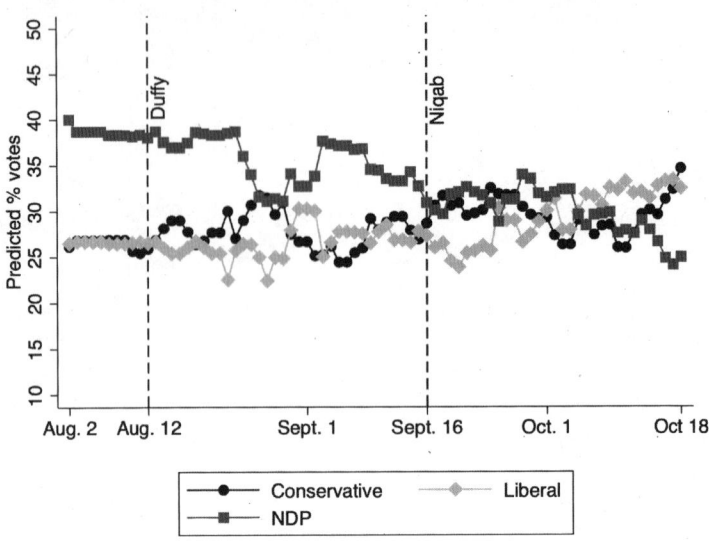

Figure 3.6 Campaign dynamics in British Columbia

was followed by a very gradual and constant decline throughout the last five weeks of the campaign.

One of the biggest questions of the campaign is whether the NDP decline was the result of the so-called niqab issue. The issue divided the parties and received considerable media attention (see chapter 6). Thomas Mulcair's stance in favour of allowing women to wear the niqab during citizenship oaths led to considerable opposition in Quebec, where the issue was most strongly debated and many supported the ban. If this issue caused Quebeckers to turn away from the NDP, and if the issue led, in turn, to the decline in voter support for that party, then the NDP drop should have been steepest in Quebec. Indeed, this seems to be the case: support for the NDP in Quebec went from about 43 per cent in mid-September to about 25 per cent by election day. The decline in NDP support in Ontario and British Columbia during the same period was more muted, about 8 points in each province.

In order to conclude that the niqab issue was the crucial factor in the NDP decline, we should see the decline starting earlier in Quebec than elsewhere. Again, this seems to be the case. The NDP's loss of support in Quebec started around 16 September, the day the Conservatives announced their appeal, and produced a drop of about

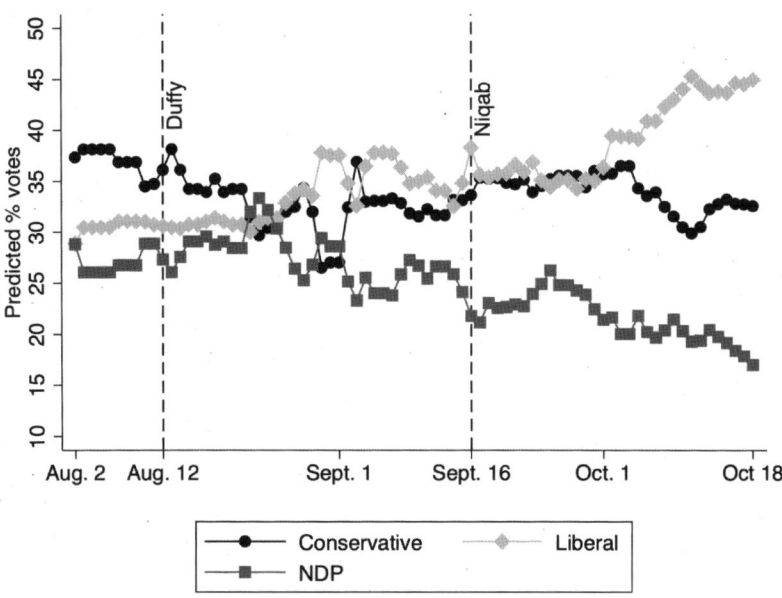

Figure 3.7 Campaign dynamics in Ontario

10 points for the NDP in late September.[7] The party's decline in Ontario and British Columbia, however, began in early October.

The evidence suggests that the niqab was an important factor in Quebec. Logically, that loss should have benefited the Conservatives and the Bloc, which both took anti-niqab stances. Yet we see little evidence of that for the Conservatives. The party that saw the biggest gain in Quebec during that period was the Bloc (from 14 per cent to 20 per cent), but the Conservatives seem to have gained only a few points (from 17 per cent to 20 per cent). As for the Liberals, their support appears not to have moved much during that period. These dynamics raise the question of why the niqab appeared to hurt the NDP but not the Liberals, even though they were on the same side of the issue. The impact of the niqab issue will be examined in greater depth in chapter 8.

One final issue to consider in light of these polling results is how to explain the NDP's continuous decline throughout October to the benefit of the Liberals. The fact that the movement is very gradual suggests that it is not due to any specific event, such as the niqab, but a symptom of something larger.

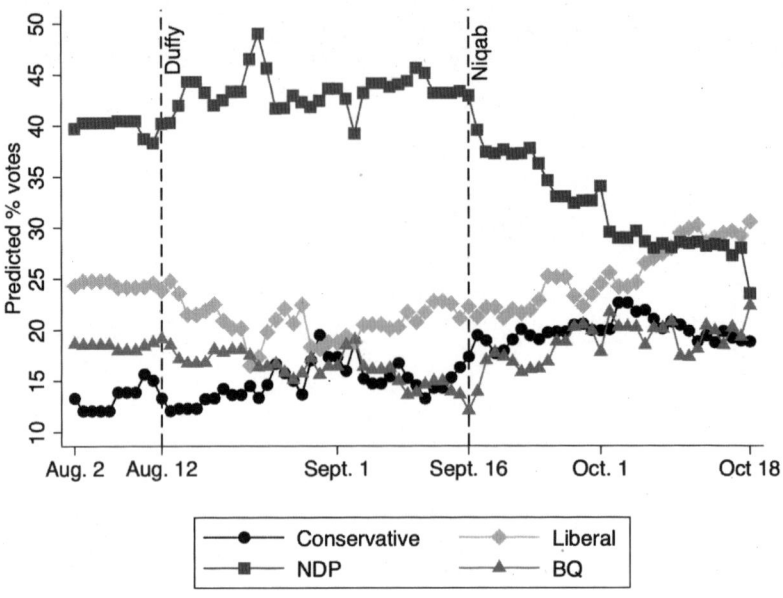

Figure 3.8 Campaign dynamics in Quebec

One interpretation is that many voters, especially in Ontario, abandoned the NDP for the Liberals as it became obvious that only the latter could defeat the Conservatives. We cannot directly test that interpretation with these data (see chapter 8 for a more elaborate discussion). We observe, however, that the Liberal gains in Ontario during the month of October came at the expense of the Conservatives as well as the NDP, which suggests an alternative explanation: that it was simply the image of the Liberal Party and of Justin Trudeau that was constantly improving in the last three weeks of the campaign. The explanation is even messier in British Columbia since, in that province, both the Conservatives and the Liberals appear to have made gains at the expense of the NDP. Furthermore, the polls started to show the Liberals systematically ahead of the NDP nationally as early as 21 September 2015.[8] But this shift in support varies provincially. The NDP descent in British Columbia began only in early October. We cannot rule out the possibility that it took some time for voters to take stock of the information provided by the polls, but two facts raise doubts about the validity of that interpretation: the evolution of vote intentions in Ontario and British Columbia was very gradual in October, and support for the Conservatives was not stable during that month.

At least one clear lesson can be drawn from our review of polling results: campaigns do matter. The Liberal Party started in third position and finished first, with a majority of the seats, while the party that was leading at the beginning of the campaign finished a distant third. What is even more striking is the fact that, with one possible exception, the campaign dynamics did not appear to be triggered by any specific campaign event. The Liberals appeared to be gaining ground and the NDP losing support every day throughout the month of October. We see no evidence that any of the debates had a noticeable impact, nor the Duffy trial (except temporarily in Ontario), nor the Liberal announcement about running deficits, nor the story about the drowned Syrian boy that prompted outrage and promises about refugees. It appears that there was just a late and steady movement toward the Liberals in October.

There is one exception, of course, and that is the effect of the niqab issue in Quebec. The evolution of the polls suggests that this hurt the NDP, and this is a reminder that symbolic issues have the potential to powerfully affect party support. Furthermore, the relationship between non-Muslim and Muslim Canadians remains a thorny issue that may have profound political consequences. At the same time, we must admit that it is not clear that this issue was the defining moment of the campaign, as many NDP strategists appear to believe. The impact on vote choice, as reported in chapter 8, is relatively modest.

This brings us to a final observation about provincial variation. We have seen that the evolution of party support between 2011 and 2015 was mostly similar across the three provinces, but the verdict is different with respect to campaign dynamics. The Duffy trial appears to have had some effect but only in Ontario, and the niqab issue only in Quebec. Meanwhile, support for the Conservatives seems to have increased in British Columbia and decreased in Ontario during the month of October. Polling evidence suggests that the campaign war was, to a great extent, a series of provincial battles.

CONCLUSION

The change in Liberal support from the 2011 election to the 2015 election was dramatic. The Liberals saw an increase of 20 percentage points between the two elections, a huge (and one might say unexpected) shift. Our analysis of polling results from 2011 to 2015 helps us to identify that the biggest shift occurred with the election of Justin Trudeau as the leader of the party, which led to a 10-point jump in Liberal vote intentions. The Liberals remained ahead in the polls for eighteen months. The trend was halted with the unprecedented provincial NDP victory in Alberta, which catapulted the federal NDP into first place and relegated the Liberals to third place. Knowing this, the eventual Liberal majority government outcome is all the more impressive. It took a long and successful campaign for the Liberals to re-establish themselves as the strongest party in the country.

It is tempting to attribute the Liberal victory to the personal popularity of Justin Trudeau. The crucial initial jump in Liberal support took place immediately after his election as leader of the party. Furthermore, the Liberal surge in the last weeks of the campaign was probably the result of Trudeau convincing many Canadians that he was ready to govern. But it would be misleading to give all the credit to one person. The Liberals were able to make big gains because of weaknesses among their competitors. Particularly important is that the Conservatives did not enjoy any honeymoon after their 2011 victory, and at no point in time were they able to go over their high-water mark of 33 per cent support. Clearly, the polling numbers show that many Canadians were dissatisfied, or at least fatigued, after almost ten years of Conservative government. The weakness of the NDP was perhaps less obvious at the beginning of the campaign, but the fact that the election of Mulcair produced only a modest and temporary boost to the party is notable. The fallout of the niqab issue, which hurt the NDP during the campaign rather than the Liberals, suggests that the NDP support in Quebec was still recent and fragile because NDP supporters in the province had not yet developed strong loyalties to the party. Focusing on leaders and national poll results also masks something that was going on at the constituency level. As Cross (2016a) has documented, Liberal Party efforts to rebuild their local associations were paying off with an increase in membership numbers, recruitment of high quality candidates, and an increase in the number of financial donors.

In the end, the 2015 election reproduced the traditional provincial differences in party support. The Conservatives remained very weak in Quebec, and Ontario remained the Liberal stronghold (outside Atlantic Canada). Some of the most dramatic (and surprising) aspects of the 2011 outcome – Conservative strength in British Columbia and NDP strength in Quebec – receded from the landscape. The outcome of the 2015 election seems to suggest that the 2011 election was an outlier: the traditional party system survived, and with it, the regional variation that Canadians have come to expect. Our goal is to better understand whether that variation is simply "Canadian" or whether it is the product of strategic decisions on the part of the parties and media. The polling results show that only certain events seemed to move vote intentions – the elections of Trudeau and Mulcair, the NDP victory in Alberta, the Duffy trial, and the niqab issue – but the dynamics in the provinces varied little with other campaign events. In the next chapters, we consider whether the parties and media should be implicated.

4

Names and Faces

Now that the scene has been set, we can move to the meat of this book: investigating the role of the parties, media, and voters as they relate to different provincial vote outcomes. In this chapter and the next, we focus on the parties and how they campaigned for votes. We start off at the ground level: understanding the campaigns waged by local candidates. While most media attention is on the national level campaign, it is important to remember that there were 338 discrete campaigns waged at the local level. Canada's single-member plurality electoral system dictates that winning an election requires success in a plurality of these discrete contests.[1] Each contest has a different cast of candidates, voters, and local circumstances. Our interest here is in how these local campaigns relate to the national campaigns in terms of emphasis on issues, party, and personality, and how they differ from one another. In doing so, we continue our focus on differences among the provinces. If local candidates and their supporters are all working from the same script, we should find little difference in terms of the issue emphasis or localization/personalization of constituency campaigns. However, if voters are receiving different messages in different regions of the country, it is quite plausible that these are delivered through the constituency-level campaigns.[2]

As noted in previous chapters, over the course of the past two decades, researchers have commented on the regionalization of Canada's electoral politics. The argument, distilled to its core, is that an era of pan-Canadian politics, characterized by the nationalizing effects of television and a preoccupation with national policy, came to an end circa 1990 and was replaced by regionally defined politics (Carty 1992; Carty, Cross, and Young 2000). As Young and Archer

(2002, 1) suggest, "Canada's party system lost its pan-Canadian veneer in the 1990s." The new party system was characterized by the rise of Reform and the Bloc Québécois, each with significant electoral strength in particular regions of the country. The result of the change was a series of elections in which different parties were the main players in different provinces characterized by an "increasingly differentiated pattern of regional political arrangement" (Young and Archer 2002, 3). One consequence of this was that parties no longer crafted pan-Canadian messages but, rather, tailored their messages and strategies to the regions where they were competing and to the different opposition they faced in each. As Cross suggested, "The parties do not enter the campaign prepared to engage in a general dialogue with all Canadians. Instead, they wish to pursue a focused dialogue with selected voters in selected ridings" (Cross 2002b, 123).

Given the subsequent changes to the party system, on its surface the 2015 campaign more closely resembled the pre-1990 period than the intervening elections. Competition across the country was once again dominated by the three national parties, with the Bloc Québécois maintaining some support in Francophone Quebec but reduced to a shell of its former self. Of course, as we saw in the previous chapter, the parties did not enter the election in their usual positions – the NDP was riding high in the polls and appeared poised to finally have a real shot at forming government. Nonetheless, the outcome reproduced dynamics that would have seemed normal to political observers in the mid-1980s.

What looked like a revival of the pan-Canadian era at the aggregate level could mask substantial variation on the ground. We do not know, for example, the degree to which the parties ran national campaigns or whether they pursued different strategies in different provinces. Knowing this is crucial to our research objective – if the parties had a national strategy that did not vary, then the case for voter preferences shaping the provincial variation in outcomes is much stronger. To evaluate this, we are particularly interested in whether the content of the parties' communication with voters varied by region. And, within the regions, was there consistency between the messages of the central campaigns and those of the parties' local candidates?

This chapter focuses on the local campaigns organized and run by candidates and their supporters. For the most part, candidates have significant discretion as to how they orchestrate their local efforts and the messages they convey to voters. In their study of the 2008 federal election, Cross and Young (2015) found a significant degree of personalization in local campaigns. In this chapter, we are interested in whether the relationship between local and national campaigns varies regionally and in the extent to which local candidates personalize or localize their campaign, thereby distinguishing it from that of their party, its leader, and local campaigns in other regions. We make use of a survey of federal candidates in each of our three provinces to provide a first-hand understanding of what the candidates did and did not do.[3] In chapter 5 we move on to examine the degree of regionalization of the parties' central campaign efforts and the extent to which these parallel their candidates' efforts on the ground.

FEDERAL-PROVINCIAL PARTY RELATIONS

As citizens of a multi-level polity, Canadians experience both provincial and federal elections, but in contrast to many federal states, there is asymmetry between the provincial and federal party systems (for more details, see chapter 1). Furthermore, the relationship between the two varies across the provinces. While some have argued that provincial and federal politics exist in two separate worlds (see Blake 1985), it will become clear from the discussion in this chapter that provincial political dynamics can influence federal outcomes.[4] Most of the existing literature on this subject concerns organizational and personnel ties between the federal and provincial parties and largely ignores the effect that one party system may have on the other. The latter is the focus of our interest.

It is not unheard of for provincial politicians to participate in federal campaigns. Perhaps the most prominent example in recent elections was Newfoundland and Labrador's Premier Danny Williams campaigning aggressively against the Harper Conservatives in the 2008 federal election (MacCharles 2008). Despite being a Progressive Conservative, the premier believed the re-election of the Harper government to be antithetical to his province's needs. While it is impossible to isolate the effect of this provincial intervention on the federal vote, it is widely credited as being a significant factor in the federal Conservatives' vote share in the province dropping from 42.7 per cent in the previous election, just two years earlier, to 16.5 per cent, while also losing all their seats in the province. This clearly was a provincial anomaly: the Conservatives' vote and seat shares increased in the remainder of the country.

While there was no such dramatic provincial involvement in the 2015 election, Ontario Liberal Premier Kathleen Wynne did campaign vigorously on behalf of her federal counterparts to a degree that was unprecedented in the province in recent decades (see Reevely 2015). Writing about Wynne's federal campaign interventions, Jeffrey (2016, 82) concludes that, "Justin Trudeau would owe at least some of his success to his provincial counterpart." The federal Conservatives were clearly aware of the potential of Wynne's involvement, as they responded by directly criticizing the provincial Liberals, running television advertisements arguing that the federal Liberals were "the same Liberals who crippled Ontario under a mountain of debt, taxes and wasteful spending" (Ellis 2016, 42–3).

That provincial politics can influence federal campaigns is also evident in the views of candidates in the 2015 election. Consistent with the polling evidence concerning the impact of the NDP victory in Alberta (chapter 3), only one-third of candidates surveyed believed that provincial politics has no effect. The degree of the effect, however, varies among the provinces. Not surprisingly, given the symmetry in terms of cross-level party relations in the province, candidates in Ontario were the most likely to report that provincial politics had an effect on their election result (see table 4.1). Almost three-quarters of the candidates in Ontario believed there is a provincial effect compared with fewer than six in ten in British Columbia and Quebec. Similarly, half of Ontario candidates reported that the most recent provincial election had an impact on their 2015 campaign result, again compared with four in ten in British Columbia and three in ten in Quebec. These data suggest that a full understanding of federal elections requires that some attention be paid to the political context at the provincial level.

The variance in, and the potential significance of, the interplay between the provincial and federal parties is also evident at the campaign and organizational levels. One in five federal Ontario candidates reported that a provincial party leader campaigned for them in 2015, contrasted with fewer than one in ten candidates in the other two provinces. Similarly, 35 per cent of Ontario candidates reported that an elected member of the provincial legislature campaigned for them, compared with 25 per cent of British Columbia candidates and only 15 per cent of those running in Quebec.

In British Columbia, where the federal and provincial NDP have significant strength and at times relatively close ties, we can observe

Table 4.1
Importance of provincial politics to federal campaign

	In your experience how important were provincial politics to the success of your campaign?			
	Canada	Ontario	British Columbia	Quebec
very (%)	11.6	10.9	0	6.7
somewhat (%)	28.4	31.5	27.3	18.3
a little (%)	27.4	29.3	29.5	33.3
not at all (%)	32.7	28.3	43.2	41.7
N	303	92	44	60
	Did the most recent provincial election results impact on your campaign results?			
	Canada	Ontario	British Columbia	Quebec
Yes (%)	45.3	49.5	39.5	31.7
N	302	93	43	60

the effect of provincial party dynamics on the federal campaign. Sixty per cent of federal NDP candidates in the province reported that a member of the provincial legislature campaigned for them, ten times higher than the number for any other party in the province and 50 per cent higher than for the party in Ontario. However, only 13 per cent of these same candidates reported having the provincial party leader campaign for them (contrasted with 23 per cent of the party's Ontario candidates). This probably reflects the internal turmoil within the provincial party at the time. After a disastrous provincial election result in 2013, the party acclaimed a new leader in 2014 who was not yet well-known in the province and had little political capital to offer federal candidates. This illustrates how shifting dynamics in provincial politics can influence federal campaigns.

That NDP candidates received proportionately greater provincial support is evidenced by the finding that 87 per cent of the party's British Columbia candidates reported having received organizational assistance from their local provincial party, compared to 20 per cent for the Liberals, and none for the Conservatives. Similar patterns emerge in Ontario where six in ten New Democrats, four in ten Liberals, but only one-quarter of Conservatives reported having received provincial party organizational assistance. These differences, both cross-party and interprovincial, reflect both the current dynamics of provincial politics and the degree of formal organizational connections between parties at the two levels (see Pruysers 2014, 2015).

The important take-away from this discussion is that federal elections are not held in a vacuum, completely removed from provincial politics. The relationship between the two levels differs both among the provinces and over time. For decades, in the twentieth century, Ontario voters supported Progressive Conservatives provincially while regularly electing large numbers of federal Liberals. Many commentators suggested this was at least partially a strategic decision by voters to keep a balance between the two levels. Turning this around in 2015, Wynne and Trudeau argued that having Liberals in power at both levels would result in stronger ties and a better relationship between Queen's Park and Ottawa. Wynne campaigned aggressively for the Liberals and was a target of Conservative advertisements in the province. While we cannot be certain of the effect, candidates reported that provincial politics and recent campaigns do influence the results of federal elections. This suggests that whatever the nature of the parties' campaigns themselves, there are different federal campaign dynamics at play across the country. For example, one of the issues of paramount importance to Wynne was federal government cooperation in an expansion of Ontario's public pension plan, an issue with little or no saliency in Quebec and British Columbia. To the extent that voters associated her with the federal campaign, this issue may have factored into federal vote choice, even if the federal parties themselves never mentioned it. The federal nature of Canadian politics, enhanced by the differing provincial party systems, thus contributes to creating a regional dimension to federal elections.

When federal candidates reported that recent provincial elections had an impact on their vote result, this effect would usually be unique to their province, as only the most extraordinary provincial election resonates elsewhere in the country. As discussed in the previous chapter, however, an exception would appear to be the 2015 Alberta election won by the New Democrats. While this surprising result seemed to provide a boost to NDP polling numbers across the country, the effect seems to have been short-lived (outside of Alberta and BC where the NDP was on the rise) and to have waned by the time of the vote in the 2015 federal election (see McGrane 2016).

LOCAL CAMPAIGN FOCUS

While Canadian federal election campaigns are often spoken about as unitary events, they are, as suggested above, in reality a collection of 338 separate contests. Ballots differ in each electoral district, listing only the names of the local candidates and their party affiliation. Votes are counted separately within each district: the local candidate with the most votes is elected. One result of this is vibrant local campaigns largely organized and orchestrated by the local candidates and their bands of local supporters (Carty and Eagles 2005, Cross 2016a). While the national parties organize a campaign largely built around their leader and attempt to create party brands, local campaigns make a series of independent judgments regarding their campaign focus. The question is how these decisions do, or do not, differentiate the local campaign from that run by the national party, and in particular whether this varies across provinces. In other words, are the local campaigns in one region delivering messages different from those received by voters in other regions?

Party versus Candidate Focus

Two important decisions are the relative weight the local candidate will give to her political party versus to herself and the degree to which the local campaign will focus on the party leader. Our candidate survey data indicate that interparty differences in the relative emphasis on the leader were greater than intraparty regional differences. Conservative candidates placed significantly less emphasis on Harper in their local campaigns than did Liberal candidates on Trudeau and New Democrats on Mulcair. This almost certainly is a reflection of public opinion polling throughout the campaign. Although not obvious from the polling data in chapter 2, Harper regularly trailed the other leaders by as many as 20 percentage points in terms of job approval (see, for example, Forum 2015b). Thus, it is not surprising that on a zero to ten scale, where ten represents placing as much emphasis on the leader as possible, Conservative candidates report a mean score of 4.3, compared with 6.1 for New Democrats, 6.7 for Liberal candidates, and 7.6 for the Bloc. The high number for the Bloc is consistent with their weak organizational strength at the local level (the party's local associations had significantly atrophied in the period following its 2011 electoral drubbing) and the return of their popular leader, Gilles Duceppe.

While voter evaluations of the party leaders did vary somewhat from province to province (see chapter 8), these are not systematically reflected in the degree of emphasis candidates placed on their leader. Harper's approval with voters did not vary significantly by province, nor did the degree to which candidates highlighted him in their campaigns. However, there are regional differences for the other leaders. For example, as shown in table 4.2, Liberal candidates in Quebec placed a significantly greater focus on Trudeau than did candidates in Ontario and British Columbia. Similarly, NDP candidates in Ontario emphasized Mulcair in their campaigns to a markedly greater degree than did their colleagues in Quebec and British Columbia.

Interestingly, these strategic decisions, at the provincial level, do not seem to match up with popular support for the leaders in the opinion polls. Considering voter evaluations of the leaders around the campaign midpoint (mid-September), Trudeau's approval ratings were 38 per cent in Quebec, 46 per cent in Ontario, and 50 per cent in British Columbia (Forum 2015b). Yet, it was Liberal candidates in Quebec who placed the greatest emphasis on the leader. Mulcair had his strongest ratings in Quebec with 57 per cent approval compared with 45 per cent in Ontario and 49 per cent in British Columbia, yet NDP candidates in Ontario reported focusing on the leader to a greater extent.

Local candidates also differed in terms of the emphasis they chose to place on themselves as opposed to their party. Here we do find significant differences both among and within parties. Overall, NDP candidates placed greater emphasis on their party affiliation than did their opponents. This is consistent with findings from earlier elections and to a certain extent probably reflects the ideological nature of the party (Cross and Young 2015; Cross and Young 2002). In 2015, this was buttressed by the party's strong position in opinion polls up to the midpoint of the campaign. As shown in table 4.3, again on a zero to ten scale, with ten representing full emphasis on the party and zero on the candidate, New Democrats fall on the party side of the spectrum with an overall mean of 5.7, compared with 5.3 for the Liberals and 4.9 for the Conservatives. The lower Conservative score probably reflects the weakness of the party brand in 2015. The Bloc is again an outlier, at 8.0, reflecting its extreme campaign reliance on the leader and party brand as opposed to local organizational strength.

There appears to be a relationship between the local candidates' relative emphasis on their party and their view as to how the last provincial election impacted their electoral chances. For example, New Democrats were least likely to focus on the party brand in British Columbia where 53 per cent of their candidates believed the recent provincial election, in which the party fared surprisingly poorly, hurt

Table 4.2
Degree of emphasis local candidates placed on their party leader (mean values)

	Canada	Ontario	Quebec	British Columbia
Conservatives	4.3 (120)	4.4 (38)	4.6 (21)	4.4 (18)
Liberals	6.7 (71)	6.3 (24)	7.8 (12)	6.5 (10)
New Democrats	6.1 (104)	7.2 (31)	6.3 (19)	6.1 (16)
Bloc Québécois			7.6 (9)	

Note: Cells report mean values on a 0 to 10 scale, where 10 represents "as much as possible" and 0 represents "as little as possible." The number of respondents is reported in parentheses.

Table 4.3
Degree of emphasis local candidates placed on their party brand relative to themselves (mean values)

	Canada	Ontario	Quebec	British Columbia
Conservatives	4.9 (120)	4.7 (37)	4.9 (21)	5.2 (18)
Liberals	5.3 (71)	5.0 (24)	6.3 (12)	4.2 (10)
New Democrats	5.7 (105)	6.5 (31)	5.1 (20)	5.0 (16)
Bloc Québécois			8.0 (9)	

Note: Cells report mean values on a 0 to 10 scale, where 10 represents the party and 0 represents the local candidate. The number of respondents is reported in parentheses.

their chances for victory. This contrasts with only 26 per cent of Ontario New Democrats sharing that sentiment. Similarly, Conservative candidates focused more strongly on their party in British Columbia where only 6 per cent believed the provincial election was a drag on their chances, contrasted with one-quarter of their candidates in Ontario where the party badly lost the 2014 election that many had predicted it would win. And, for the Liberals, the strong focus on the party in Quebec may in part reflect the fact that fewer than one in five candidates felt the most recent provincial election hurt their chances contrasted with four in ten Liberals in British Columbia and Ontario (this, in turn, could be a product of the disconnect and ideological distance between the PLQ and the federal Liberals.) That Liberals were the most likely to focus on the party in Quebec and were least likely to do so in British Columbia is also not surprising given that the federal Liberal Party has traditionally been weak in British Columbia, and there is little transfer in terms of support between the provincial and federal parties. For the Conservatives, only in British Columbia did candidates, on average, focus more on the party than on themselves.

Clearly, our analysis reveals that across all parties, local campaigns in the three provinces differed from one another in terms of the relative focus on the party. Furthermore, this appears to be largely a strategic decision made by local candidates reflecting their perception of the local strength of the party brand. The implication is that not all voters experienced the campaign the same way. Some voters received campaign communications focused on a party label and leader, while others received more local, candidate-centred appeals.

CAMPAIGN ISSUE EMPHASIS

Local candidates also make decisions regarding the issues on which they wish to communicate with voters. One decision is whether to stick to the policy script of the national campaign or to highlight other issues that might be specific to their local electorate or to their province. Consistent with earlier studies, a majority of candidates in 2015 reported that they did deviate from their party's national policy emphasis by also highlighting local and provincial issues (Cross and Young 2015). With little variance among parties, eight in ten candidates reported that they raised issues during their campaign that were specific to their province, and a similar number reported raising issues of local concern that were not part of the national campaign. This, of course, means that different issues were highlighted by candidates in different parts of the country. In fact, fostering a local campaign issue focus appears to be something of a strategy of the national campaigns. Approximately six in ten candidates in all three parties reported that they received training or advice on campaign messaging and strategy from their party that was specific to their province or region. Campaigning to appeal on both national and local issues accords with the two-dimensional strategy outlined in chapter 2 (Elias et al. 2015). Although each *party* is competing nationally, voters are electing *individual* members of Parliament to represent their local constituency. This raises the possibility that voters in different regions are receiving somewhat different messages from candidates who share the same party label.

This local and provincial focus does not happen to the same extent, however, in all parts of the country. Candidates in the province of

Ontario were significantly less likely to engage in these activities than were their counterparts in British Columbia and Quebec. This seems consistent with the notion that Ontario traditionally has had the weakest distinct political identity and tends to mirror the federal system (Cross et al. 2015). By contrast, federal election campaigns in Quebec have long been distinct from the rest of Canada in terms of campaign discourse and advertising. To a lesser degree, campaigns in Western and Atlantic Canada have typically taken on a more regional cast. These trends are apparent in the 2015 election.

As illustrated in table 4.4, approximately three-quarters of candidates in British Columbia and Quebec reported having received region-specific campaign training compared to slightly more than half of Ontario candidates. Nine in ten Quebec candidates raised issues specific to their province compared to three-quarters of British Columbia candidates and two-thirds of their Ontario counterparts. Similarly, close to nine in ten Quebec and British Columbia candidates raised issues not broached by the national campaign, compared with three-quarters of Ontario candidates. These data illustrate the regional nature of federal campaigns across the country, with candidates raising unique provincial and local issues that are not part of the national discourse and that, by definition, almost certainly differ from the issues raised by local candidates in other parts of the country. While occurring everywhere, this focus on regional issues is strongest in Quebec and significantly weaker in Ontario.

LOCAL CANDIDATES' POLICY VIEWS

While considering the extent to which local campaigns differ from their national counterparts, and the degree to which they vary regionally, it is also worth considering the importance and nature of local candidates' policy views in relation to their campaign efforts. The data in table 4.4 suggest that candidates routinely raised issues of importance to their province and local community that were distinct from those raised by the national campaigns. These might not be contrary to the positions staked out nationally, but they do add an additional, local dimension to the local campaign. In this section, we build on this finding to consider whether candidates' *personal* policy views were important in securing their party's nomination and how often they discussed them with voters during the general election campaign. Again, these personal policy views may not be contrary to

Table 4.4
Local candidate emphasis on provincial and local issues (per cent engaging in each activity)

	Canada	Quebec	Ontario	British Columbia
Raised issues specific to their province	80.2 (283)	87.9 (58)	67.1 (85)	76.3 (38)
Raised local issues not raised by national campaign	80.1 (307)	88.5 (61)	77.4 (93)	86.4 (44)
Received regional/provincial specific training on strategy and campaign messaging	63.5 (307)	75.4 (61)	53.8 (93)	70.5 (44)

Note: The number of respondents is reported in parentheses.

the party's position, but this type of personalized campaigning has the potential to introduce significant variation within a party. We thus consider the general ideological disposition of candidates to see how these views might differ from their party's positions and whether this varies by province.

Party nominations in Canada largely take place at the local level. Would-be candidates recruit their personal supporters to join the party and, together with traditionally relatively small numbers of existing party members, these local activists choose the parties' candidates. The rules for candidate selection are consistent across the country with the national parties setting the regulatory framework (Pruysers and Cross 2016). While most observers point to candidates' recruiting capacity and their ties to civil society groups as key factors in securing a nomination (Carty 1991), less attention is paid to the role policy positions may play (for an exception, see Cross 2004, 2002a).

Candidates in all three major parties reported that their policy views were important to their obtaining their party's local nomination for the 2015 campaign. As illustrated in table 4.5, more than four in ten candidates across the country reported that their policy views were very important, and fewer than one in ten reported they were not at all important. While candidates' views were important in all three provinces under investigation, the pattern revealed above regarding Quebec continues as half of the respondents in this province said their views were very important compared to fewer than four in ten in British Columbia and Ontario. And, it is again in Ontario where candidate-distinct views appeared to be of least significance, suggesting greater consistency with the national campaign than in the other provinces.

Table 4.5
Importance of policy views to securing party nomination (percentages reported)

How important were YOUR policy views to securing your party's nomination?				
	Canada	Ontario	Quebec	British Columbia
Very	43.6	34.9	50.8	39.5
Somewhat/a little	47.8	53.0	42.4	55.8
Not at all	8.7	12.0	6.8	4.7
N	289	83	59	43

That candidates believe their policy views were important to their securing the nomination is a significant finding as it confirms two things. First, candidates are comfortable communicating their personal views during the nomination campaign, regardless of their congruence with the federal party. Second, candidates take policy positions that are likely to be part of their general election campaign. To test how frequently candidates communicated about their own policy views, we asked them how often these came up when canvassing general election voters. As illustrated in table 4.6, more than one-third of candidates reported this occurred frequently or very frequently, with only one-quarter responding that their views were rarely or never discussed. Taken together, these data suggest that candidates often set out their own policy views during nomination campaigns and discuss them with voters during the general election.

Interestingly, once again there is a divide between Quebec and the other provinces. Candidates in Quebec reported discussing their personal views with voters significantly more often than did those in other provinces. Almost one-quarter of Quebec candidates reported doing so very frequently compared with fewer than one in ten in British Columbia and Ontario, and this is consistent for all of the parties competing in these three provinces.

Given that candidates were regularly talking with voters about their personal policy views, it is important to consider how these views compared with their party's candidates in other provinces and with their party brand generally. As a proxy for candidates' views on particular issues, we consider their general ideological position. Candidates were asked to place themselves and their party on an 11-point scale with zero representing far left and ten far right. The results in table 4.7 suggest that the ideological disposition of candidates within parties

Table 4.6
Communication of policy views during voter canvassing (percentages reported)

| | How often did YOUR (as opposed to your party's) policy views come up when you were canvassing voters? | | | |
	Canada	Ontario	Quebec	British Columbia
Very frequently	11.6	6.5	23.0	9.1
Frequently	25.7	26.9	19.7	· 25.0
Occasionally	38.3	34.4	34.4	38.6
Rarely	22.4	30.1	18.0	25.0
Never	2.0	2.2	4.9	2.3
N	303	93	61	44

Table 4.7
Left-right ideological placements of candidates and their parties (mean values)

| | Where do you place your political views? | | | |
	Canada	Ontario	Quebec	British Columbia
Conservatives	7.2 (114)	7.1 (38)	7.7 (22)	7.3 (18)
Liberals	4.3 (67)	4.1 (24)	4.9 (12)	4.0 (10)
New Democrats	2.6 (97)	2.3 (31)	2.9 (19)	2.8 (16)
Bloc Québécois			3.3 (7)	
	Where do you place your party?			
	Canada	Ontario	Quebec	British Columbia
Conservatives	7.7 (113)	7.8 (38)	8.2 (22)	7.6 (18)
Liberals	4.3 (67)	4.0 (24)	4.6 (12)	4.6 (10)
New Democrats	3.4 (97)	3.3 (31)	4.0 (20)	3.7 (15)
Bloc Québécois			3.9 (7)	

Note: Cells report mean values on a 0 to 10 scale, where 0 represents the most left and 10 represents the most right. The number of respondents is reported in parentheses.

did not differ dramatically by province though, in each case, there is one group of provincial candidates who did place themselves at a noticeably different point on the scale than their out of province colleagues. The largest difference is for Liberal candidates from Quebec, who placed themselves almost a full point to the right of their British Columbia and Ontario counterparts (though still slightly to the left of the scale's midpoint). Ontario New Democrats were to the left of their British Columbia and Quebec colleagues, and Quebec

Conservatives were to the right of candidates from the other provinces. This suggests that in their discussions with voters, these candidates articulated policy positions somewhat distinct from those discussed by their fellow candidates in other parts of the country.

Conservative candidates viewed their party as being a half point to the right of themselves. Liberals placed their party at the same point as themselves. The most significant difference is with New Democratic candidates who, on average, placed themselves almost a full point to the left of their party. This likely reflects the shift toward the centre taken by the national campaign in 2015. This finding suggests that at least for the Conservative and New Democratic parties, the two most ideological parties, there were significant differences in left/right policy perspectives between candidates and their parties. Further, it suggests that when Conservative and NDP candidates were talking to voters about their personal policy views and perhaps when highlighting other issues that were not part of the national campaign, the conversations are likely to have veered away from the message delivered by the party and, to some extent, varied among provinces.

Local Campaign Policy Emphasis

We can also consider the relative importance of issues in local campaigns across the country. While we find some regional differences in candidates' views when it comes to which issues were of local importance, there is significant cross-provincial consistency. Candidates were asked to rank six issue topics by importance to their local campaigns. In all three parties, the economy and leadership were ranked as the two most important issues nationally and no lower than third in any of the three provinces we focus on. This is accompanied by some notable interparty differences. For example, social programs were ranked as least important by Conservative candidates, while they were third in importance for Liberal and NDP candidates. Refugee policy was ranked last, in terms of campaign importance, for candidates of these two parties, while it was ranked fourth for Conservatives.

As illustrated in table 4.8, there is considerable interprovincial consistency within parties. For Conservatives, the ordinal ranking for five of the six issues never varies by more than one placement. The economy and leadership were always ranked first or second, the issue of taxes was consistently third, refugee policy was either fourth or fifth, and social programs were consistently fifth or sixth. Only government

Table 4.8
Candidates' ranking of relative issue importance in their local campaign

	Economy	Leadership	Taxes	Refugee policy	Government corruption	Social programs
CONSERVATIVES (110)						
Canada	2	1	3	4	5	6
Quebec	1	2	3	4	6	5
British Columbia	2	1	3	5	4	6
Ontario	1	2	3	4	5	6
LIBERALS (64)						
Canada	1	2	4	6	5	3
Quebec	1	3	4	5	6	2
British Columbia	1	2	5	6	3 (tie)	3 (tie)
Ontario	1	2	3	6	5	4
NEW DEMOCRATS (94)						
Canada	1	2	4	6	5	3
Quebec	2	1	5	6	3 (tie)	3 (tie)
British Columbia	1	2	5	6	4	3
Ontario	1	2	5	6	4	3

Note: Rankings are by province separately for each party.

corruption shows modest variance ranking fourth in British Columbia, fifth in Ontario, and sixth in Quebec. The fact that Conservative candidates in Quebec ranked this issue last suggests there was little residue of the Chrétien-era corruption allegations that rocked the Liberal Party in the province for most of the past decade.

While still significant, there is less interprovincial consistency for the Liberals. The economy was ranked the most important issue in all three provinces, and leadership ranked second or a close third. There is a difference for social programs with the issue ranking second in Quebec, third in British Columbia, and fourth in Ontario. This may well reflect the party's attempt to attract the left-leaning Quebec voters who had voted for the NDP in 2011. There is also some variance in the relative importance of tax policy, with the issue ranking third in Ontario, fourth in Quebec, and fifth in British Columbia. The government corruption issue also ranges from third in importance in British Columbia to fifth in Ontario and sixth in Quebec. The greater range among Liberals probably reflects their tradition of being a brokerage party and thus more ideologically flexible than their opponents (Carty 2015, Carty and Cross 2010), which should make it easier for candidates to highlight different issues and perhaps stake out distinct policy positions.

We find the greatest consistency within the NDP, which probably reflects the stronger ideological cast of the party. The economy, leadership, and social programs are the top three issues in all regions followed by government corruption, taxes, and refugee policy in that order, in all three provinces.

CONCLUSION

Consistent with the imperatives of the single-member plurality electoral system, Canadian elections take place at two levels: the national campaigns waged centrally by the party and the local campaigns largely organized and orchestrated by constituency candidates and their bands of supporters. Both of these campaigns take place in a federal state with largely distinct party systems at the provincial and national levels. To best understand the types of local campaigns waged in the 2015 election, we went right to the source – a survey of the candidates themselves. The candidate data reviewed above suggest that local campaigns do vary, in terms of issue and brand focus, both from one another and from the national campaigns, and that some of this variance is regionally based. This does not appear to be a source of significant tension between the two levels, as evidenced by the fact that a significant number of local candidates reported receiving regionally tailored campaign training and advice from their central party. Parties acknowledge that electoral success requires winning a plurality of votes in a plurality of these local contests and accordingly give their candidates significant leeway in crafting their local campaigns. This is consistent with the stratarchical nature of party organization that Carty (2002, 2004) and Cross (2006, 2016b) have identified as a key feature of party organization in Canada (see chapter 2).

Thus, the results from this chapter suggest that the campaigns experienced by voters can vary substantially across provinces. The fact that parties are focused on winning, and thus integrate region-specific campaigning into their strategies, opens up the possibility that election campaigns are different across the country. Parties allow, and perhaps even encourage, their constituency candidates to emphasize issues with local and regional saliency. This necessarily results in voters in different regions receiving somewhat different campaign messages. This should not be overstated, however, as the data clearly suggest that candidates across our provinces prioritized similar policy areas in their campaign communications.

As already discussed, provincial political competition varies substantially, with parties of the same name having different levels of success and also different relationships with the federal parties. This variation seems to be echoed in the ground campaigns waged in the 338 ridings across the country. Perhaps, then, the variation in federal election outcomes by province simply reflects party strategies.

5

Multi-Pronged Attacks?

In a federal election, the parties' campaigns are fought at two separate levels. In the previous chapter, we viewed the election through the prism of the local campaigns waged in the 338 geographically based electoral districts. In this chapter, we shift our focus to the national campaigns. That is, the campaigns waged by the parties' national offices and their leaders. Here, we are interested in determining whether the national effort (parties' messages and allocation of their campaign resources) is tailored to regional sensitivities. We saw in chapter 4 that many candidates reported receiving guidance on how to tailor their campaigns to address local and regional concerns. Is there evidence of similar regional sensitivity at the national level? Additionally, we consider whether the focus of the national campaigns matches that of their local candidates in terms of issue focus.

Three types of data are used in this chapter to provide a thorough evaluation of our research question. First, we examine the party leaders' tours to consider where they campaigned and which issues they focused on. Carty and Eagles (2005, 99) refer to leaders' tours as being "at the centre" of the parties' campaigns, and they find a significant, though modest, boost to the electoral fortunes of candidates whose leaders visit their riding during the campaign[1]. Not surprisingly, leaders' tours are highly scripted events (Flanagan 2010). Parties send their leaders to areas of the country where they believe the attention generated by the visit will result in an electoral premium leading to victory in the local constituencies. Locales are also chosen to bring attention to particular issues. As Cross et al. (2015, 74) note: "In successful campaigns, these events are carefully selected and scripted to highlight the issues that a party wishes to focus voter attention on with the knowledge that much of the media's campaign coverage focuses on the leader's daily activity" (see also, Mughan 2000; Poguntke and Webb 2005; and Garzia 2011). Carty and Eagles (2005, 100) also note that leaders' tours offer one of the best opportunities in which "a party's national and electronic-air campaign intersects with and reinforces the constituency-level ground war waged by partisan activists at the grassroots."

That the leader's tour remains a key component of each party's campaign strategy is evident from the amount of resources they expend on them. As illustrated in table 5.1, the parties spend approximately one-sixth of their entire election budget on the tour. This is the second largest amount after the combined total for television and radio advertisements.

We were able to track the leaders' whereabouts through most days of the election campaign. Given that this was the longest campaign in recent history and was called unexpectedly early, it is perhaps not surprising that each leader spent some days away from the campaign trail. We tracked the leaders' activities in several ways. First, the page on the CBC website "Map: Tracking the Leaders" (www.cbc.ca/news/multimedia/map-tracking-the-leaders-1.3081740) was reviewed. This tool indicates the provinces visited by the leaders for most days of the campaign. A general online search of news sources for each day resulted in identification of additional campaign stops. It was more challenging to identify the topic of the leaders' comments at each stop. Again, we used the CBC site and supplemented this with newspaper searches. The *Toronto Star* was systematically searched for each day of the campaign and, when a leader was in British Columbia, this was supplemented by a search of that day's *Vancouver Sun;* similarly, stories in the *Montreal Gazette* were reviewed for days the leader was in Quebec and the *Ottawa Citizen* for visits to Ontario. When these sources turned up no information regarding the substance of a particular campaign stop, a more general online search was conducted, and information was occasionally found, primarily from the *Huffington Post* and CBC *News.* In all, we were able to track Trudeau's activities for sixty-four days, Harper's for fifty-seven, and Mulcair's for sixty. On most of the other days, we were able to find news accounts reporting that the leader was not campaigning. We were also able to find news accounts of the leaders' remarks for most of their public events. Of course, we are limited to considering the content of their remarks as reported by the media. It is quite likely that these

Table 5.1
Amount spent by the major parties on 2015 leaders' tours

	Amount spent on tour in Canadian $	Amount spent on tour as % of total election expenses
Liberals	7,014,377	16.3
Conservatives	7,035,929	16.8
New Democrats	5,893,666	19.8

Note: Data from parties' disclosure reports to Elections Canada.

capture the principal content of what was said but not necessarily every issue that was mentioned. There is, however, no reason to believe that the media would not report on the events objectively (particularly by region, which is our primary concern). While the media might be tempted to bias election coverage to appeal to regional interests (see chapter 6), we expect such tailoring would have to do with emphasis in analyses and opinion pieces rather than coverage of actual events.

Second, we analyze the parties' press releases, again to examine the issues that were emphasized and the extent to which they referenced specific regions in these campaign communications. All three parties issued press releases throughout the campaign. While regularly posted on the parties' web pages, these are not likely to have been read by many voters beyond committed partisans. Instead, the intended readership is the news media. The objective is to raise issues the campaign desires to bring to the media's attention, either highlighting positive aspects of their record or criticizing those of their opponents.[2] By tracking the parties' webpages, we were able to collect and analyse 601 press releases issued during the campaign: 255 from the Liberals, 239 from the NDP, and 107 from the Conservatives.

Finally, we look at social media activity of the parties and leaders. We include data from both Facebook and Twitter. This information provides an alternative take on the issues that were prioritized, by considering an avenue of direct contact that is far less formal than press releases and far less expensive than leader visits. It also provides a point of comparison for the types of issues that are emphasized in other campaign activities. While social media does not have the same regionalized component as other types of data that we include here, we nonetheless find it useful to include as it reflects one of the largest growing segments of political communication, and understanding how leaders and parties communicate on these platforms is integral to understanding their communications strategy, which does have regionalized aspects.

WHERE THE LEADERS CAMPAIGNED

That the three provinces we focus on in this study were of central importance to the campaign is evident from the number of days each leader spent campaigning in them. We find that Trudeau campaigned in the three provinces of Ontario, British Columbia, and Quebec on fifty-six days, or 88 per cent of the days for which we record him as campaigning. Harper spent forty-five days in these provinces (79 per cent of his campaign time), while Mulcair spent forty-nine days, representing 82 per cent of his days on the trail. Note that the three provinces combined represent only 71 per cent of the 338 seats up for grabs in the election. The disproportionate attention probably represents the leaders' desire to be in major media centres (particularly those in the three largest cities: Toronto, Montreal, and Vancouver) and also the competitive nature of elections in these provinces, as all three parties made serious plays for seats in each of them.

In their study of the 2000 election campaign, Belanger, Carty, and Eagles (2003, 454) find that "Canadian parties can and do adopt different but strategically comprehensible geographies in planning and managing their leaders' campaign." Similarly, in a study of the 2011 Ontario provincial election, Cross et al. (2015) find strong evidence of parties employing different regional strategies in constructing their leaders' tours. Table 5.2 shows clear differences in the strategies of the three national parties in terms of the concentration of their efforts in each province in 2015. These seem largely compatible with the competitive positions of the parties at the outset of the campaign. The Conservatives and New Democrats focused on British Columbia considerably more than did the Liberals. While the province had only 12 per cent of the seats up for grabs in the election, both party leaders were there during 20 per cent of the campaign days. This probably reflects what Carty and Eagles (2005) term a defensive strategy (see chapter 2) – given that both parties had a significant number of seats in the province – and that both recent elections and early polling suggested competitive races. The Conservatives won twenty-one of the province's thirty-six seats in 2011, the NDP won twelve, and the Liberals won only two. Perhaps equally important, the Liberals were second in only four of these contests compared to

Table 5.2
Number of days in which leader made a campaign stop in each province
and as per cent of total campaign days tracked for each leader

	BRITISH COLUMBIA		ONTARIO		QUEBEC		Total days in these provinces	
	Days	%	Days	%	Days	%	Days	%
Trudeau	8	13	35	55	15	23	56	88
Harper	11	19	33	58	11	19	45	79
Mulcair	12	20	21	35	19	32	49	82
Share of total seats	12%		36%		23%			

Note: The leaders sometimes campaigned in more than one of these provinces in a single day, thus the 'total' column is less than the sum of the three province-specific columns.

nineteen for the NDP. Polling at the start of the campaign showed the NDP with a significant lead in the province (with 44 per cent of the vote) and a realistic chance to add significantly to their seat total (Forum Research, 2015a).

While the Liberals won only eleven seats in Ontario in 2011, they have traditionally been highly competitive in the province, finishing second in forty-six ridings in that election, and in 2015 they had strong support from the provincial Liberal government (see chapter 4). The party clearly saw winning back a large number of its previously held Ontario seats as key to a successful campaign effort, and thus expended considerable time in the province. We can also interpret the disproportionate Conservative effort in Ontario as a response to the Liberal challenge and an effort to maintain as many of the seventy-three Conservative seats won in 2011 as possible. The party was not poised to make significant gains elsewhere, thus holding on to their Ontario seats was crucial to their chances for victory. It is interesting that the NDP campaign spent significantly fewer days in Ontario than did its opponents. The party had won twenty-two seats in the province in 2011 and was tied with the Conservatives for first place in polling at the campaign's outset. However, despite the party's national breakthrough in 2011, it did not win significantly more seats in Ontario than in previous elections (twenty-two compared with seventeen in 2008). This paled beside the party's seat breakthrough in Quebec and may well have dampened expectations for the province, particularly given the Liberals' revitalization. It is worth noting, however, that the party did spend a proportionate amount of time in the province; it just did not overemphasize its presence in Ontario as its competitors did.

Instead, the NDP clearly focused on maintaining its strength in Quebec. Having won fifty-nine of the province's seventy-five seats in 2011 (representing almost 60 per cent of the party's total MPs) and holding a strong lead in pre-election polling, it is not surprising that Mulcair spent a disproportionate amount of his time campaigning in the province. The NDP leader spent nineteen days (32 per cent) campaigning in Quebec even though it represented fewer than one-quarter of the total seats. The Conservatives had only modest hopes for gains in the province, beginning in fourth place and having no recent history of significant success. Harper did make some efforts, particularly in the Québec City region, and these paid off with modest gains, winning an additional five seats. The Liberals, however, were the big winners in the province. Liberal gains in voter support in Quebec appear to have come late in the campaign, and thus it is not surprising that we find Trudeau to have made a disproportionate number of his visits to the province as the campaign progressed, visiting it only four times in the first month compared with eleven visits in the next month and a half.

PROVINCE-FOCUSED PRESS RELEASES

We now turn to consider whether there is evidence of regionalized campaigning in party press releases, which are important indicators of strategic party activity. Our first area of inquiry is how often a press release is used to bring attention to one of the three provinces that are the subject of our study. To assess this, the releases were hand coded to determine whether they specifically mentioned at least one of British Columbia, Ontario, Quebec, or a specific geographic region or city in one of these provinces (for example, the Niagara peninsula or the Lower Mainland).[3] As illustrated in table 5.3, overall, slightly more than one-quarter of the parties' releases include a reference to at least one of these provinces. In terms of variance among parties, the Liberals were almost 50 per cent more likely to reference one of these provinces than were the Conservatives. The Conservatives were most likely to be regionally generic and to present their policy arguments in a national form, which might be taken as a form of position avoidance when it comes to the territorial dimension (see chapter 2).[4]

Table 5.3
Number of party press releases referencing any combination of the three provinces:
British Columbia, Ontario, Quebec

	British Columbia	Ontario	Quebec	Any of the 3 provinces
Liberals (255)	16 (6.3%)	34 (13.3%)	44 (17.3%)	76 (29.8%)
Conservatives (107)	8 (7.5%)	10 (9.3%)	9 (8.4%)	22 (20.6%)
New Democrats (239)	12 (5.0%)	35 (14.6%)	23 (9.6%)	64 (26.8%)
Total (601)	36 (6.0%)	79 (13.1%)	76 (12.6%)	162 (27%)

Note: Total press releases issued by party reported in parentheses in column.

The additional regional focus in Liberal releases is largely a result of references to Quebec, as the party was about twice as likely to mention that province than were its opponents. For both the Conservatives and the NDP, Ontario was mentioned most often, while for the Liberals Quebec references were most common.

Beyond consideration of whether a province is mentioned, we also examine whether a press release refers to provincial politics and whether it deals with an issue in a province-specific context. As shown in table 5.4, only 37 of the 601 press releases referenced either a provincial party or clearly were about a provincial political issue. Three-quarters of these (28) related to Quebec. The Conservatives were again the least likely of the three parties to raise province-specific issues. The relatively large number of Liberal references to Quebec politics is a result of their frequent criticisms of Mulcair's record in the Quebec National Assembly and particularly as provincial environment minister. The Liberals were very critical of his role in the bulk water export issue and highlighted this in many of these releases. The Liberals also accused him of opposing investments in small businesses and generally being anti-Albertan during his time in provincial politics.

It is unusual for politicians with significant careers in provincial politics to lead federal Canadian parties and this may be an illustration of why that is. They are open to criticism for positions taken on their parochial provincial stages that may not play well on the national scene. On the other hand, the NDP also referred to Quebec provincial politics significantly more often than to the politics of the other provinces. In this case, they almost always were praising Mulcair's tenure in the National Assembly, highlighting his work on the environment and support for the province's strong social programs such as the

Quebec Pension Plan and child-care provision. The NDP was on the offensive in Ontario, using several press releases to criticize the Liberal Wynne government as corrupt, referencing scandals it was embroiled in. The Wynne government also came under fire from the Conservatives as two of its releases criticized the province's plan to expand its pension scheme.

**EXAMPLES OF PARTY PRESS RELEASES
REFERENCING PROVINCIAL POLITICS**

September 14, 2015, Conservative release references "British Columbia's disastrous experience with an NDP government in the 1990s." (https://www.conservative.ca/harper-outlines-balanced-budget-low-tax-plan-to-protect-canadas-economy/).

October 1, 2015, Liberal release argues that "Thomas Mulcair failed as Quebec Environment Minister. Mulcair advocated for the mass export of fresh water, tried to sell off pristine parkland and made headlines for his inaction on greenhouse gases." (https://www.liberal.ca/thomas-mulcair-is-no-friend-of-the-environment-2/).

October 8, 2015, NDP release quotes Mulcair, "As a former Cabinet Minister in Quebec, I've seen how investments in child-care can boost the economy and give families a much-needed break." (https://www.ndp.ca/news/ndp-statement-national-day-action-early-childhood-educators-and-child-care-workers).

The most important take-away from table 5.4, however, is that the federal parties did not make many references to provincial politics in their press releases. Altogether, all of the releases that mentioned provincial politics amounted to only 6 per cent of the total. This is interesting given that, as reported in the previous chapter, a significant number of local candidates reported that provincial politics had an impact on their federal electoral chances.

We are also able to consider whether an issue with national saliency is raised in a province- or region-specific manner. An example of this type of subsuming strategy (see chapter 2) might be a press release making reference to the need for government investment in the manufacturing sector and then tying this into a plan to provide a stimulus to the automobile industry in southern Ontario. This is a

Table 5.4
Number of party press releases referencing provincial politics

	British Columbia	Ontario	Quebec	Any of the 3 provinces
Liberals (255)	0	1 (0.4%)	17 (6.7%)	18 (7.1%)
Conservatives (107)	1 (0.9%)	2 (1.9%)	2 (1.9%)	5 (4.7%)
New Democrats (239)	1 (0.4%)	4 (1.7%)	9 (3.8%)	14 (5.9%)
Total (601)	2 (0.3%)	7 (1.2%)	28 (4.7%)	37 (6.2%)

Note: Total press releases issued by party reported in parentheses in column.

concept that is challenging to define and code, and so we do not attempt to provide comprehensive data. However, a review of the releases indicates that similar to the findings reported above, a disproportionate number of these press releases, for all three parties, related to Quebec, although, again, the Conservatives were significantly less likely to make this sort of regional appeal than were the Liberals or New Democrats.

ISSUE FOCUS BY PROVINCE

Leaders' Tours

Beyond the regions and provinces the parties visit and highlight in their press releases, the actual content of the visits is important. We therefore consider what issues each party referenced. Reflecting the tradition that daily news coverage of the campaign often revolves around the leaders' activities, parties give great consideration to the exact venue of the visit and the subject of their leaders' remarks. The two are often used to complement one another. For example, a speech on the need for greater investment in mental health may well be made at a hospital, while one regarding the need to train high-tech workers will probably occur either on the campus of a post-secondary institution or on-site at a high-tech firm.[5] Of interest to us is whether the parties talked about different sets of issues in the different regions. In the past, parties have been criticized for both talking about and actually taking different positions on the issues in different regions. Indeed, the Liberals issued several 2015 press releases criticizing Mulcair for doing just this during the 2015 campaign. This type of regionalized campaigning, however, was probably more common before the age of national broadcasts of the leaders' remarks, which have made it easier to immediately contrast their statements in different regions (Carty et al. 2000). Nonetheless, it is possible (and perhaps probable) that the parties continue to emphasize different issues in different regions, tailoring their remarks to the specific concerns of voters in the locale they are visiting. Carty and Eagles (2005, 102) nicely capture this sentiment when they write that

> we expect that a party leader's campaign period visit to a particular area will do more than simply exploit an appropriate backdrop for policy announcements aimed at the national media. These visits also play an important role in conveying the leader's attentiveness to and empathy with the distinctive concerns of a community's voters ... In this context, leaders' tours provide a vehicle for the parties to reinforce and massage particular messages to suit a geographically dispersed and differentiated electorate.

It is worth considering a few brief examples of this for each leader. When visiting Quebec on 10 August 2015, Trudeau criticized the NDP's proposed child-care plan as being meaningless for Quebecers as it was redundant given the province's own plan. On 3 September in Montreal, he talked about the need for increased infrastructure spending and highlighted the aging Champlain Bridge and the generally poor condition of the city's transportation network. When in the Maritimes on 8 September, he talked about reversing changes to employment insurance brought in during the Harper government. When in British Columbia on 10 September, he criticized the Harper government for its approach to pipelines. And, on 14 October, in Hamilton, Ontario, he blamed the Harper government for troubles in the region's steel industry.

Trudeau was not alone in discussing issues of particular salience to the regions he visited. In Toronto, on 3 August, Harper criticized the Ontario provincial government's plans for an expanded pension scheme. In British Columbia, on 21 August, he highlighted his government's support for Pacific salmon habitats and for a national marine conservation area. In Northern Ontario, on 2 September he discussed his government's support for tax credits for resource development. On 6 October, in Oshawa, Ontario, he announced a new fund to help the area's struggling auto sector.

Mulcair followed suit, for example, by discussing subway expansion into Scarborough while visiting Toronto on 13 August 2015, employment insurance issues in New Brunswick on 22 September, rail safety on 16 October in Lac Mégantic, and the automotive industry in southern Ontario on 9 September.

In table 5.5, we categorize the subject of the leaders' remarks in each province according to the issue categories used in the previous chapter. The data reveal both some striking similarities and some significant differences across parties and provinces. The first observation is that the economy generally was a frequent subject of the leaders' remarks in all three provinces. It was, in fact, the most common issue reported for each of the three leaders in each of the provinces. This is consistent with the findings in the previous chapter that show this issue was generally considered by candidates to be the most important issue in their local campaigns.

The most notable differences at the party level are the Conservatives' emphasis on taxes (four times greater than the NDP's overall and three times greater than the Liberals'), and the NDP's greater focus on social policy programs and government corruption. This too is consistent with the finding that local Conservative candidates ranked taxes as being more important to their local efforts than did those from the other parties. The Liberals do not vary from the other parties, though their lack of emphasis on the issue of government corruption, when compared to the NDP, is notable.

Within parties, we do find some variance by province. For the Liberals, social policy and programs were far more important in British Columbia than in the other provinces. This may reflect their competition with the NDP for centre-left voters in the province, as Mulcair also appears to have emphasized the issue in his visits to the province, while Harper did not. Similarly, Trudeau is reported to have discussed refugee policy in Quebec more frequently than in the other provinces. And, it is only in Quebec that Liberal candidates did not rank this issue last in terms of importance (see chapter 4).

For the Conservatives, the issues of the economy and taxes dominated reports of Harper's campaign stops in Ontario compared with those in Quebec and British Columbia. Refugee policy played heavily in British Columbia as did the issue of government corruption in Ontario. However, given that Harper's comments on the corruption issue were defensive in nature (usually relating to the Duffy Senate scandal) it is likely that these were in response to reporters' questions

Table 5.5
Per cent of campaign days in province for which news reports indicate leader discussing issue

	British Columbia	Ontario	Quebec	In all 3 provinces
		LIBERALS		
N	8	35	15	56
Economy	63 (1)	54 (1)	67 (1)	61 (1)
Taxes	13 (Tie 3)	26 (Tie 2)	13 (Tie 3)	21 (3)
Leadership	13 (Tie 3)	9 (5)	7 (6)	9 (5)
Social policy/programs	50 (2)	26 (Tie 2)	13 (Tie 3)	27 (2)
Refugee policy	0	11 (4)	27 (2)	14 (4)
Government corruption	0	6 (6)	13 (Tie 3)	7 (6)
		CONSERVATIVES		
N	11	33	11	45
Economy	46 (1)	70 (1)	46 (Tie 1)	71 (1)
Taxes	27 (Tie 2)	61 (2)	46 (Tie 1)	60 (2)
Leadership	0	9 (6)	18 (3)	7 (6)
Social policy/programs	0	27 (3)	0	20 (Tie 3)
Refugee policy	27 (Tie 2)	18 (4)	0	20 (Tie 3)
Government corruption	0	15 (5)	9 (6)	13 (5)
		NEW DEMOCRATS		
N	12	21	19	49
Economy	75 (1)	71 (1)	67 (1)	71 (1)
Taxes	0	10 (5)	32 (3)	16 (4)
Leadership	8 (4)	5 (6)	11 (6)	8 (6)
Social policy/programs	50 (2)	33 (2)	37 (2)	39 (2)
Refugee policy	0	14 (4)	21 (Tie 4)	14 (5)
Government corruption	25 (3)	24 (3)	21 (Tie 4)	25 (3)

Note: More than one issue category can be included each day, thus column percentages exceed 100. Ordinal rankings for each province reported in parentheses. N represents total number of campaign days spent in each province.

and not the planned subject of the prepared event. This highlights that parties and leaders have only limited control over the subject of news reports. While they may attempt to orchestrate their events around a particular subject and complementary location, there is no guarantee that reporters will not ask about other issues and report on those instead of what is being highlighted by the leader. Conservative candidates' ranking of leadership as the second-most important issue in these provinces is also not reflected in these findings. This issue seems underrepresented for all three leaders' tours and may reflect the media's reporting of the substantive issues discussed by the leaders as opposed to any framing of them that may highlight leadership qualities. However, as discussed below, the parties' national press releases often discussed policy issues in ways that highlighted their own leaders' strengths or criticized their opponents. We consider those now.

Press Releases

The parties' press releases offer another opportunity to examine the issues each party wished to bring attention to during the campaign. The advantage of examining press releases instead of reports of leader visits is that press releases are unmediated communications. In table 5.6, we report the subject of releases that made specific reference to one of the three provinces.

While the results in table 5.6 illustrate some differences among parties, perhaps most notable is the substantial consistency within each party and across the provinces. As was the case with the leaders' tours, the economy was the most popular issue for all three parties. Similarly, taxes were once again a more prominent issue for the Conservatives than for their opponents, and social policy issues were more likely to be raised by the NDP and Liberals.

The leadership issue featured more strongly in the press releases of all three parties than it did in reports of the leaders' tours. This appears to result from a common framing of issues in the press releases in terms of either criticism of an opposing leader or praise for the party's own leader. For example, the Conservative's release on 20 September 2015 argues that "Under the proven leadership of Prime Minister Harper, Canada's manufacturers came through the global recession…" (https://www.conservative.ca/prime-minister-harper-announces-new-support-for-manufacturing/). The phrase "Under the proven leadership of Prime Minister Harper" recurs frequently in the party's releases. Similarly, the party is often critical of the other leaders as illustrated in their 1 September release arguing that "Justin hasn't

Table 5.6
Per cent of party press releases in which issue was discussed for releases referencing one of these three provinces

	British Columbia	Ontario	Quebec
	LIBERALS		
N	16	34	44
Economy	63 (1)	74 (1)	77 (1)
Taxes	25 (3)	32 (4)	23 (4)
Leadership	13 (4)	35 (3)	30 (3)
Social policy/programs	31 (2)	44 (2)	39 (2)
Refugee policy	0	0	2 (5)
Government corruption	0	3 (5)	0
	CONSERVATIVES		
N	8	10	9
Economy	63 (Tie 1)	60 (Tie 1)	67 (1)
Taxes	63 (Tie 1)	60 (Tie 1)	56 (2)
Leadership	38 (3)	60 (Tie 1)	22 (Tie 3)
Social policy/programs	25 (4)	20 (4)	22 (Tie 3)
Refugee policy	13 (5)	0	0
Government corruption	0	0	0
	NEW DEMOCRATS		
N	12	35	23
Economy	58 (Tie 1)	57 (1)	74 (1)
Taxes	25 (3)	17 (4)	17 (4)
Leadership	17 (4)	34 (Tie 2)	22 (3)
Social policy/programs	58 (Tie 1)	34 (Tie 2)	35 (2)
Refugee policy	0	3 (6)	4 (Tie 5)
Government corruption	0	9 (5)	4 (Tie 5)

Note: More than one issue category can be coded for a single press release, thus column percentages exceed 100. Ordinal rankings for each province reported in parentheses.

thought through this issue and has shown time and again that he is not capable…" (https://www.conservative.ca/prime-minister-harper-announces-support-for-manufacturing-jobs-in-canada-2/).

In terms of regional differences, in the case of all three parties, press releases mentioning Quebec were the most likely to reference the economy; however, the economy was also the most common issue raised regarding all three provinces. For the NDP, social policy was a common issue and was significantly more likely to be raised in releases referencing British Columbia; however, the issue is ranked no lower than a tie for second in any province. This too is consistent with Mulcair's tour as he is reported to have discussed this issue set more frequently than his opponents and to have done so disproportionately in British Columbia. Refugee policy and government corruption were not often mentioned in the party's releases.

For the Conservatives, issues across provinces were quite consistent, with the economy and taxes being most prevalent. The most significant interprovincial difference for the party was on the leadership issue – which was substantially more likely to be raised in releases mentioning Ontario. Refugee policy and government corruption were rarely raised. For the Liberals, there is little difference in issues among the provinces, though the leadership issue was less often raised in releases referencing British Columbia.

In sum, the party press releases do not seem to be particularly tied to region. There are cases where they bring attention to regional issues or cast national issues in a regional perspective, but these are in the clear minority. There are relatively few references to provincial politics, and only one in four makes any reference to one of the country's three largest provinces.

SOCIAL MEDIA PRESENCE

Since the 2008 election, social media outreach has risen in popularity and importance for political parties interested in reaching a younger and a more tech-savvy audience. While social media imposes certain constraints on communication – namely the necessarily short-form messaging style – parties who fail to adopt social media exclude themselves from a robust online political network. Thus, examining the social media presence of parties gives us a window into a specific type of campaign effort. In order to account for parties' and leaders' communication on social media, we look at party and leader activity on two platforms: Facebook and Twitter. Though these are not the only social media platforms that were in use during the campaign (parties have also adopted Instagram, YouTube, and Flickr accounts),

Facebook and Twitter are the most active platforms and the two most prominent on the parties' websites.

Facebook

Facebook, the social media and networking site that originated in 2004, was the first social media platform to be adopted by mainstream political parties in Canada (see Small 2012). While it has since been surpassed by Twitter as the social media platform of interest in politics, Facebook remains a necessary platform for parties to engage with voters. Unlike Twitter, Facebook permits longer-form communication; though posts are generally brief, they are not subject to the same character limits as Twitter. Facebook also permits embedded videos, more links to external sites, and more visible two-way interaction through the process of posting and commenting. As a platform, Facebook also engages a different demographic than Twitter and helps leaders and parties cast a broader social media net around potential supporters.

We monitored the five major parties' Facebook accounts throughout the campaign and captured the text of all original party posts. We did not collect videos or capture comments that were posted in response to these posts; however, our data enable us to comment on how often parties and leaders posted on their Facebook pages and the thematic content of those posts. Compared with Twitter (see below), Facebook was a low-engagement platform. Over the seventy-eight-day campaign, the Conservatives posted 107 Facebook updates, the Liberals posted 165, the NDP 125, and the Greens 151. The Bloc were even less active on Facebook, posting only ninety-six original comments throughout the campaign. Leaders (or their media teams) were a bit more active on this platform: Trudeau's Facebook page had 270 posts, Harper's had 302, and Mulcair's 308, while Duceppe and May's pages featured 127 and 72 posts, respectively.

Three topics received the most coverage: the economy, energy-related matters, and social policy. The economy received the most attention from Stephen Harper (257 posts) and the Conservative Party (65 posts). This comes as no surprise since the Conservatives campaigned largely on their stewardship of the economy and the perception that it would be in the safest hands with the experienced leadership of Stephen Harper. Harper, in particular, was also particularly expressive on the issue of taxes, with a total of ninety-one posts on the subject. Compared with Trudeau's and Mulcair's single posts on taxes, Harper was clearly using social media as a means to articulate a fiscally oriented agenda. Few other topics gained any prominence. The Greens posted comparatively more on energy-related issues, and Mulcair and Trudeau vied for the most posts on social policy, but few observable patterns on public policy are evident from the data.

Twitter

What leaders and parties tweet, and indeed whether they tweet or not, is also part of campaign strategy. Since 2008, Twitter has provided an unmediated platform for communications that are timely and targeted. They can also reach followers quickly as they are retweeted and circulated. While tweets cannot be geographically isolated, they do provide an idea of the topics that are considered shareable and therefore important to communicate.

To begin, consider figures 5.1 and 5.2, which show the volume of tweets sent by leaders and parties during the campaign. Note that the following analysis reflects original tweets authored by the leader and party and does not include retweets. Trudeau sent approximately fifteen hundred tweets from his account, followed by May with about twelve hundred, and Mulcair with approximately one thousand. On the other hand, the very low volume of tweets by Harper (122) and Duceppe (216) suggest that either they did not prioritize outreach via Twitter or they did not think messages would effectively reach supporters on Twitter. The volume of party tweets changes the story slightly. The Green, Liberal, and NDP parties are still the most active, but this time the Green Party leads its competitors with a total of 935 tweets. The overall volume of tweets by parties (2625), however, is much lower compared to those sent from leader accounts (3994).

What did the leaders and parties using Twitter write about? We looked at specific core issue mentions by parties and leaders (crime, the economy, the environment, foreign affairs, public safety, social policy, and taxes) and campaign issues (the Duffy trial, energy, Indigenous Peoples, marijuana, niqab, refugee, and trade). Tables 5.7 and 5.8 contain the details.

With respect to core issues, the economy was mentioned the most frequently by each leader. Over the course of the campaign, the economy was tweeted about 161 times by Trudeau, 87 times by Mulcair, and only 56 times by Stephen Harper (though Stephen Harper, using

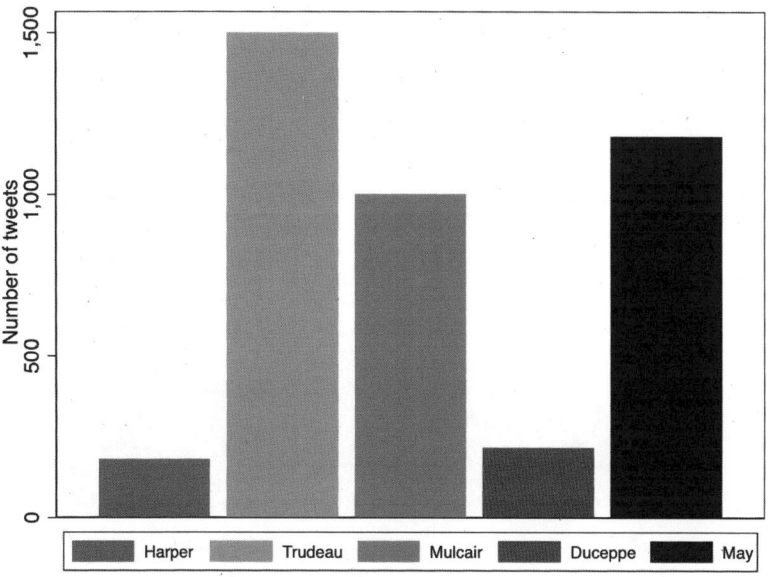

Figure 5.1 Number of tweets by party leader

his @pmharper account, rarely took to Twitter during the campaign).
The parties themselves were more prolific, with the Liberals tweeting
277 times about the economy, the Conservatives 156 times, the NDP
171 times, and the Greens 148 times. The next most common issue
was social policy, but the mentions were far fewer (206 across all the
leaders, though no mentions from Stephen Harper). The mentions by
leaders were very similar in volume to their parties, although there
was a difference in terms of how often taxes and the economy were
mentioned. These seem to be issues that parties communicated about
more than leaders.

In terms of campaign issues, refugees and energy issues were mentioned the most often in party tweets, although again in relatively
small numbers. The mentions of these issues also seem to correspond
to concerns that arose over the course of the campaign, such as refugees after the Kurdi picture was made public at the beginning of
September. Not surprisingly, the leader tweets followed the same
pattern. These patterns suggest that the parties were not using Twitter
extensively as a communication platform for policy related matters.
Rather, the platform was used largely to coordinate events, draw

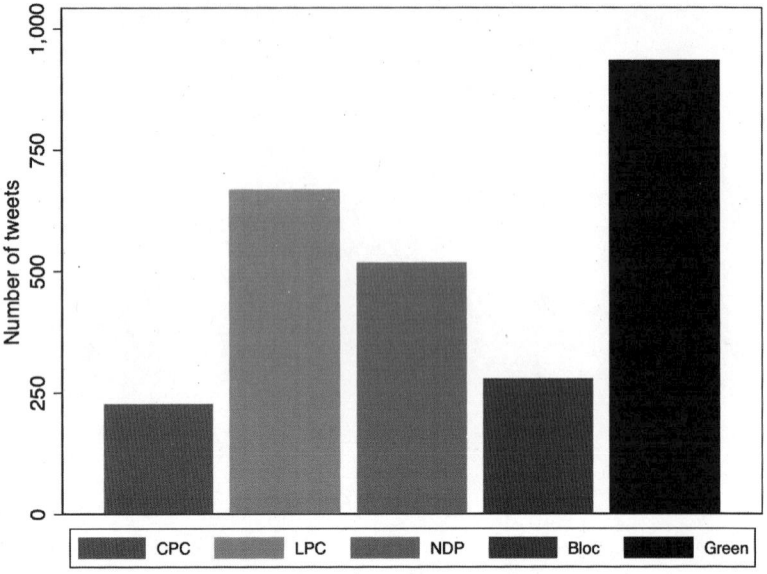

Figure 5.2 Number of tweets by party organization

attention to leader visits, and generally cheer on local candidates or the party itself.

CONCLUSION

The various types of data (party leaders' tours, press releases, and social media activity) reviewed in this chapter suggest that there was far less of a regional cast to the 2015 election, at least in terms of the parties' strategies, than in campaigns at the beginning of the century. While, as discussed in the previous chapters, there are somewhat distinct political cultures and patterns of party competition in the regions, with the exception of Quebec, party competition at the federal level looked fairly similar across the country with the Liberals, Conservatives, and NDP competing nearly everywhere. Even in Quebec, where the Bloc continues to compete (though in a much-weakened state), the three national parties all made serious efforts. The party leaders did tailor their messages to the local scene when possible. However, with only modest differences among the three provinces, they and their parties consistently emphasized similar

Table 5.7
Core issue tweets, by leaders and parties

	Harper	Trudeau	Mulcair	Duceppe	May	Total leader tweets	CPC	LPC	NDP	BQ	Green	Total party tweets
Crime	0	4	4	0	11	19	0	7	9	2	2	20
Economy	56	161	87	6	197	507	156	277	171	4	148	756
Environment	1	30	23	2	47	103	1	34	33	3	38	109
Foreign affairs	4	10	6	0	23	43	13	14	11	1	11	50
Public safety	3	9	7	0	16	35	8	11	6	0	6	31
Social policy	0	123	40	0	43	206	7	112	64	1	19	203
Taxes	15	9	4	0	10	38	39	28	13	0	8	88

Table 5.8
Campaign issue tweets, by leaders and parties

	Harper	Trudeau	Mulcair	Duceppe	May	Total leader tweets	CPC	LPC	NDP	BQ	Green	Total party tweets
Duffy	0	1	1	0	11	13	0	9	10	0	2	21
Energy	1	14	5	0	73	93	3	37	28	4	65	137
Indigenous peoples	0	14	21	0	38	73	0	40	26	0	23	89
Marijuana	0	5	0	0	2	7	2	7	0	0	0	9
Niqab	0	3	3	2	10	18	0	5	3	3	2	13
Refugee	1	30	7	0	46	84	2	48	20	0	25	95
Trade	6	4	4	0	40	54	1	5	23	2	29	60

issue sets. Given Quebec's distinctiveness, it is not surprising that it was in regard to this province that a regional dimension was most likely to emerge.

While each of the major parties in 2015 made its own strategic decisions on where to focus resources, our analysis of the leaders' tours shows that all three campaigned extensively in Ontario, Quebec, and British Columbia. However, the amount of a leader's time spent in each province did vary significantly in accordance with the strategic importance of that province to the party's electoral strategy. And while different parties focused on different issues reflecting their policy priorities (for example, social programs for the NDP and taxes for the Conservatives), the differences among regions are not particularly stark. There is little evidence, in examining the parties' campaign press releases, leaders' visits, and social media activity, that there were attempts to focus extensively on different issues in different parts of the country. Contrary to the variation revealed in our analysis of local campaign strategies, the federal campaigns really did seem to be focused on a national war.

6

Framing the Fight

Through their national and local campaign efforts, parties reach out to voters in many ways. However, even in the age of social media, parties are able to connect directly with only a relatively small number of voters; most of their communications are still mediated by the press. Generally, it is the media's representation of what the candidates did and said that typically reaches the voters. For that reason, media are an important part of any election campaign story. In this chapter, we turn the focus of our investigation into the regional character of federal elections to consideration of the media's role.

What gets reported, and how, matters because it influences the campaign discourse and has the potential to influence votes. Newspapers – both in print and online – and television news broadcasts are two of the most important sources of election information for voters. Social media may be increasing in popularity, but mainstream media are still the most common external sources of political content circulated on social media (Charlton and Brin 2017; Gregg 2017). While parties devote considerable effort and resources to trying to influence campaign news coverage, the media are not simply a vehicle for party propaganda. Information is mediated through the voices of journalists and editors, resulting in a version of the campaign that is presented to the public for consumption. Observing media agenda setting and framing is crucial to understanding how individuals respond to issues, parties, and party leaders (see Soroka et al. 2009; Trussler and Soroka 2014; Gidengil 2014). If a party wants to make a campaign about the environment, but the media insist on reporting on the economy, there is little the party can do beyond preaching to the narrow segment of their base that pays close attention to party communications.

In a federal election, there is another aspect of the media to consider: variation in reporting around the country. National news sources, of course, have a readership and viewership across the country, but there are also a number of local and regional sources that are the preferred choice of many voters. Depending on patterns of consumption and independence, news sources have the potential to articulate different views of campaigns as they unfold. National news may focus on issues of national importance (e.g., the economy) and party leaders, while regional newspapers may provide details of local candidates, leaders' visits to the region, and issues of importance to the area. In other words, local media may tailor details of national and provincial campaigns to the interests of local readers. Just as we saw in chapter 4 with the campaigns of individual candidates, regional variation can be introduced into a national campaign when messages are tailored for specific constituencies. Indeed, as noted in chapter 2, Deacon, Wring, and Golding (2006) found evidence of regionalization across the UK in the issue agendas of print and broadcast media.

This chapter focuses on understanding how the campaign was covered in the media during the 2015 campaign, whether coverage varied across the three provinces, the focus (leadership, issues, or horserace), and the tone of coverage. We investigate two distinct types of media coverage: newspapers (national and local/regional) and televised news (in Montreal, Toronto, and Vancouver). The content of what Canadians read and watched during the campaign may have had a considerable impact on the information upon which they based their vote. If that is the case, then evidence of geographic variation in the presentation of issues and parties may help explain regional variation in the vote.

SHAPING THE CONTEST

To understand what the election campaign looked like to the voter, we need to consider how the media reported it and who their target audience is. There is little doubt that the landscape of Canadian media has changed considerably since the introduction of online newspapers, social media, and news aggregators. Canadians have been connecting with electoral politics online since the 2004 and 2008 elections (Small 2008), and the movement to online news monitoring has only gained strength since. Subscriptions to print newspapers have dramatically declined, though their online counterparts have picked up a good portion of their audience share.[1] That said, television remains the main news source for a plurality of Canadians (29 per cent), though it is closely followed by Facebook (21 per cent), and news websites (14 per cent) (Blevis and Coletto 2017). In fact, social media's position as a primary news source for Canadians more than doubled between 2015 and 2017, according to Abacus Data (Blevis and Coletto 2017). Of course, these trends are more reflective of the behaviour of younger Canadians, while older Canadians still rely predominantly on television to access news, with CTV ranking as the most-watched Canadian television network for sixteen years running (Newswire 2017). In line with this shift to televised and online news comes a change in the ways Canadians access news. Almost 80 per cent of Canadians over eighteen own a smartphone and, according to Charlton and Brin (2017), almost 30 per cent of Canadians regularly employ them to access the news (a further 53 per cent regularly access news through their computer, and approximately 25 per cent use a tablet).

Both the frames and the tone used by reporters could dramatically alter the messages delivered by candidates and parties. This type of mediation of politics is well-documented across elections (Goodyear-Grant 2013; Nadeau et al. 2008; Mendelsohn 1998). Existing research has demonstrated that the media prefer headline-grabbing stories, and to some extent this has pushed coverage to be more about the horserace aspect of the campaign, that is, which party or candidate is polling first, the margins between the candidates, and so forth, rather than the substantive issue proposals that are advanced by the political parties (Soroka and Andrew 2009). Coverage of leaders is also popular; following what leaders (as the public faces of the parties) do and say (and where) is an easy way of feeding a relatively surface-level demand for campaign information (see Bittner 2011; Gidengil 2008). Issue coverage is also potentially important to the vote decision, particularly as it relates to evaluations of leader and party competence and positive associations between parties and issue handling (Bélanger 2003).

We first consider coverage in print media. Figure 6.1 shows the overall proportion of each type of coverage across national (*Globe and Mail, National Post, The Canadian Press* wire service, and Radio-Canada) and regional (British Columbia, Ontario, and Quebec) newspaper stories[2] collected during the campaign period, from 4 August to 19 October 2015. In all, we examine news stories from twenty-nine regional newspapers: eleven in Ontario, ten in Quebec, and eight in British Columbia. Stories were coded using a dictionary-based, computer-assisted coding package (Lexicoder) according to whether they mentioned public opinion polling (the horserace), issues, or party leaders.[3] Despite research suggesting that horserace coverage should dominate, figure 6.1 demonstrates that coverage of issues and leaders was far more prominent during the 2015 election campaign. Almost three-quarters of the stories in our sample included issue or leader mentions, while fewer than one-quarter covered the horserace. Perhaps this lack of focus on the horserace is unsurprising given the length of the campaign. At seventy-eight days, the 2015 election campaign was the longest on record in over one hundred years. Given the volatility of the polls and the number of undecided Canadians, it may have been the case that reporters were less likely to rely on the horserace when so much appeared to be subject to change during the campaign. Typically, campaign coverage was characterized by low but sustained levels of poll reporting as part of broader analyses that were focused on leaders and issues. This was true for both local and national coverage, which makes sense, as we would not necessarily expect there to be a national/regional dimension to the use of polling information given its widespread availability across news organizations that have both national and local news holdings. Nonetheless, horserace coverage may have been more salient, and therefore prevalent in the media, in regions where the election was likely to be particularly close or where there were dramatic changes in party standings in the polls from the previous election. That we do not observe such variation in horserace coverage across regional and national coverage suggests that regional horserace information was available less frequently than coverage of the national contest owing to the media's concentration on the favourability of party leaders and parties as a proxy for many of the regional races.

Did the type of coverage vary by the geographic focus of the newspaper? As noted above, regional papers may be more likely to focus on aspects of the campaign that concern their readership more directly. One can imagine, for example, that discussions of language rights might be more prominent in Quebec papers than in British Columbia papers. We thus consider the focus of news stories across the various media outlets. Figure 6.1 demonstrates that the story does not change much when we consider regional coverage separately from national news coverage. A slightly larger proportion of regional media focused

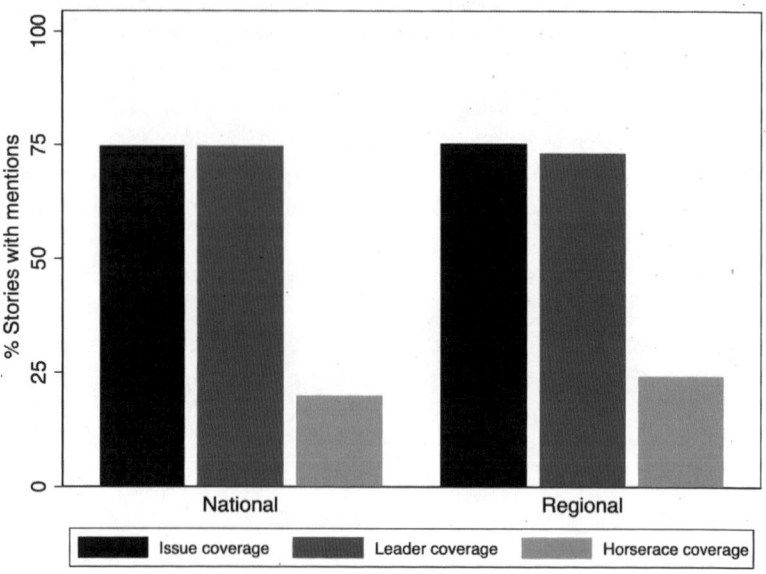

Figure 6.1 Proportion of coverage type (print news)

on issues than leaders, but both the national and regional papers gave far less attention to the horserace than they did to leaders and issues.

Breaking the sample down further by province, the comparative lack of horserace coverage is once again clear, but figure 6.2 shows some interesting variation with respect to issue and leader coverage. Both Ontario and British Columbia print news sources emphasized coverage of issues, whereas leader coverage edged out issue coverage in Quebec. On closer examination, it turns out that the greater emphasis on leaders in the province was only apparent in the French-language press. This focus on the leaders might have been due to contextual factors such as the sudden and dramatic rise of the NDP in Quebec in 2011, the focus on Mulcair's leadership, and hometown coverage of Trudeau. Interestingly, it is also consistent with the local campaigns' emphasis on the party leaders reported in chapter 4. For all three national parties, the emphasis on the party leader by Quebec-based newspapers surpassed the national average.

To examine television news, we collected CTV evening news broadcasts in Vancouver, Toronto, and Montreal for a two-month period during the campaign from 18 August to 19 October 2015.[4] Out of a

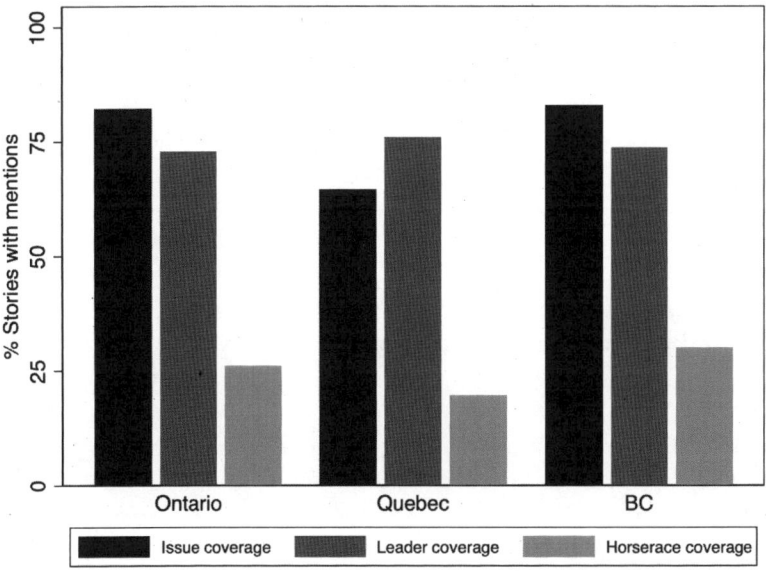

Figure 6.2 Coverage by province (print news)

total of 469 individual stories across the three cities' broadcasts, 317 (68 per cent) mentioned an issue, 365 (78 per cent) mentioned leaders, and 161 (34 per cent) mentioned the horserace. These numbers are closely aligned with those we observed for newspapers: the horserace did not dominate coverage. Horserace coverage increased toward the end of the campaign, but this is not surprising, as poll results would be prominent later in the campaign when many voters were making their decisions and there were few new policy positions to be announced by the parties (see Soroka and Andrew 2009).

DISSECTING THE ISSUE FRAME

The analysis above suggests that the picture of the election campaign that was transmitted to voters through the press often featured coverage of the election issues, especially in British Columbia and Ontario. The next step, then, is to consider which issues were discussed and to what extent. We illustrate this for newspapers (table 6.1) and broadcasts (figure 6.3), breaking down the issue coverage by topic. First consider print news (we rank the topics in both the national and

provincial presses for convenience). Recall that one of the reasons to
look at newspaper coverage regionally is to understand whether those
media outlets tailored their coverage to their audiences. There is some
evidence of this in table 6.1. Nationally, as well as across the three
provinces, the economy received the most coverage, while democratic
reform received the least. Given that three of the five major parties
supported changing the electoral system, one might have expected
this topic to receive greater coverage. The remainder of the topics
received varying degrees of coverage; in some cases (such as refugees
or the niqab) the levels of coverage in British Columbia and Ontario
mirrored the national levels, whereas for other issues (such as the
Mike Duffy trial), it was Quebec coverage that most closely resembled
the national level. However, the Quebec press was clearly an outlier
when it came to the amount of attention paid to the niqab issue. Only
the economy received more attention in the province's press.

Considering the discussion in chapter 5, it is not surprising that the
economy appears to have dominated news coverage of the campaign.
It was by far the most common subject of the leaders' events and was
also at the top of the list of issues discussed in the parties' press
releases. Interestingly, the Conservative's emphasis on tax policy is
not reflected in the newspapers' campaign coverage.

Turning to broadcast news, figure 6.3 shows the number of issue
mentions by city. What is immediately obvious is that social policy
(including health care, education, and family-related policies) dominated televised coverage of the campaign. Given the focus on economic
issues in the newspapers, leaders' events, and party press releases, this
finding is striking. We suspect that it reflects the different audiences
for each type of media. Social policy issues may be more central to
the considerations that inform television viewers' votes. At the same
time, the nature of social policy coverage may be more relatable than
coverage of economic issues and might lend itself to short, pithy
soundbites and visuals that work well in televised news.

The economy is the second-most covered issue in all three cities,
but there is variation in the amount of coverage from city to city for
the remaining issues. Crime and taxes were covered more often in
Vancouver while security and taxes received more coverage in Toronto.
In Montreal, taxes, security, the refugee crisis, the environment, and
democratic reform all received a significant amount of coverage. In
both Toronto and Montreal, though, coverage of these issues trailed
far behind social policy and the economy. Overall, then, the results

Table 6.1
Proportion of issue coverage devoted to different topics (print news)

	NATIONAL		BRITISH COLUMBIA		ONTARIO		QUEBEC	
	%	Rank	%	Rank	%	Rank	%	Rank
Crime	7.2	4	6.4	5	4.5	9	2.9	11
Duffy	7.7	3	3.7	11	5.5	5	11.9	3
Economy	30.0	1	29.5	1	31.9	1	24.0	1
Democratic reform	0.3	14	0.4	14	0.6	14	0.1	14
Energy	6.8	5	8.6	3	5.1	6	4.1	8
Environment	4.8	8	5.2	9	4.5	9	6.0	6
Foreign affairs	5.3	7	5.8	6	6.5	4	3.1	10
Indigenous peoples	4.6	9	5.5	8	4.0	11	6.0	6
Marijuana	1.3	13	1.9	12	1.2	13	1.4	12
Niqab	4.2	10	4.4	10	4.4	10	15.9	2
Public safety	3.8	11	4.4	10	4.9	8	4.3	7
Refugees	10.5	2	9.5	2	10.6	2	9.1	4
Social policy	6.4	6	7.5	4	9.7	3	6.2	5
Taxes	4.2	10	5.7	7	5.0	7	1.3	13
Trade	2.8	12	1.5	13	1.8	12	3.9	9
Totals	100		100		100		100	

show that there is less variance across provinces than there is across media types. Someone who consumes only television news (from CTV, at least) would have a different understanding of key issues in the election than someone who only reads newspapers.

How does the coverage of issues in both media types compare to actual campaign events? Clear variation could indicate active behaviour on the part of the media to set the agenda for the election. Figure 6.4 presents data about newspaper coverage and assuages this concern, as coverage of the issues responded to happenings in the campaign. For example, the prominence of the Duffy trial in the early days of the campaign reflects the timing of Nigel Wright's testimony, and the spike in coverage of the refugee crisis at the beginning of September followed the release of the photo of Alan Kurdi on 3 September 2015.

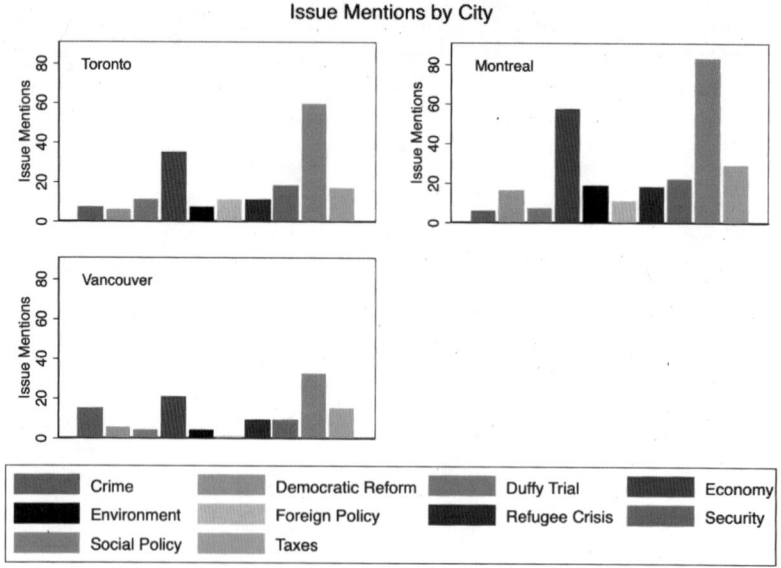

Figure 6.3 Issue mentions by city (broadcast news)

Similarly, coverage of trade surged far later in the campaign as news coverage was dominated by discussions of the Trans-Pacific Partnership agreement early in October. The debate over the proposed ban on wearing the niqab during citizenship ceremonies re-emerged after the Supreme Court refused the government's appeal on 15 September.

The same events prompted spikes in coverage in all three provinces, but how strongly the press responded varied depending on the issue and the province. Notably, the Duffy trial and the niqab issue were far more important in Quebec than in British Columbia or Ontario, with the trial accounting for more than half of the issue mentions early on in the campaign, and the niqab accounting for nearly half of the daily issue coverage around 24 September 2015. Quebec coverage also emphasized the refugee crisis in the week following Labour Day to a greater degree than the other provinces. All told, Quebec newspapers, in general, were more prone to coverage of salient events as they happened.

Turning to broadcast news, we divided the coverage of issues into the periods before and after Labour Day (7 September 2015), which many thought marked the start of the campaign in earnest (see

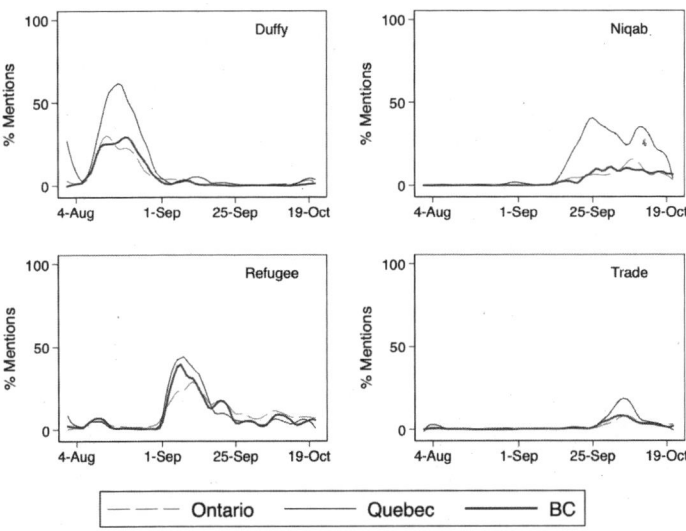

Figure 6.4 Trends in print media campaign issue coverage by province (print news)

table 6.2). For ease of interpretation, the ranking of each issue in terms of the frequency of its coverage is indicated in parentheses.

Broadcast news data, similar to the print data, show some interesting movement in issue coverage over the course of the campaign. The Duffy trial, not surprisingly, dropped substantially in terms of the volume of coverage it received after the trial was completed at the end of August. Crime became somewhat more prominent in Toronto and especially in Vancouver, as did security and the economy, while the environment lost prominence in televised news coverage. Democratic reform, foreign policy, taxes, and the refugee crisis received almost the same amount of coverage in both time periods, although there is some interesting variation by city. In Montreal, democratic reform went from ranking eighth to ranking fifth in the volume of coverage. Coverage of taxes decreased slightly in Montreal and Vancouver, while the refugee crisis only lost prominence in Montreal. Overall, however, the relative attention to the various campaign issues seems fairly similar across the cities. Whether they were watching TV news in Vancouver, Montreal, or Toronto, voters would have been receiving approximately the same sort of campaign information, but this information would not have mirrored what was in the newspapers.

Table 6.2
Proportion of issue coverage by city, pre- and post-Labour Day (broadcast news – frequency ranking in parentheses)

	TORONTO		MONTREAL		VANCOUVER	
	Pre-Labour Day	Post-Labour Day	Pre-Labour Day	Post-Labour Day	Pre-Labour Day	Post-Labour Day
Crime	0.0 (7)	5.3 (6)	3.8 (7)	0.6 (9)	7.7 (5)	13.4 (3)
Democratic reform	1.9 (6)	4.4 (7)	0.0 (8)	8.5 (5)	0.0 (7)	6.1 (6)
Duffy trial	20.8 (2)	0.0 (9)	7.5 (4)	0.6 (9)	11.5 (4)	1.2 (7)
Economy	18.9 (5)	21.1 (2)	23.8 (2)	20.3 (2)	15.4 (3)	19.5 (2)
Environment	3.8 (5)	2.6 (8)	6.3 (5)	6.2 (7)	11.5 (4)	1.2 (7)
Foreign policy	1.9 (6)	5.3 (6)	3.8 (7)	4.0 (8)	0.0 (7)	1.2 (7)
Refugee crisis	3.8 (5)	7.9 (5)	7.5 (4)	6.8 (6)	7.7 (5)	8.5 (5)
Security	3.8 (5)	10.5 (3)	5.0 (6)	10.2 (3)	3.8 (6)	8.5 (5)
Social policy	34.0 (1)	33.3 (1)	27.5 (1)	33.3 (1)	23.1 (1)	29.3 (1)
Taxes	11.3 (4)	9.6 (4)	15.0 (3)	9.6 (4)	19.2 (2)	11.0 (4)
Total	100.0	100.0	100.0	100.0	100.0	100.0

COVERING THE LEADERS

As discussed above, press coverage frequently mentioned the party leaders, but did some leaders receive more coverage than others and did the amount of coverage they received vary across the three provinces? Given the close ties between leaders and their parties, receiving more – or less – media coverage could reflect a province's partisan complexion, but it could also influence the popularity of the leader (and party) in that province. For that reason, examining the coverage given to the party leaders across the campaign and across the country is an important aspect of understanding how the election played out in print media in different regions.

Figure 6.5 tracks the number of mentions for each party leader in newspaper stories across the entire campaign (all regional and national news). Some obvious trends emerge: first, then-prime minister Harper received the most mentions for the majority of the campaign. It is

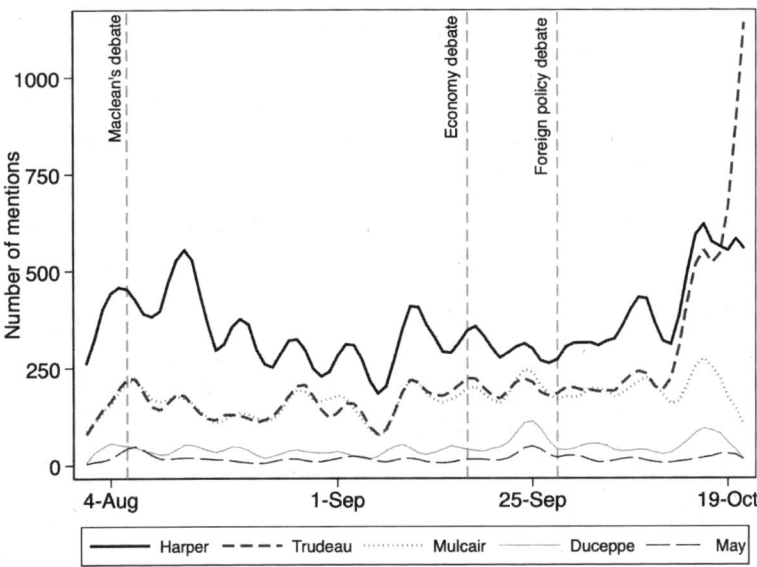

Figure 6.5 Leader coverage across the campaign (print news)

hardly surprising that Harper, as the incumbent prime minister and the leader with the most to lose in the campaign, was able to sustain the media's interest. Even more striking is the dramatic spike in coverage of Trudeau in the final days. The race for second is equally telling: until mid-October, both Trudeau and Mulcair received about the same amount of coverage but, in the final weeks of the campaign, coverage of Trudeau surged while Mulcair's shrank. In the critical closing weeks of the campaign, the press clearly perceived the Liberal leader to be Harper's chief competition, mirroring his party's rise in the polls.

Unsurprisingly, leaders of the two smaller parties, the Bloc and the Greens, were covered far less than their Conservative, Liberal, and NDP counterparts. Duceppe's party only contested seats in one province, so the fact that he received more coverage than Elizabeth May, whose Green Party was running candidates across the country, is noteworthy. The lack of coverage of the Green Party is yet another example of a longstanding pattern of media coverage: "hopeless cases get hopeless coverage" (Robinson and Shehan 1980, 76). Duceppe's coverage reflects the Bloc Québécois's status as a major contender in Quebec, but it is also a salutary reminder that media attention does not necessarily translate into electoral success, given that the Bloc captured only ten seats in the province (though that does represent an increase from the number they had captured in the previous election).

There appear to be relatively few differences in levels of reporting on leaders across regions other than the (understandably) higher rate of coverage of Duceppe in Quebec (see figure 6.6). Harper tended to be covered with less frequency in Quebec than he was in Ontario and British Columbia, but overall trends in the rate of coverage were consistent across provinces. The same is true for Trudeau and Mulcair. Most interesting is the clear upturn for Trudeau in the final weeks of the campaign in all three provinces, accompanied by the downturn in the volume of coverage of Mulcair and Harper.

Next consider television coverage. Table 6.3 tracks the number of stories that contain a leader mention in each city by month to consider how they varied over the course of the campaign. Recall that the amount of televised coverage that mentioned leaders was quite high at 78 per cent of all election stories – comparable to issue mentions at 68 per cent.

Not unexpectedly, the data show that mentions of leaders increase over the course of the campaign, a probable side-effect of an increase in the number of stories about the campaign in general. However, looking across the leaders, it is striking how similar the trends are to the print media. Mentions of Trudeau became more prominent in all three cities as election day approached; Harper marginally edged out his competitors, receiving the most coverage of the campaign; Mulcair also received significant coverage, particularly in Montreal where he dominated the other leaders in the middle of the campaign; and Duceppe received a significant bump in attention toward the end of the campaign in Montreal. That he did not receive more mentions earlier, given the historic strength of the Bloc in Quebec, is interesting and probably a commentary on how the expectations of that party's performance changed over the course of the campaign, as well as the fact that the party would likely be of less interest to the network's English-speaking viewers.

PARTIES

Were the same trends visible in the coverage of the parties? We should be mindful that while leaders and parties are tightly linked in Canadian politics, they are not identical. It is possible that coverage of the

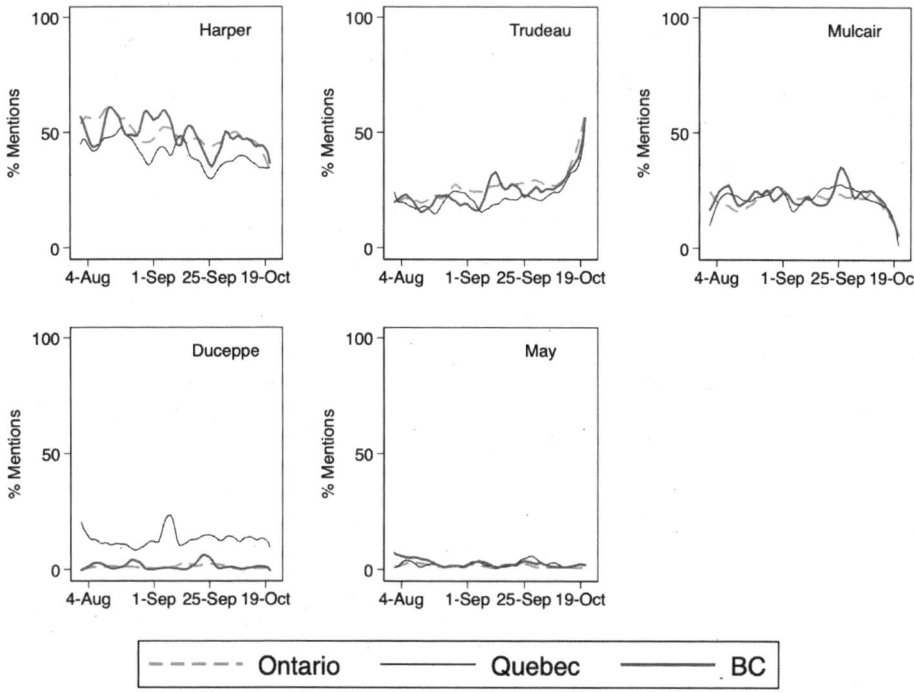

Figure 6.6 Leader mentions across the campaign by province (print news)

parties deviated from that of the leaders, particularly if we expect that star candidates or ministers struggling to keep their seats may have engendered some regionally focused coverage. Further, leaders may be worthy of mention for something unrelated to their party's stance. Finally, coverage might follow public opinion polls, with more attention being paid to the parties that are the most popular among voters. The data presented in chapter 3 show that, initially, the Conservatives were leading in the polls; thus, it makes sense that the incumbent government would receive the most lead mentions. But looking at the number of mentions over the course of the campaign reveals a good deal of variation in how attentive the media were to the parties, and how that varied across regions.

Figure 6.7 tracks party mentions by province over the campaign in newspapers. It is immediately clear that party and leader mentions can vary quite a bit, and that regional variation in party coverage also shows some startling trends. Quebec stands out with many more mentions of the Conservatives and far fewer of the Liberals throughout

Table 6.3
Number of stories containing a leader mention by month of campaign
(broadcast news)

	Harper	Trudeau	Mulcair	Duceppe	May
TORONTO					
Aug	27	19	19	0	0
Sept	29	25	24	2	2
Oct	27	31	20	2	1
MONTREAL					
Aug	15	12	15	4	0
Sept	31	29	33	3	5
Oct	35	37	23	11	0
VANCOUVER					
Aug	9	5	5	1	0
Sept	20	17	18	0	2
Oct	25	24	18	0	2

much of the campaign. Quebec also led in the number of mentions of the NDP, probably driven by the prominence of the party going into the 2015 campaign, the constant rhetoric of the "Orange Wave," and the speculation around its sustainability that occupied the minds of reporters during the campaign. The shift at the end of the campaign, away from the Conservatives and NDP and toward the Liberals, was dramatic. It seems that the province's press finally picked up on the trends in vote intentions that had been evident since late September (see chapter 3).

Looking across the three provinces, the trends in Ontario and British Columbia were similar to one another, but varied considerably from those observed in Quebec. Print coverage of the campaign in Ontario and British Columbia appears to have increasingly pitched the campaign as a contest between the Liberals and Conservatives. While the NDP figured in coverage at roughly the same level as the Liberals and the Conservatives early in the campaign, their slow, but consistent,

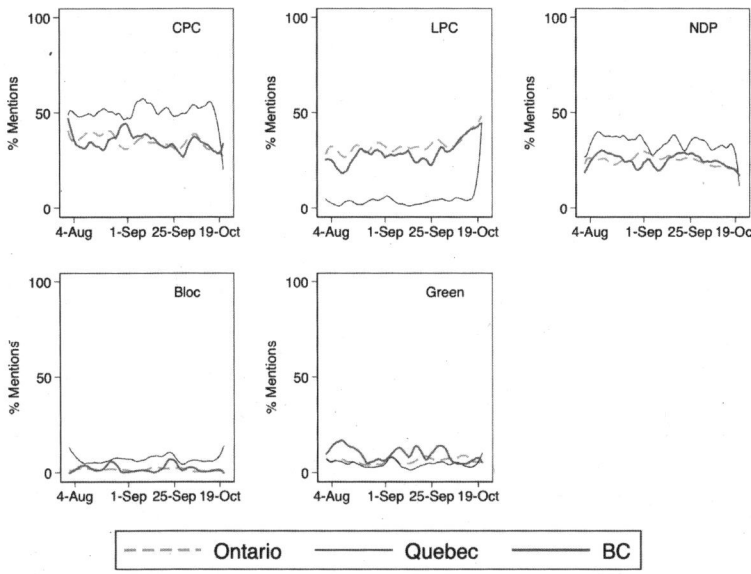

Figure 6.7 Party mentions across the campaign by province (print news)

decline throughout the last eight weeks of the campaign put them clearly in third place in terms of media coverage. Interestingly, the British Columbia and Ontario press appeared to be quicker than their Quebec counterparts to pick up on the steady increase in Liberal vote intentions and, starting on 10 October 2015, the Liberals began to routinely displace the Conservatives as the most covered party.

Figure 6.8 shows the broadcast news coverage of the main parties by month and city. Many of the same trends observed in the print media are present, such as greater NDP coverage in Quebec and a two-way race in Toronto and Vancouver toward the end of the campaign. The incredible shift toward covering the Liberals, especially in Quebec, is also clear. The general trend across all three cities points toward an imbalance in coverage of the Conservatives and Liberals, with the Conservatives having far more coverage in August and September but the Liberals catching up in October when their popularity began to pick up. Only in Montreal did anything approximating a three-way race emerge (which is unsurprising given the heightened interest in Mulcair and the NDP in the province), although coverage

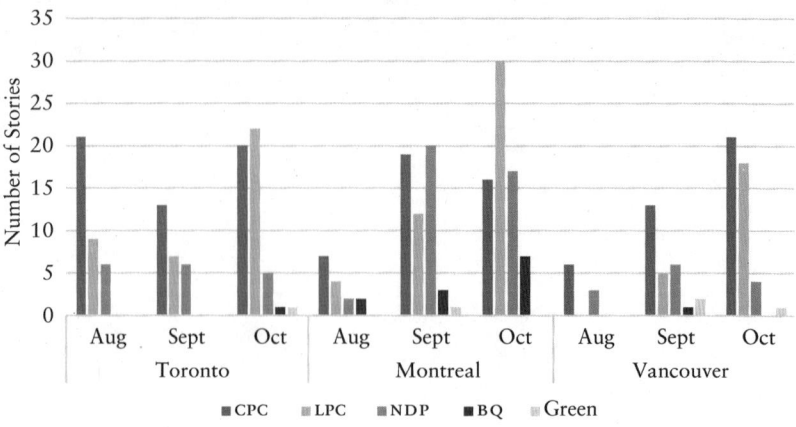

Figure 6.8 Party mentioned most by city (broadcast news)

largely focused on the Liberals in the final weeks of the campaign, with the NDP and Conservatives duelling for second place.

TONE

The volume of leader and party mentions are important metrics of party success because mentions tend to build knowledge and recognition among voters. But, arguably, the tone of coverage matters as much (if not more). If a leader receives a lot of coverage, but none of it is positive, then it is hard to envision a situation in which the coverage is a benefit to the leader's election performance. Indeed, there is evidence that the tone of coverage can influence leader evaluations and vote intentions, at least among those who are paying attention to the news (Dobrzynska, Blais, and Nadeau 2003; Johnston et al. 1992; Mendelsohn and Nadeau 1999). Therefore, coding and analyzing the tone of leader references is essential to understanding how a leader's performance may have helped or hindered the party's electoral fortunes.

We measured tone in news stories using a simple calculation of the proportion of positive words less the proportion of negative words (see Young and Soroka 2012). Figure 6.9 compares the net tone of leader coverage during three different periods of the campaign. It shows some striking variation. Coverage of Harper was consistently negative, just as coverage of Mulcair, Duceppe, and May was

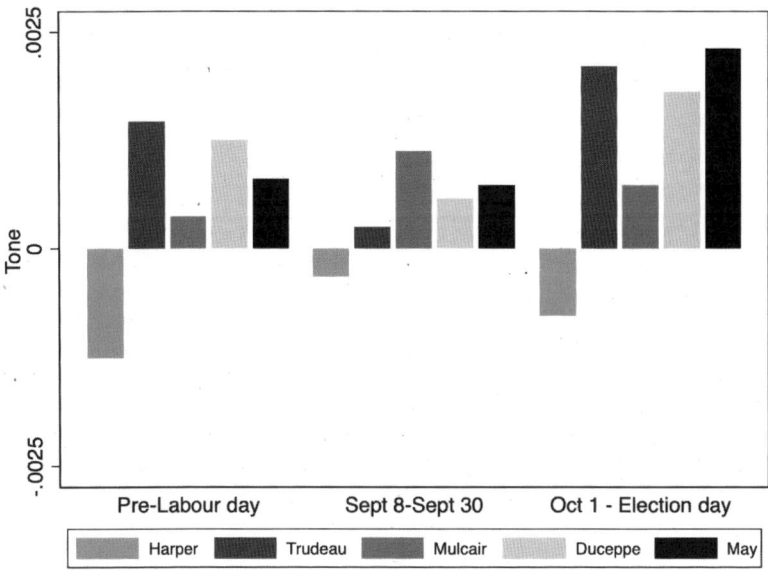

Figure 6.9 Tone of leader coverage by campaign period (print news)

consistently positive. The tone of Trudeau's coverage was far more variable: while it was generally quite positive in the early days of the campaign, it was somewhat more negative during the middle weeks of the campaign and then rebounded in the final weeks, outperforming Harper and Mulcair. This late positioning held across the three provinces, but resulted from different paths. In Ontario, Trudeau's coverage became consistently more positive over the course of the campaign. In Quebec, it rebounded to end at a higher level than it was pre-Labour Day. In British Columbia, however, Trudeau's coverage ended up less positive than it was at the outset of the campaign.

In the televised media data, we manually classified each leader's coverage as positive, negative, or neutral. Neutral coverage is any coverage that was neither outright positive nor negative for the leader, or coverage that was roughly balanced between negative and positive reporting of the leader.

In Toronto, Trudeau received the most positive coverage, with Mulcair coming close behind, while Harper received the most negative coverage, pointing to an uphill battle for the sitting prime minister (see table 6.4). Yet, all three leaders were primarily referred to in

Table 6.4
Tone of leader coverage by city in both percentage and number (N) of stories (broadcast news)

MONTREAL

	Harper		Trudeau		Mulcair		Duceppe		May	
	%	N	%	N	%	N	%	N	%	N
Positive mentions	12	10	42	33	21	15	17	3	40	2
Neutral mentions	50	40	51	40	48	34	55	10	60	3
Negative mentions	38	31	7	6	31	22	28	5	0	0

TORONTO

	Harper		Trudeau		Mulcair		Duceppe		May	
	%	N	%	N	%	N	%	N	%	N
Positive mentions	19	16	41	31	38	24	0	0	0	0
Neutral mentions	52	44	52	39	52	33	75	3	100	3
Negative mentions	29	25	7	5	10	6	25	1	0	0

VANCOUVER

	Harper		Trudeau		Mulcair		Duceppe		May	
	%	N	%	N	%	N	%	N	%	N
Positive mentions	17	9	50	23	46	19	100	1	50	2
Neutral mentions	57	31	43	20	46	19	0	0	25	1
Negative mentions	26	14	7	3	7	3	0	0	25	1

neutral terms. While this may reflect a conscious effort by televised broadcasts to be balanced, it appears that Trudeau and Mulcair both received more favourable televised coverage than their main opponent. As for May, all coverage was neutral in tone, but was scant when compared to the other leaders (a mere three stories).

The story in Montreal was very different. Most leaders received a large proportion of neutral coverage, but both Harper and Mulcair received far less positive coverage in the Montreal broadcasts than Trudeau. As in Toronto, the Liberal leader received very little negative coverage (only 7 per cent of the stories that referenced his candidacy). This may seem surprising given his father's mixed legacy in Quebec, but as our data are limited to an English-language network, findings from French-language news may have been more critical.

While Duceppe received more negative coverage than Trudeau, he fared better than Harper and Mulcair. In contrast to Toronto, May received some positive coverage in the Montreal news broadcasts. Indeed, her coverage was more positive than all of the other leaders' save Trudeau, but once again she received so little positive coverage (only two stories).

Finally, in Vancouver, the real competition appears to have been between Trudeau and Mulcair, with Mulcair receiving only marginally less positive coverage than Trudeau. On the other hand, Harper fared poorly, with the largest proportion of negative coverage and the least positive coverage. Meanwhile, in contrast to Toronto and Montreal, May received almost as much negative coverage (as a proportion of her total coverage) as Harper, though once again, of course, she received little coverage overall (four stories), even in the province where it was expected that she would make the greatest gains.

The tone of leader mentions is by far the most regionally varied of all aspects of televised news coverage considered here. This is not surprising, given that some of the leaders had a hometown advantage in the three cities we examine. On the other hand, there is one strikingly consistent pattern across all three cities: the tone of Harper's coverage was more negative than the other major party leaders. To what extent this was matched in voters' perceptions, and in turn may have influenced their vote choice, remains to be analyzed in the following chapter.

LOCAL CANDIDATES

There is one more aspect of media coverage to consider: to what degree were local candidates featured in the news broadcasts? Local candidates campaign tirelessly for their constituency seats, as we saw in chapter 4, and often stray from the party message when campaigning to emphasize local or regional concerns. To what extent do the local media assist in these efforts?

In figure 6.10 we compare the number of mentions of local candidates in broadcast news programs by city with the number of leader mentions. The Montreal English-language broadcast news paid much more attention to local candidates than the broadcasts in Toronto or Vancouver, but in all three cities leaders attracted far more coverage than local candidates. For example, Trudeau received seventy-five mentions over the course of the campaign in Toronto, compared with

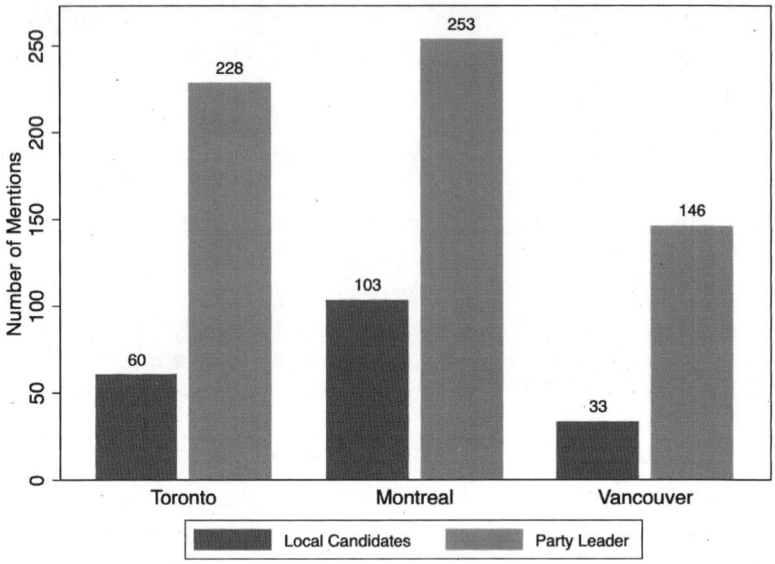

Figure 6.10 Local candidate vs party leader mentions by city (broadcast news)

just nineteen for local Liberal candidates. Mulcair was mentioned seventy-one times in Montreal but the local N D P candidates only received thirty-one mentions. Meanwhile, Green candidates were not mentioned even once in the Vancouver broadcasts, even though British Columbia was the one province where the Greens polled in double digits. These findings further support the long-held notion that leaders, not local candidates, are the face of electoral campaigns. However, another take on the data would be that local candidates show a significant amount of local coverage. Major cities are less likely to see a focus on local candidates (of which there can be many), so the fact that local candidates were mentioned in between a fifth and a third of stories is notable.

CONCLUSION

Our analysis of media coverage of the 2015 Canadian election campaign has revealed some interesting, and somewhat unexpected, findings. In terms of media coverage of the election overall, the low level of horserace coverage is surprising given the conventional wisdom in the academic literature. On the other hand, it is reassuring that issue coverage is prominent, given the importance of issues in democratic decision making. The relatively equal coverage of issues and leaders suggests that newspapers were providing commentary on the leaders as much as they were reporting on matters of policy importance to Canadians. This may reflect the importance of federal elections for picking a prime minister (Bittner 2011). The Canadian parliamentary system intertwines parties with leaders at the local and national level, and it is not surprising that the media would report on the individuals who may lead the country.

Most importantly for our overall research agenda, we find only modest variation in issue coverage by province in the print and broadcast media. Our data do *not* show that the media played a role in either creating or emphasizing different views of the election issues. We did, however, find that the issues that were covered varied by the type of media, with social policy coverage on television challenging the prominence of economic reporting in newspapers. As one might expect, we find that the prominence of issues matches with their temporal nature.

We see far more variation in the amount, tone and regional distribution of leader coverage, and, notably, not all parties and leaders were treated equally by the media. The tone of leader coverage varied the most strikingly by province, placing certain party leaders – namely Trudeau and Mulcair – at a clear advantage over the sitting prime minister. Finally, despite the local nature of the broadcasts, local candidates received little attention in any of the three cities. These nuances of how campaign information was transmitted to voters would not have been revealed if we had only considered national coverage. To what extent this variation may have affected the attitudes of voters in different provinces and translated into voter support remains to be examined in the next chapter. Whatever the case, the fact that we find evidence of variation means that any analysis of voters must be cognizant of the potential for differential media coverage to have an impact on vote choice.

PART THREE

Influencing Voters

7

Influencing the Masses

The purpose of this chapter is to consider whether media environments and media choices influenced party, leader, and issue evaluations in 2015. As noted in chapter 1, we are trying to understand whether there are systematic factors underlying the provincial variation in vote outcomes. One place to look for such factors is with the parties; another is with the media's portrayal of the issues, the leaders, and the parties. We have seen that campaign coverage varied across the three provinces. It would seem only logical that this variation could help us understand the variation in the outcome of the election. After all, why would the political parties invest so much effort in crafting their media strategies if they did not believe that media coverage influences election outcomes? It may be surprising to learn, then, that the consensus in the academic literature is that media effects are mostly limited and indirect.

Research on media effects began in the 1920s with the premise that the media have massive effects on public opinion, creating "pictures in our heads" that shape how we understand events (Lippmann 1922). The dominant metaphor in the early years likened the media to a hypodermic needle that injected ideas into the minds of the audience. This view changed abruptly in the 1940s when Lazarsfeld and his colleagues found minimal evidence of media effects on campaign dynamics (Lazarsfeld, Berelson, and Gaudet 1948). Beginning in the 1960s, a more nuanced view emerged. Researchers increasingly came to see the power of the media lying not in telling people *what* to think but in telling them what to think *about* (Cohen, 1963, 13). According to this limited effects paradigm, the media can influence people's interpretations of events through the way stories are framed, they can influence people's issue priorities by giving some issues more extensive coverage than others, and they can influence the weight that people give to various considerations when deciding their vote.

The advent of the rolling cross-section survey design made it possible to link media coverage and opinion dynamics on a daily basis. Studies using this design have found some evidence of direct effects on leader evaluations and vote intentions, but they have been unable to show that media coverage affected actual vote choice (see Dobrzynska, Blais, and Nadeau 2003). Even the evidence for the media's agenda-setting power is mixed (Gidengil 2014). Voters are not blank slates. They have predispositions and perceptual biases that affect how they process media messages.

Our expectation, then, is that we will uncover only limited evidence of media effects. However, this is not a conclusion that should be taken for granted. It is necessary to provide a systematic analysis. Demonstrating media effects is notoriously difficult. Finding that leaders who received more positive coverage are more popular with voters or that voters prioritize issues that received the most extensive coverage is actually very weak evidence of media effects. These correlations between patterns of media coverage and public opinion could simply "indicate that the media were successful in matching their messages to audience interests" (McCombs and Shaw 1972, 184–5). On the other hand, the absence of such correlations can be taken as prima facie evidence of the limited nature of media influence.

Here we merge data on media consumption patterns from our survey of citizens in British Columbia, Ontario, and Quebec with the media data presented in the previous chapter. The survey asked a number of questions about media consumption, which we use to create a picture of the information environment of each respondent. We outline the most common information sources in each province, and then consider whether a voter's information environment is related to how she feels about the issues, the leaders, and the parties. We also consider whether expectations of the election outcome varied with media use. Although the horserace was not a dominant part of the media story until just before the election, the tone of coverage may have shaped expectations throughout the campaign.

CAMPAIGN INFORMATION ENVIRONMENTS

In chapter 2 we discussed existing research about the regionalization of media coverage. There is mixed evidence: to some extent, media outlets are consistent in their coverage, but there is variation by issue

(Gidengil 2014), the scope of the outlet (national vs. local; Doyle 2002; Soderlund et al. 2012), and the type of reporting (event-driven vs. detailed; Graber 2009). How and in what form one consumes elections news, then, has the potential to influence voter learning, issue priorities, and in turn, vote choice.

However, we know little about patterns of media consumption across the Canadian provinces. Canada is served by two national newspapers (the *Globe and Mail,* owned by Woodbridge, and the *National Post,* owned by Post Media), four national television chains (CTV, CBC/Radio-Canada, Citytv, and Global), and one additional network operating in Quebec (TVA, owned by Quebecor). Importantly, all five networks are owned by different media conglomerates (Bell, CBC/publicly funded, Rogers, Corus, and Quebecor). This variation in outlet ownership can theoretically produce further differences in content and presentation of information, which would probably result in voters being presented with different (albeit only slightly in some cases) versions of the campaign depending on which and how many of these news sources they followed.

Looking at the results of our survey, we observe that there is some provincial variation in media consumption in our sample. Televised news watching is more common than newspaper reading in all three provinces.[1] We see this in Quebec especially, where 86 per cent of respondents indicated they followed televised news about the election, compared with 75 per cent in Ontario and 81 per cent in British Columbia. Newspaper use was highest in Ontario at 50 per cent, compared to 31 per cent in Quebec and 46 per cent in British Columbia. However, there is little variation in what type of news people pay attention to. When the survey respondents were asked how often they read, watched, or listened to national and regional/local news (ranked on an 8-point scale from "never" to "several times a day"), the median of the responses corresponded to "once a day" for each question across all three provinces.

Nonetheless, when we look at the print sources that voters were attentive to, the predominance of regional/local (broadsheet, tabloid, and commuter) over national newspapers in both British Columbia and Ontario is striking (see figure 7.1). In Quebec, we coded *La Presse* and *Le Devoir* as national papers given their prominence as French-language news sources across the country, but even there we still see a good deal of reliance on regional papers.[2] It is logical, then, to suspect that newspaper readership may contribute to attitudinal differences across provinces.

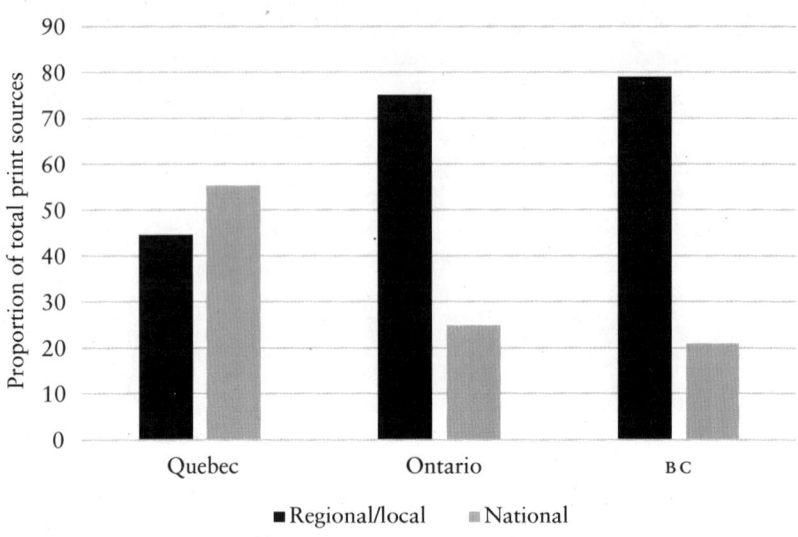

Figure 7.1 Types of print sources by province

Yet, we suspect that attentiveness to media is not an either/or proposition. In fact, many individuals who are attentive to televised news may also be attentive to newspapers, either in print or online. Among respondents who ranked their attention to news about the election in newspapers or on television as 6 or higher on a 0 to 10 scale, table 7.1 shows that those who reported high newspaper attention also frequently cited television news among their primary election news sources. Similarly, the consumption of print sources was generally higher for those who paid more attention to television news. However, it is clear that high-attention newspaper readers were much more likely to name television sources than high-attention television viewers were to name regional/local or national print sources (more than 80 per cent compared to less than 50 per cent and less than 25 per cent, respectively). Moreover, even low-attention newspaper readers frequently named television news as one of their primary news sources. Clearly, more respondents relied on television news for campaign information than relied on print sources, and many of those who paid little attention to television news were not turning to newspapers instead. Trends hold across the provinces, though the proportions vary.

Table 7.1
Media consumption by attention type and level, across provinces and media format (percentage)

| | NEWSPAPER ATTENTION | | | | | |
| | Low | | | High | | |
	Quebec	Ontario	British Columbia	Quebec	Ontario	British Columbia
TV	82.1	68.7	79.4	91.1	82.9	85.3

| | TELEVISION ATTENTION | | | | | |
| | Low | | | High | | |
	Quebec	Ontario	British Columbia	Quebec	Ontario	British Columbia
Regional/local print	15.0	35.7	34.9	19.9	49.0	43.5
National print	15.5	15.5	14.6	23.2	21.3	14.1

THE EFFECTS OF MEDIA ENVIRONMENTS

While we know that Canadians vary in their consumption of news media, it is much less clear whether attentiveness to regional/local or national media environments in the 2015 Canadian election had an effect on the outcome. Given the tendency to vote based on assessments of party and leader competence and issue salience (see Bélanger 2003; Bélanger and Meguid 2008), we begin our evaluation by looking at aggregate information on issues, party ratings, and party leader evaluations from our survey data.

We focus on respondents who reported high television and newspaper attention to election news since they are the most likely to have been influenced by media coverage. Table 7.2 shows the most important election issues identified by these respondents, divided by type of information source. Recall from the previous chapter that there were some, but not major, differences in the media agenda between the provinces.

The table reveals that there are few differences in issue priorities between high-attention newspaper readers and high-attention television viewers across the provinces. Most importantly, the top three issues (the economy, health care/social programs, and taxes) are identical across the provinces, regardless of medium. This is hardly surprising given the overlap between high-attention newspaper readers

Table 7.2
Most important issues, by province and media format (percentage)

	QUEBEC		ONTARIO		BRITISH COLUMBIA	
	TV	Newspaper	TV	Newspaper	TV	Newspaper
Economy	34	35	39	40	37	35
Healthcare/social programs	28	28	22	20	23	25
Taxes	15	15	15	15	11	12
Security of Canadians	7	6	7	7	6	5
Environment	7	7	4	4	8	9
Childcare	3	3	1	1	1	1
Other	3	4	6	6	6	3
Democratic reform	2	1	4	4	5	6
Foreign policy	1	1	2	2	1	2
Crime	0	0	1	1	1	1

and television viewers. Interestingly, those who paid attention to election news on television were no more likely to list social programs as the most important issue than were newspaper readers despite its prioritization in televised news (as observed in chapter 6). This underlines the limited agenda-setting power of the media when it comes to issues that relate to people's day-to-day concerns (Gidengil 2014; Soroka 2002).

We also find little to suggest that a respondent's information environment was associated with clear differences in attitudes toward the parties. Figure 7.2 presents party ratings on a 0 to 10 scale by province and information source among high-attention respondents. The figure illustrates that, in most cases, individuals within each province rated the parties very similarly, regardless of media format. Ratings of the Liberals and NDP were uniformly high, while Conservative ratings seem to reflect the overall negativity felt toward that party, as detailed in the previous chapters. The ratings for the Bloc and the Green Party are as expected, with the Greens enjoying their greatest popularity in British Columbia.

In figure 7.3 we present the corresponding ratings of party leaders. Similar to what we observed across party ratings, high-attention television viewers and high-attention newspaper readers do not

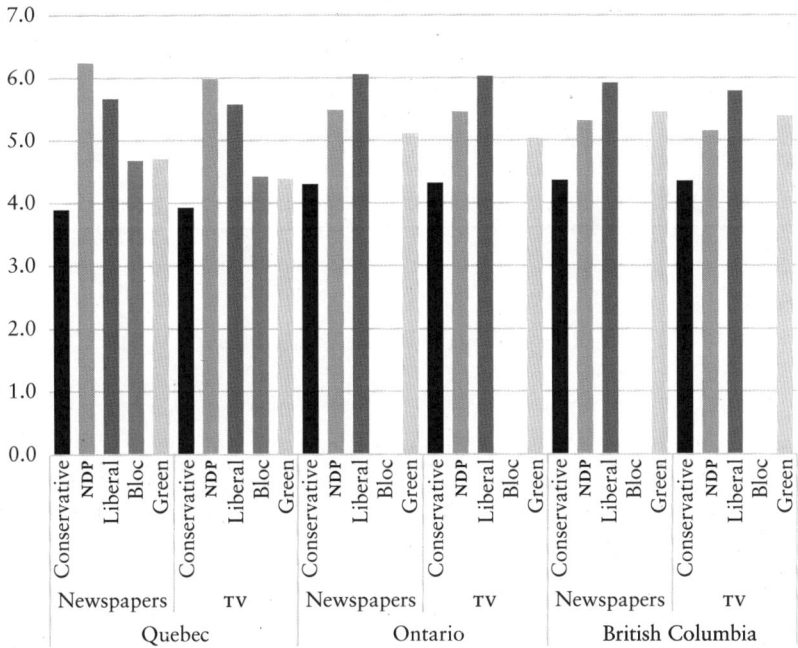

Figure 7.2 Party ratings, by province and media format

evaluate the leaders very differently. The only cross-provincial differences appear to be the uniformly higher ratings for May in Ontario and British Columbia, compared with Quebec, and lower ratings for Mulcair in British Columbia.

It is useful to compare these results to the data on the tone of newspaper and television coverage in chapter 6. On television, for example, we found similarities across the provinces in the tone of coverage of both leaders and parties. While then-prime minister Harper's coverage was the least positive, his main challenger by the end of the campaign, Trudeau, was rated the most positively. These patterns are reflected in figure 7.3 except in Quebec, where NDP leader Mulcair, who figured more prominently there, was more highly rated than Trudeau by high-attention newspaper readers and television viewers. We cannot necessarily infer, though, that the leader ratings were influenced by their coverage in the media.

We can also look at the expectations that respondents held about the outcome of the election. Table 7.3 shows the proportion of high-attention respondents who thought that each party was likely to win

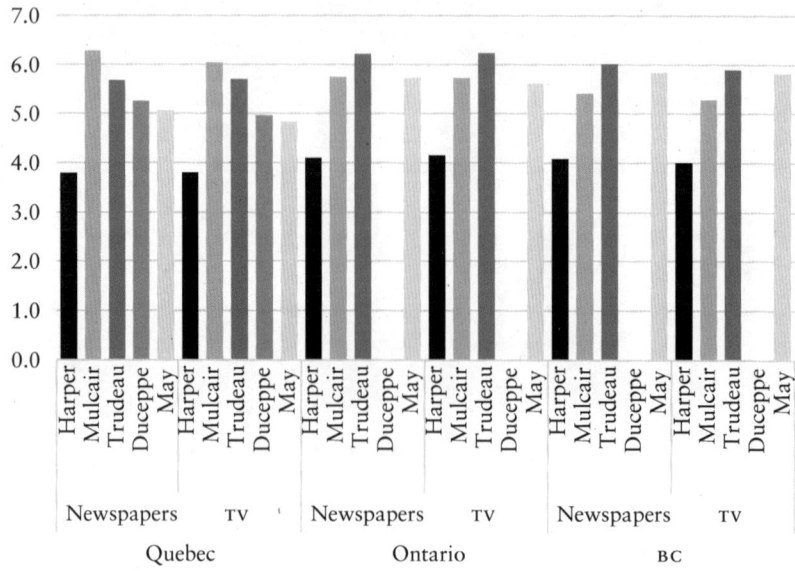

Figure 7.3 Party leader ratings, by province and media format

the most seats in the election, by province and by media type. There is consensus about the likely winner in Ontario and Quebec but in BC the expectations are split more evenly between the Conservatives and Liberals. Even in settings where the pre-campaign context was very different, there appears to be cross-provincial agreement about the strength of the Liberals, although the closeness of the race varied across provinces. The results are similar across media types.

Finally, we can turn to regression analyses to get a fuller picture of how formats and sources may have affected evaluations of the parties and their leaders. Table 7.4 shows the effects of self-reported attention to different types of news (national and regional/local) and high newspaper and television attention on party leader ratings. Each variable was coded to be dichotomous. For the different types of news, those reporting they read or watched the news at least once a day were considered "highly attentive." For the different sources, as above, those scoring 6 or higher on the 0 to 10 scale were classified as "highly attentive." Controls for sex, age, language (French), university education, type of community (rural, town/small city, and suburban), election interest, and party identification were included but are not shown.[3]

Table 7.3
Expectation of party performance by media format (percentage)

	TELEVISION VIEWERS (High attention)			NEWSPAPER READERS (High attention)		
	Quebec	Ontario	British Columbia	Quebec	Ontario	British Columbia
Conservative	32.0	38.8	42.7	32.3	39.4	42.1
NDP	20.2	8.6	16.6	23.0	9.7	16.0
Liberal	45.9	52.3	40.6	43.0	50.6	41.9
Bloc	2.0	0	0	1.7	0	0
Green	0	0.3	0.2	0	0.3	0

There are few significant effects at the $p<0.05$ level. In Ontario, respondents who paid attention to national news rated Trudeau and May more highly. Higher attention to regional/local news advantaged Harper in British Columbia. However, given that the tone of Harper's coverage was negative, it is risky to infer that this effect was a result of media exposure per se. The effects of newspaper and television attention are more varied. Newspaper reading was associated with more positive evaluations of Trudeau in British Columbia, Mulcair in Quebec and Ontario, Duceppe in Quebec, and May in Ontario. As might be expected, Trudeau fared well with high-attention television viewers in all three provinces. Mulcair also did well with television viewers, but only in Ontario, as did Harper in British Columbia. Unsurprisingly, Duceppe was also rated favourably by television viewers in Quebec.

We found similarly mixed results when we considered party ratings (results not shown). National news attention was associated with more positive Liberal ratings in Ontario and Bloc ratings in Quebec, and regional/local news attention was associated with more positive Conservative ratings in British Columbia and Liberal ratings in Ontario. Newspaper attention had positive coefficients for the Liberals in BC and the NDP and Bloc in Quebec. Consuming high levels of televised campaign coverage was positively related to evaluations of the Conservatives in British Columbia, the Liberals in Ontario and British Columbia, and the Bloc in Quebec. Individually, these findings correspond with some of the general trends observed

Table 7.4
Coefficients for ordinary least squares (OLS) regressions looking at influence
of high attention to media on leader ratings, controls not shown

		QUEBEC Coefficient (Robust SE)	ONTARIO Coefficient (Robust SE)	BRITISH COLUMBIA Coefficient (Robust SE)
HARPER	National	-0.13 (0.23)	-0.39 (0.23)	0.29 (0.23)
	Regional/ local	0.22 (0.22)	-0.34 (0.22)	0.64 (0.22)**
	Newspaper	0.24 (0.23)	-0.00 (0.21)	0.31 (0.22)
	TV	0.34 (0.24)	0.15 (0.23)	0.46 (0.22)*
TRUDEAU	National	0.24 (0.21)	0.48 (0.22)*	-0.22 (0.23)
	Regional/ local	0.03 (0.21)	0.35 (0.21)	0.05 (0.22)
	Newspaper	0.16 (0.20)	0.25 (0.22)	0.54 (0.20)**
	TV	0.48 (0.22)*	0.76 (0.22)***	0.53 (0.22)*
MULCAIR	National	-0.22 (0.19)	0.20 (0.18)	-0.11 (0.21)
	Regional/ local	-0.10 (0.19)	-0.02 (0.17)	0.07 (0.21)
	Newspaper	0.45 (0.19)*	0.36 (0.17)*	0.33 (0.20)
	TV	0.21 (0.20)	0.45 (0.17)**	0.32 (0.21)
DUCEPPE	National	0.41 (0.21)		
	Regional/ local	0.06 (0.21)		
	Newspaper	0.77 (0.22)***		
	TV	0.53 (0.23)*		
MAY	National	0.09 (0.18)	0.45 (0.19)*	-0.07 (0.20)
	Regional/ local	-0.17 (0.18)	0.06 (0.18)	0.00 (0.19)
	Newspaper	0.34 (0.18)	0.38 (0.18)*	-0.06 (0.19)
	TV	0.16 (0.19)	0.28 (0.18)	-0.06 (0.19)

* p<.05; ** p<.01; *** p<.001

in the previous chapter, but there are no clear patterns in these results, other than the positive relationship between television viewing and evaluations of Trudeau.

We can also use regression analysis to take an in-depth look at the impact of specific media sources. The surveys asked individuals to indicate their primary media source(s), allowing us to create indicators for national and regional sources.[4] We then entered these variables into regressions to map the relationship between the tone of coverage in specific sources and ratings of each major party and leader, controlling for the following: age, sex, education, language, type of community, election interest, and party identification. This enables us to test the hypothesis that different media sources will have different effects on voters' evaluations of parties and leaders. We calculated tone for each media source using the Lexicoder Sentiment Dictionary written by Young and Soroka (2012). Tone for each article is calculated as a proportion of positive words over negative words (the number of positive words less the number of negative words divided by the total number of all words) (see Young and Soroka 2012, 215). The validity of the automated tone score is discussed in depth in Young and Soroka (2012, 219), who have found that automated coding of tone performs as well as human coders. Figures 7.4 and 7.5 display the significant ($p < 0.05$) coefficients of the different media sources on leader and party ratings. The vertical axis indicates the sources and the direction of the tone, to enable us to see whether a positive tone is associated with a positive effect.

Some media sources do seem to affect leader evaluations – but perhaps not as one would expect. Most notable is that the majority of effects are in Ontario. Only in one case (*Le Devoir* for Trudeau) did the source of coverage have a significant effect in Quebec. In addition, in several cases the effect of a media source on leader support was opposite to the tone it conveyed to the reader. For example, the *Toronto Sun's* coverage of Trudeau was net positive, but that was nevertheless associated with a negative effect on his ratings among *Sun* readers in Ontario. Similarly, the *National Post's* coverage of Harper was net negative, but the effect was positive on *Post* readers. The absence of effects of regional news on Harper evaluations in British Columbia is at odds with our previous analysis, but this may be because of the strong Liberal and NDP presence in the province's main urban centres. These results suggest that readers' evaluations of leaders are typically not swayed by media consumption – even from their primary news sources. This is relevant because it speaks directly to claims that the media have too much influence on voters or sway voters despite their personal preferences.

Figure 7.5 reveals similar effects on party ratings. Again, we observe cases in which the direction of effect is opposite to that of the tone taken by the media source. Note that we do not see opposite effects across provinces for the same source in any of the significant cases.

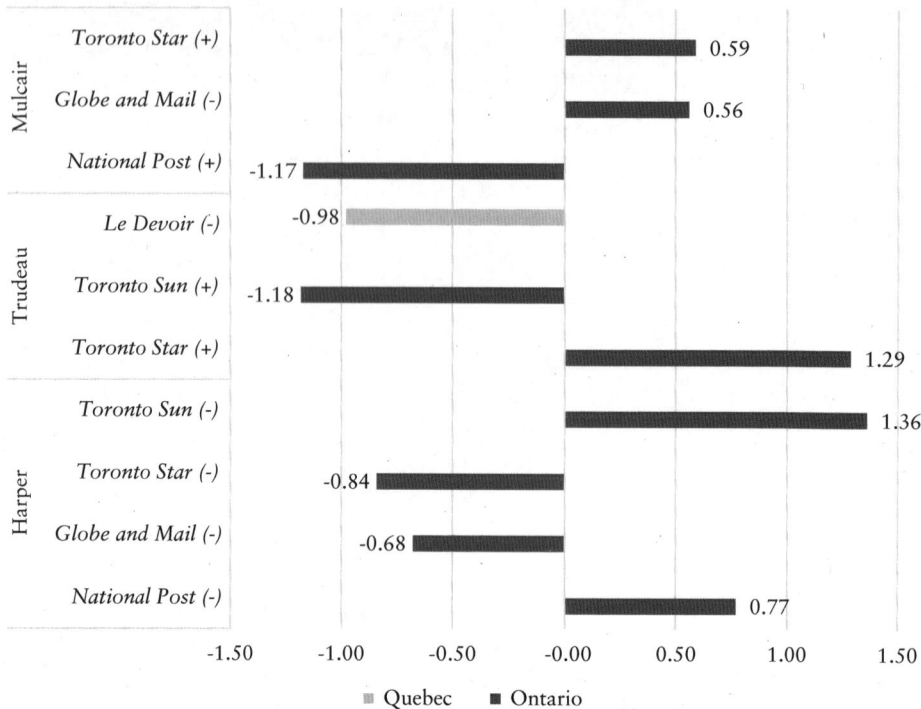

Figure 7.4 Media consumption effects on leader ratings (OLS coefficients)

CONCLUSION

When we bring together information on media coverage of parties and party leaders and the corresponding evaluations of citizens who are attentive to these media, we see similar evaluations of parties and leaders regardless of the type of media consumed, and despite the differences in coverage between the two media formats. One obvious reason for these similarities may be that voters are influenced by several factors besides the media. Also, we identified a group of people who are attentive to both television and print news. Therefore, there is likely to be a fair amount of cross-pollination between information environments, which makes disentangling the effects of a single media source in a specific region far more complicated than a content analysis of different media types might suggest.

Our findings are consistent with the limited effects literature: citizens are not blindly swayed by the tone of media coverage. Existing

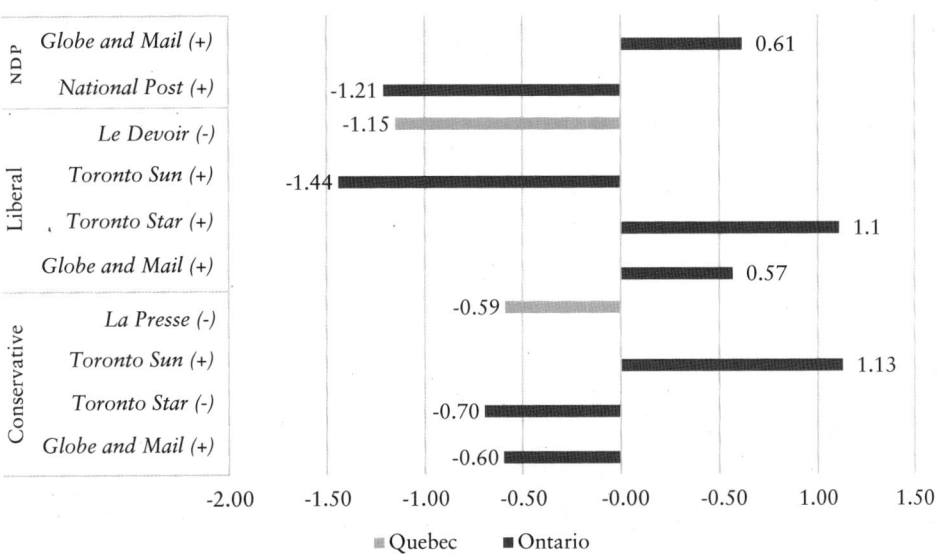

Figure 7.5 Media consumption effects on party ratings (O L S coefficients)

research has documented that individuals can counter-argue information that is contrary to their own opinions and pay greater attention to information that supports their position (see Taber and Lodge 2006). This seems to be reflected in our results. For example, the finding that evaluations of Harper were positively related to consuming media that had a negative tone suggests that individuals countered the information.

Overall, we find very little evidence of regionally differentiated media coverage in the 2015 Canadian election. Furthermore, although there were certainly differences in the election outcome across the provinces, we see little to indicate that media coverage and consumption were responsible for these differences.

8

The Final Battle(s)

As we saw in chapter 1, there were substantial differences in party fortunes across the three provinces in the 2015 Canadian election. We also found that socio-demographic variation and provincial politics did not fully explain those differences. In the chapters that followed, we considered whether strategic choices made by candidates or parties or regionalized media coverage could account for the observed provincial vote outcomes. Our reasoning was that if voters in the three provinces were exposed to different messages, provincial outcomes could differ even if voters themselves had similar interests and concerns. However, we have found little evidence of such systematic variation. Therefore, in this chapter, we turn to consider the final possible explanation: variation among the voters themselves. To evaluate this explanation, we conduct quantitative analyses using citizen survey data. This is the most appropriate method available to researchers to understand the individual-level correlates of vote choice in a population.

In essence, we are continuing the analysis we began in chapter 1 by ascertaining whether the vote calculus varied across the three provinces. In that chapter, we looked at social background characteristics and found that differential effects explained far more variation in vote outcomes than compositional differences, but we did not take the next step of identifying those differential effects. We take up that task here.

Examining differential effects has a number of other benefits. First, it enables us to determine whether similar vote shares masked important differences in the vote calculus employed by voters in different provinces. When investigating the impact of region on election outcomes, it is only natural to focus on the differences, but this provides only a partial picture of differences in voting behaviour. As we saw in chapter 1, both the Liberal and NDP vote shares were very similar in British Columbia and Quebec, yet it is very likely that those outcomes were driven by different factors.

Second, evaluating the contribution of differential effects enables us to consider the impact of party and media strategies on voters. We did not find much evidence of systematic variation that would account for the differences in vote outcomes. Only by comparing what we learned about party and media messages with the factors motivating voters' choice of parties can we understand the extent to which they mattered at all. For example, comparing the issues that were salient to voters in the different regions with the issues that were highlighted by the media can tell us something about the media's agenda-setting role. This cannot tell us about the direction of causality, as correlations between the media agenda and voters' issue priorities do not necessarily mean that the media set the agenda. It could instead be a matter of the media wanting to maximize their audience share by highlighting the issues that mattered to voters. In practice, there is likely to be a dynamic and reciprocal relationship between the media agenda and what matters to voters throughout the length of the campaign. Nonetheless, it is useful to highlight both the parallels and the discrepancies between the media agenda and voters' priorities and to see how these varied across the three provinces.

We can also gain insight into the success of the parties' strategies by focusing on differential effects. For example, if identifying with a party proves to be a more important factor in the vote in a particular province, it could indicate how successful the party has been in mobilizing its core supporters. Conversely, if identifying with its competitors has a weak effect, it may speak to the party's success in inducing defections. Similarly, we can see whether strategies like playing up leadership or downplaying the economy appear to have paid off.

Our analyses are based on a series of regression models. Our modelling approach aims for comprehensiveness rather than parsimony. We estimate a series of block recursive models that incorporate all of the major explanatory factors. The relevant explanatory factors are conceptualized as a series of blocks, and the blocks are entered in the models according to their presumed proximity to the vote (Gidengil et al. 2012). Entering the blocks of variables in stages makes it possible to estimate the total impact of each explanatory factor, as opposed to only that portion that is not mediated via more proximate factors. We are not assuming, of course, that all voters necessarily take account of all of these considerations. We are simply trying to capture a decision process in which voters participate to varying degrees. Explanatory factors are only retained in the models if their effects are statistically significant at p<0.10. The full results are presented in an online appendix.[1] Note that all of the effects reported in the text represent the total effects as estimated when the given factor is first entered into the model.

The first block consists of social background characteristics. As we saw in chapter 1, voters sharing the same social background characteristics often voted differently, depending on their province of residence. However, we did not investigate which characteristics had differential effects. Here, we consider a number of characteristics that have been found to influence vote choice in federal elections, including sex, age, education, income[2], language, religion, racial background, and type of community (Blais et al. 2002; Fournier et al. 2013; Gidengil et al. 2012).

The next block of variables pertains to ideological cleavages. In all three provinces, we examine the impact of views about redistribution. These tap into the traditional left-right cleavage. In Quebec we have to take account of a second cleavage. Views about sovereignty have dominated the province's politics for the past forty years.

The next variables to be added measure party identification, which we treat as a relatively stable, long-term component of the vote. Party identification can affect how voters view the issues and the party leaders (Bartels 2002; Blais et al. 2010; Gidengil et al. 2012).

The next two blocks encompass short-term factors that were salient in the election: the economy, balancing the budget, cutting taxes versus improving services, immigration, the niqab, crime, and perceived corruption as exemplified by the Duffy affair.

The final variables to be entered are the ratings of the parties' leaders.

Details of how the variables are coded can be found in the online appendix. The models are estimated using multinomial logistic regression. Given the small number of Green voters, the analysis is limited to the choice between the Conservatives, Liberals, and NDP, plus the Bloc in Quebec. We discuss the results of our analyses in terms of vote probabilities and present visualizations of some of the key findings.

WHAT EXPLAINS VOTE CHOICE?

Social Background Characteristics

Compositional differences may explain little of the vote share gaps but there were some consequential differences in the impact of social background characteristics. With one exception, the results reveal that social background characteristics were much less of an influence on voting for all three parties in Quebec. In Ontario and British Columbia, by contrast, vote choice was much more rooted in social group memberships. In and of itself, this finding suggests notable regional differences affect elections.

Predictably, in Quebec, the defining cleavage was language. The Liberals held much less appeal for Francophones than non-Francophones. The probability of voting Liberal was fully 30 points lower for Francophones. Meanwhile, their probability of voting Bloc was 24 points higher. However, this reflects the fact that hardly any non-Francophones voted Bloc. The NDP could not repeat its 2011 success but still outpolled the Bloc among Francophones (29 per cent to 25 per cent). The other social background characteristics that influenced vote choice in Quebec had much weaker effects.[3]

French-speakers in Ontario were much less likely to vote Conservative (21 points). However, given their small numbers, this is not what hurt the Conservatives. Much more damaging was the party's lack of appeal to women. There is clear evidence of the "modern gender gap" (Gidengil et al. 2013; Inglehart and Norris 2003) in Ontario: the probability of voting Conservative was 11 points lower for women and the probability of voting for one or other of the two left-of-centre parties was correspondingly higher. Women were also less likely to vote Conservative in British Columbia (7 points), but now there was only a significant sex difference in voting Liberal. Women were no more likely than men to vote NDP. Meanwhile, there was little sign of the modern gender gap in Quebec.

The Conservatives were also hurt in Ontario by their lack of appeal to voters living in the big cities. The probability of voting Conservative was 14 points lower for big-city residents. This benefited both the Liberals and the NDP. In British Columbia, on the other hand, big-city dwellers were less likely to vote NDP (8 points). Once again, this worked to the benefit of the Liberals (11 points).[4]

In British Columbia, the Conservatives were also hurt by their lack of appeal to younger voters: voters under the age of thirty-five were less likely to vote Conservative (15 points) and more likely to vote Liberal (9 points) than middle-aged or older voters. Age played out differently in Ontario where voters aged fifty-five or over were less likely than middle-aged or younger voters to opt for the NDP (10 points) and more likely to vote Conservative (6 points). Age made little difference in Quebec.

Being self-employed or employed also had opposite effects in British Columbia and Ontario. In British Columbia, these voters were more likely than other voters to vote NDP (9 points) and less likely to vote Conservative (7 points). In Ontario, by contrast, they were less likely to vote NDP (10 points) and more likely to vote Conservative (9 points) than voters who were not in the workforce.

Thus, the parties seemed to appeal to different groups across the country, despite their mostly national message. However, along with these differences, there were some notable similarities. Union membership is an example. Except for the NDP's years in the electoral wilderness between 1993 and 2000, union households have traditionally been key supporters (Archer 1985). Regaining that support was a critical factor in the party's resurgence after 2000 (Gidengil et al. 2012). There is evidence of this in both Ontario and British Columbia where voters from union households were more likely to vote NDP (11 points and 8 points, respectively) to the detriment of the Conservatives (10 points and 9 points, respectively). In Quebec, on the other hand, union membership was simply not a factor.

One of the longstanding puzzles in the literature on voting behaviour in Canada has been the lack of effect of income. Indeed, Canada has been described as a case of almost "pure non-class voting" (Alford 1963, x-xi; see also Gidengil 2002; Kay and Perrella 2012). British Columbia proved to be an exception in the 2015 election. The Conservative and NDP votes divided along the lines of income: the probability of voting Conservative was 12 points lower among voters with annual household incomes of less than $70,000 while the probability of voting NDP was 13 points higher. There was a similar pattern in Ontario, but the effects, while statistically significant, were only half the size.

Kay and Perrella (2012) have suggested that education may be a better indicator of social class than income, but it only proved to be a significant factor in Ontario where voters with only a high school education or less were more likely than voters with higher levels of educational attainment to vote NDP (9 points) and less likely to vote Liberal (13 points). The Conservative vote was unaffected, suggesting that the education effect was not a reflection of social class.[5]

The conventional explanation for the historic weakness of class voting in Canada has been that religion, like region, supersedes social class as a factor in vote choice. Catholic voters have traditionally been the key to Liberal dominance (Blais 2005), though their support wavered when the sponsorship scandal led to a decline in the Liberals' electoral fortunes (Gidengil et al. 2012; Stephenson 2010). The religious cleavage has been memorably characterized as "a moderately interesting, but strikingly peculiar, houseguest who has overstayed his welcome" (Irvine 1974, 570). Just why Catholics have long been more likely to vote Liberal than Protestants has defied explanation (Blais 2005). Issue attitudes, intergenerational transmission, the existence of a Catholic ethos in predominantly Catholic communities, and the religious affiliation of candidates and party leaders may all play a role, but none of these factors provides a compelling explanation. Whichever the explanation, the religious cleavage in both British Columbia and Ontario was a pale reflection of its former self in the 2015 election. Catholics were more likely to vote Liberal, but the effect was only 9 points in British Columbia and failed to satisfy conventional levels of statistical significance in Ontario where the support of the province's Catholics was once the bedrock of Liberal success.[6] What mattered more in both provinces was professing no religious affiliation. The probability of voting Conservative was fully 18 points lower in Ontario and 17 points lower in British Columbia for secular voters. The NDP was the major beneficiary in Ontario (12 points) but both the NDP and the Liberals benefited in British Columbia.

The other longstanding source of Liberal support has been visible minority voters (Blais 2005; Gidengil et al. 2012; Harell 2013). This was evident in both British Columbia (12 points) and Ontario (10 points). The Conservatives' efforts to woo visible minority voters did not pay off in either province. On the contrary, in British Columbia, these voters were less likely than other voters to opt for the Conservatives (9 points).

Differences in the *effects* of social background characteristics clearly mattered. This is most obviously the case in Quebec where the effect of language trumped other social background characteristics.

However, there were also consequential differences in effects between Ontario and British Columbia. On the other hand, as we saw in chapter 1, except for the gap in Conservative voting between Quebec and British Columbia, compositional differences played a very minor role in accounting for the differences in parties' vote shares across the three provinces.

IDEOLOGICAL CLEAVAGES

Not surprisingly, opinion about sovereignty was a major influence on vote choice in Quebec. When asked how they would vote on a Quebec-independence referendum, 30 per cent of Quebec respondents said that they would vote yes. This figure rose to 36 per cent among Francophones. The probability of voting Conservative was 12 points lower among those who favoured independence. However, it was the Liberal vote that was most affected by support for independence. The probability of voting Liberal was 20 points lower among pro-independence voters. Predictably, these voters were much more likely to vote for the Bloc (34 points). The NDP vote was unaffected.

As we would expect, given the importance of sovereignty, the left-right cleavage in voting was muted in Quebec (see figure 8.1). We captured the left-right dimension by asking respondents to place themselves on an 11-point scale that ranged from strongly favouring the redistribution of wealth from the rich to the poor to strongly opposing redistribution. In all three provinces, the median score was four, indicating that the median voter was a little to the left-of-centre.

Canadians may not be very good at telling left from right when it comes to politics (Gidengil et al. 2004; Lambert et al. 1986), but their vote is nonetheless structured along left-right lines (Gidengil et al. 2012). This was clearly the case in both Ontario and British Columbia. In both provinces, voters on the right were much more likely to vote Conservative than voters on the left or in the centre of the ideological spectrum. However, the two provinces diverged when it came to which party was able to capitalize on the support of voters on the left. Indeed, the patterns of support are strikingly different. In Ontario, the left-right cleavage divided the Conservatives from the Liberals. Voters on the left were more likely to vote Liberal than NDP. In British Columbia, by contrast, the left-right cleavage pitted the Conservatives against the NDP. This fits with the conventional understanding of the NDP as Canada's party of the left and is consistent with the stronger class

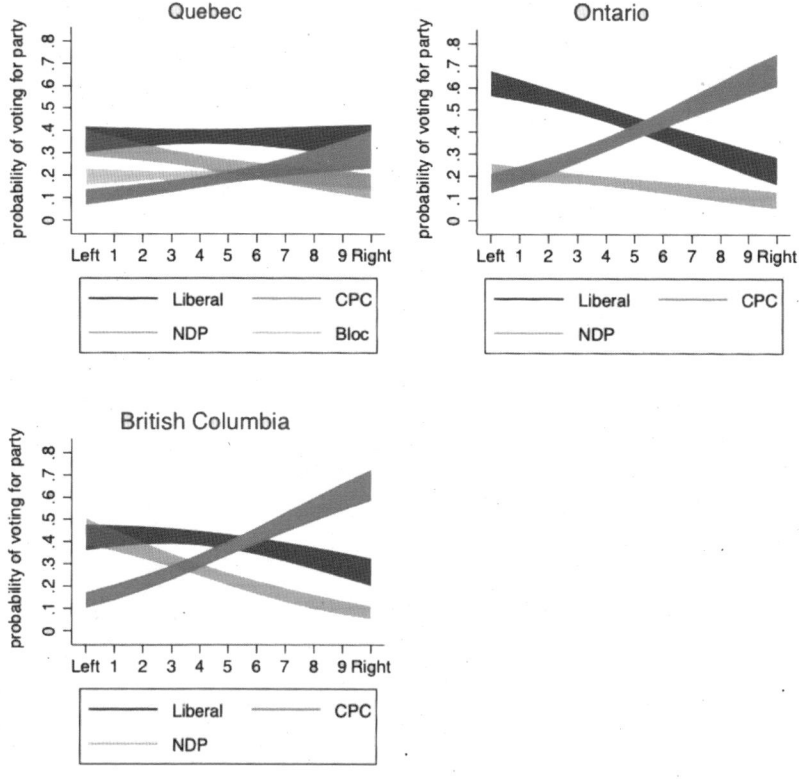

Figure 8.1 The left-right cleavage in voting

Note: The predicted probabilities were estimated on the basis of multinomial logistic regression models that controlled for social background characteristics. Voters'
positions on the left-right dimension were measured using their responses to a
question about redistribution of wealth from rich to poor.

cleavage in British Columbia that we saw above. This contrast between
Ontario and British Columbia is particularly interesting in light of
claims from some N D P members that the party moved too close to
the centre in 2015. This may have hurt the N D P in Ontario but not
necessarily in British Columbia. Note, though, that the N D P was much
less successful in appealing to voters on the left in British Columbia
than the Liberals were in attracting their support in Ontario.

The pattern is different yet again in Quebec. The left-right cleavage
was simply not a factor in voting for either the Liberals or the Bloc.
To the extent that the cleavage mattered in Quebec, it pitted the
Conservatives against the N D P. While the cleavage was much weaker

in Quebec, it is still worth noting that the NDP outpolled the Bloc
among left-leaning voters.

PARTISANSHIP

Whether Canadians have meaningful attachments to political parties
has been contested. However, evidence from the three elections held
between 2004 and 2008 suggests that a sizable number of Canadians
do have an enduring psychological attachment to a particular party.
Certainly their attachments are not immutable, but they can show
surprising resilience in the face of short-term shocks. The most compelling evidence of this comes from Liberal partisans in the wake of
the sponsorship scandal that rocked the party in the 2004, 2006, and
2008 elections (Gidengil et al. 2012). Many partisans failed to vote
for the party in those elections, but they nonetheless continued to
think of themselves as Liberals.

The challenge for any party is to mobilize its core supporters while
outpolling the other parties among non-partisans and inducing partisans of other parties to defect. None of the parties could count on
a large partisan base in any of the three provinces (see figure 8.2).
With non-partisans making up around two-thirds of the electorate
in all three provinces, the electoral fortunes of all three parties hinged
on their ability to attract the votes of non-partisans while encouraging
as many of their partisans as possible to vote for the party.

The Liberals clearly had the most appeal to non-partisans in all
three provinces (see figure 8.3). At the same time, their partisans
tended to be very loyal, though the party's mobilization efforts were
more successful in Quebec and Ontario than British Columbia. The
Liberals even managed to induce a non-trivial number of defections
from other parties in all three provinces.

The Conservatives were almost as successful as the Liberals in
mobilizing their partisan base in Ontario and outperformed the
Liberals in British Columbia. The story was very different in Quebec
where almost one Conservative in four voted for another party. With
18 per cent of Conservatives voting Liberal, these defections largely
benefited the Liberals. Even more damaging, the Conservatives had
the least appeal to the province's non-partisans, attracting only half
as many non-partisans as the Liberals. The party also failed to per-
suade many partisans of other parties to defect. Only the Bloc fared
worse in this regard. Indeed, in all three provinces, the Conservatives

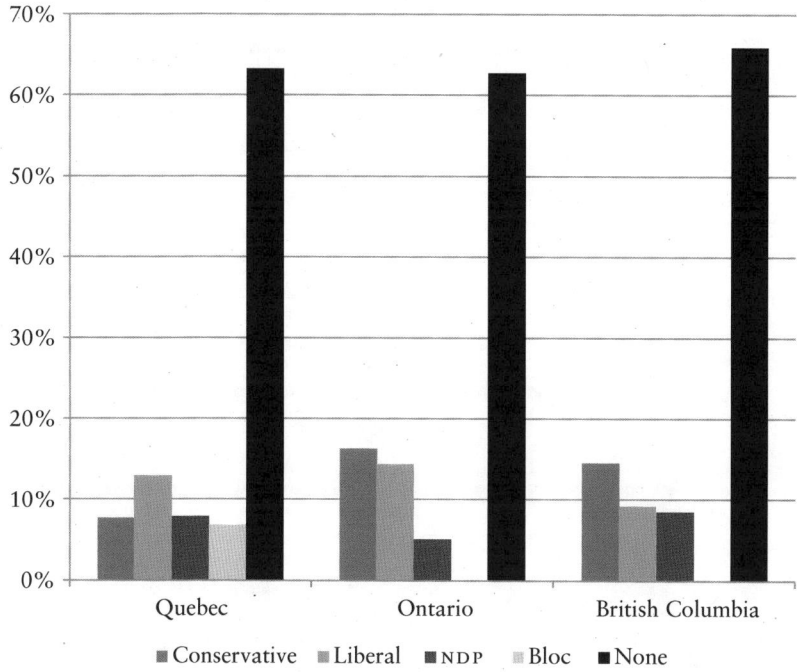

Figure 8.2 The distribution of party identification

failed to induce many partisans of other parties to defect. However, the non-partisans were the real prize and in Ontario, the Conservatives easily outpolled the N D P in this key group.

Surprisingly, perhaps, the N D P's Quebec partisans proved to be more loyal than their counterparts in Ontario and British Columbia. This may reflect the amount of time that the party's leader spent in the province (see chapter 5). Spending many fewer days in Ontario than the Liberal and Conservative leaders may have been a strategic mistake. The N D P did a much poorer job than the other parties of getting the province's partisans to vote for the party. If defectors had been as likely to vote Conservative as Liberal this would not have been so damaging, but this was not the case. The defectors voted overwhelmingly Liberal. The N D P also lagged well behind both the Liberals and the Conservatives when it came to appealing to the province's non-partisans. Combined with the small size of its partisan base and the number of defections, as well as its inability to induce defections from other parties, the N D P's lack of appeal to

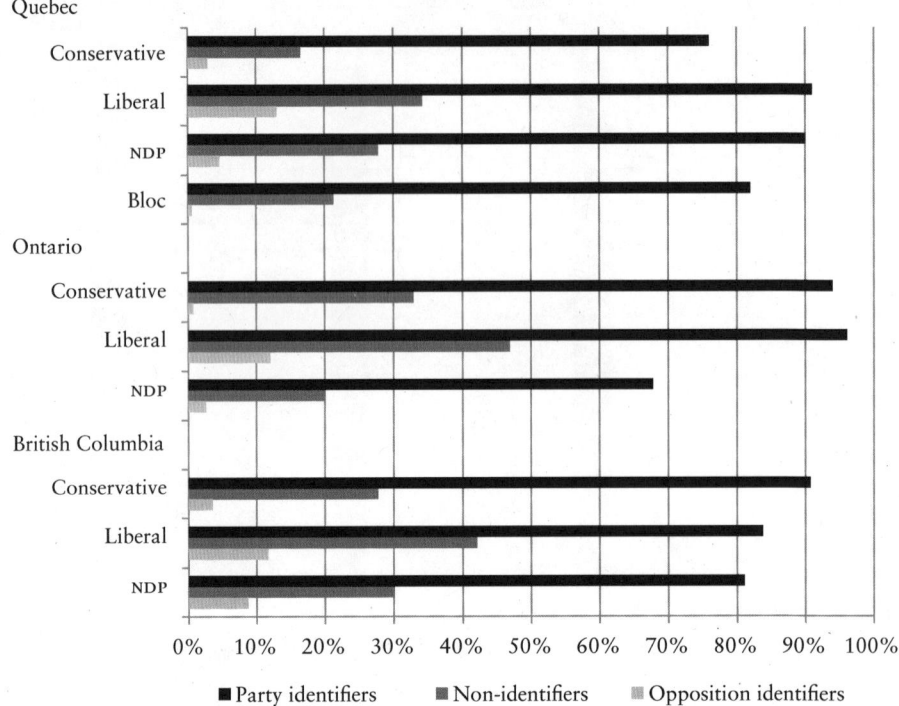

Figure 8.3 Vote choice by party identification

non-partisans is undoubtedly an important part of the explanation for the party's lacklustre performance in Ontario. The NDP was more successful in mobilizing its base in British Columbia, but one in five NDP partisans nonetheless voted for another party and, once again, that party was almost always the Liberal Party. Still, the NDP did a little better than the Conservatives in appealing to non-partisans and even managed to induce some defections from other parties.

SHORT-TERM CONSIDERATIONS

All of the factors considered so far are typically thought of as long-term influences on the vote. Their impact may vary from election to election in consequential ways, but the factors themselves are relatively immune to change. When partisans are disaffected with their party, they are as likely to declare themselves to be non-partisans as to change their partisanship (as opposed to changing their vote in a given election) (Gidengil et al. 2012). Similarly, voters are unlikely to switch from one side of the left-right spectrum to the other. Thus, these longer-term factors contribute an important element of inertia in voting behaviour even in times of electoral volatility. Other factors are likely to change in the short term. Party leaders come and go, the country's economic performance fluctuates, and unpredictable events can shift a voter's issue attitudes (and vote intentions, as we saw in chapter 3). A heinous crime can move opinion on dealing with crime in a get-tough direction, or a scandal can change perceptions of government corruption. What interests us is whether the influence of these shorter-term considerations varies from province to province.

The place to start is with voters' own positions. With one notable exception, opinion was not strongly differentiated along regional lines. This fits with the finding that policy preferences have become less regionalized in recent years (Anderson 2010; Montpetit et al. 2017). However, this does not mean that voters in the three provinces necessarily shared the same priorities when deciding their vote, nor does it mean that those priorities played into their choice of party in the same ways. On the contrary, there were some marked regional differences. What particularly interests us is how voters' priorities compared with those of the parties and the media.

As we saw in chapter 4, candidates for all three parties in all three provinces ranked the economy as the most important issue in their local campaigns, along with leadership. The economy was also the most popular issue in the press releases of all three parties and the most frequently addressed topic at all three leaders' campaign stops in all three provinces (see chapter 5). At the same time, the economy was the issue that received the most coverage in the national press and in the regional press in all three provinces, and it ranked second only to social policy in televised coverage (see chapter 6). There is every reason, then, to expect that economic evaluations would weigh heavily in voters' choice of party, regardless of province. Indeed, as we saw in chapter 7, voters who were paying a good deal of attention to campaign coverage, whether in the press or on television, were most likely to name the economy as the most important issue.

This was an issue with potential to hurt the Conservatives. Very few voters thought that the economy had improved over the previous twelve months and clear majorities in all three provinces believed that

Table 8.1
Issue attitudes (percentage)

	Quebec	Ontario	British Columbia
ECONOMY			
Worse	58	54	60
About the same	36	39	35
Better	6	7	6
BALANCED BUDGET			
Very important	34	43	41
Somewhat important	45	38	40
Unimportant	22	19	19
ANTI-NIQAB			
Yes	84	63	56
CORRUPTION			
A lot	37	35	38
Some	30	31	31
Hardly any	33	34	31

the economy had deteriorated (see table 8.1). Obviously, this was not good news for the Conservatives as the incumbent party. However, the party only paid a price in Quebec and Ontario, and the price was not very high (see figure 8.4). Indeed, it is striking how little economic perceptions mattered in British Columbia for any of the parties. There is a clear contrast with Ontario where the state of the economy was a much more salient concern for voters. What is really striking in Ontario is that negative perceptions of the country's economic performance had no effect on the likelihood of voting NDP.

The contrast between the importance attached to the economy by the candidates/parties/leaders/media and the impact on voters' choice of party might seem remarkable. The economy really only made a difference to the outcome in Ontario. However, we have to bear in mind that voters are apt to view the economy through a partisan lens (see, for example, Bartels 2002). As Campbell and his colleagues (1960, 133) argued, party identification "raises a perceptual screen through which the individual tends to see what is favourable to his partisan orientation." Indeed, this is one reason why media effects are typically limited when it comes to vote choice.

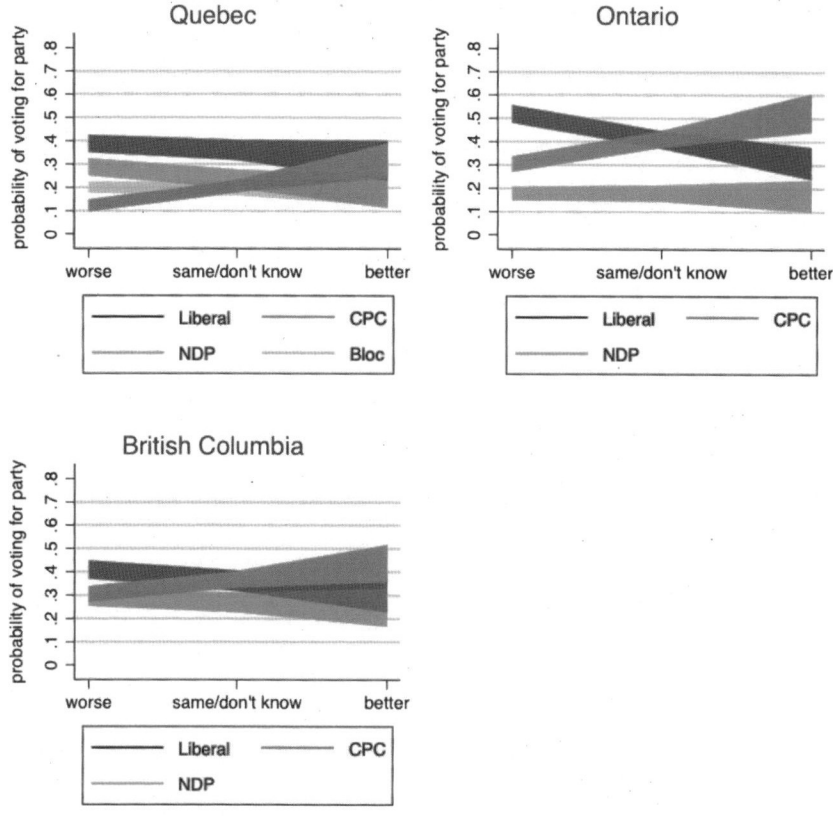

Figure 8.4 The impact of economic perceptions

Along with the economy, taxes figured prominently in reports of Harper's campaign visits, especially in Ontario. Many Conservative candidates also ranked taxes as being important to their local campaigns. Meanwhile, Mulcair's and Trudeau's campaign stops both emphasized social policy and social programs, especially in British Columbia. Opinion was close to the centre in all three provinces on the question of reducing taxes versus improving public services, with mean scores ranging from 5.0 in Quebec to 5.4 in British Columbia (where 10 indicated strongly supporting improved services). However, this issue was not a vote getter for any of the parties. It simply did not resonate with voters in Ontario and was a minor factor in British Columbia and especially Quebec. Predictably, the more voters favoured

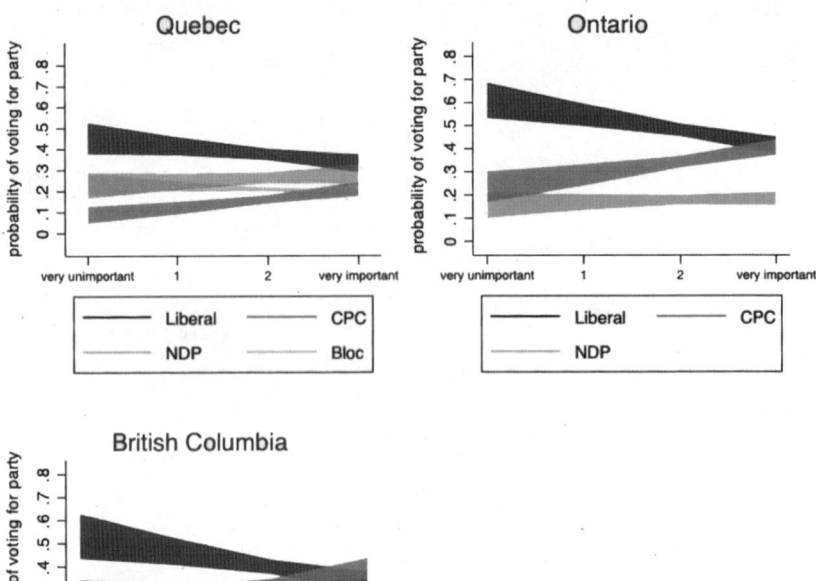

Figure 8.5 The impact of views about the federal budget

cutting taxes, the more likely they were to vote Conservative, but the effect was modest.[7] The effects on voting for the other parties were even smaller.

During the campaign, the Conservatives and the N D P both emphasized their plans to balance the federal budget. The Liberals, meanwhile, were willing to run a deficit in order to fund their policy commitments. Only one voter in five thought that this issue was unimportant, but they were more evenly divided when it came to whether balancing the federal budget was very or only somewhat important (see table 8.1). This issue did not help the N D P (see figure 8.5). On the other hand, there is no evidence to suggest that it actually hurt the party's chances in any of the provinces. Voters who thought that balancing the budget was very important were more likely to vote Conservative. This fits with theories of issue ownership (Bélanger and Meguid 2008). The

Conservatives were credible on the issue; the N D P was not. In all three provinces, the Liberals' willingness to run a deficit hurt the party's chances, but the impact was more muted in Quebec.

The niqab was not as big an issue in voters' minds as we might have expected, given the analysis of public opinion in chapter 3. This was the issue where opinion was most clearly regionalized with the vast majority of Quebeckers agreeing with the Conservative stance on the question of whether a woman should be allowed to take the oath of citizenship while wearing a niqab (see table 8.1). Our survey asked whether wearing the niqab should be allowed in this circumstance because "respect for minority rights is an important Canadian value," or not allowed because "it is inconsistent with Canadian values." There was less opposition in Ontario and British Columbia, but public opinion in both provinces was on the Conservatives' side. This was potentially a winning issue, but only if it trumped other considerations in the voters' decision calculus. The niqab issue played out differently from one province to another. This issue helped the Conservatives in British Columbia where the probability of voting for the party was 10 points higher when voters agreed with the Conservative position. The effect was only half as strong in Quebec and Ontario. The party's support for a woman's right to wear the niqab while taking the oath hurt the N D P in British Columbia, though the impact on vote choice was only modest (6 points). However, the impact on the probability of voting N D P in Quebec was very small. The issue may have hurt the N D P during the campaign, but there is no evidence that it drove Quebeckers' vote on election day.[8] It was the Liberals who appear to have paid a price in Quebec (8 points).

Once views about the niqab were taken into account, a more generalized sentiment that there should be fewer immigrants had very modest effects. The balance of opinion in all three provinces tipped slightly toward limiting numbers, with mean scores on a 0 to 10 scale ranging from a low of 5.1 in British Columbia to a high of 6.1 in Quebec. The issue did not have a significant effect on vote choice in British Columbia. In both Quebec and Ontario, the fewer immigrants voters wanted to see admitted to Canada, the more likely they were to vote Conservative, but the effect was quite weak.[9] The Liberals attracted the votes of Ontarians who favoured more immigration to Canada, but the effect was similarly weak. The effects on Liberal and N D P (and Bloc) voting were even smaller in Quebec.

The perception that there was a lot of corruption in the federal government, which may have been fuelled by the Duffy affair, was potentially damaging to the governing party. Mulcair frequently addressed the issue at his campaign events in all three provinces, though Trudeau did not emphasize the issue to the same extent (see chapter 5). Two in three voters in all three provinces believed that there was some or even a lot of corruption in the federal government (see table 8.1). This issue did hurt the Conservatives in British Columbia and Ontario but, even in Ontario, the effect was relatively modest (see figure 8.6). This helped the Liberals in Ontario and the NDP in British Columbia, but it was not a winning issue for either party. The issue was even less of a factor in Quebeckers' choice of party.

When it came to dealing with crime, there was a slight skew toward favouring tough sentences to fight crime rather than programs to rehabilitate offenders with mean scores ranging from 4.2 in Quebec to 4.6 in Ontario on a 0 to 10 scale. Predictably, this was an issue that helped the Conservatives but only in Quebec and Ontario (see figure 8.7). The issue was less salient in British Columbia with voters who favoured a get-tough approach gravitating toward the NDP and the Conservatives. Voters who favoured rehabilitation, on the other hand, were more likely to favour the Liberals in all three provinces. Once again, though, none of these effects is strong.

Indeed, overall, vote choice in the three provinces was not strongly issue driven. This was particularly true of Quebec. The salience of issues in voters' decision calculus varied depending on the party. Issue attitudes typically carried more weight in the decision to vote Conservative in all three provinces but were a relatively minor factor in NDP voting. It was the Liberals, rather than the NDP, who typically capitalized on the support of voters who were opposed to the Conservatives' issue positions. Perhaps the most telling finding to emerge here is the NDP's failure to attract voters in British Columbia and Ontario who were concerned with the deterioration of the country's economy, a finding that underscores the party's longstanding inability to capture ownership of the issue of economic management.

LEADERSHIP

Leadership is the focus of a lot of media attention. As we saw in chapter 6, Harper received the most negative coverage whereas Trudeau received the most positive coverage. Harper was the least

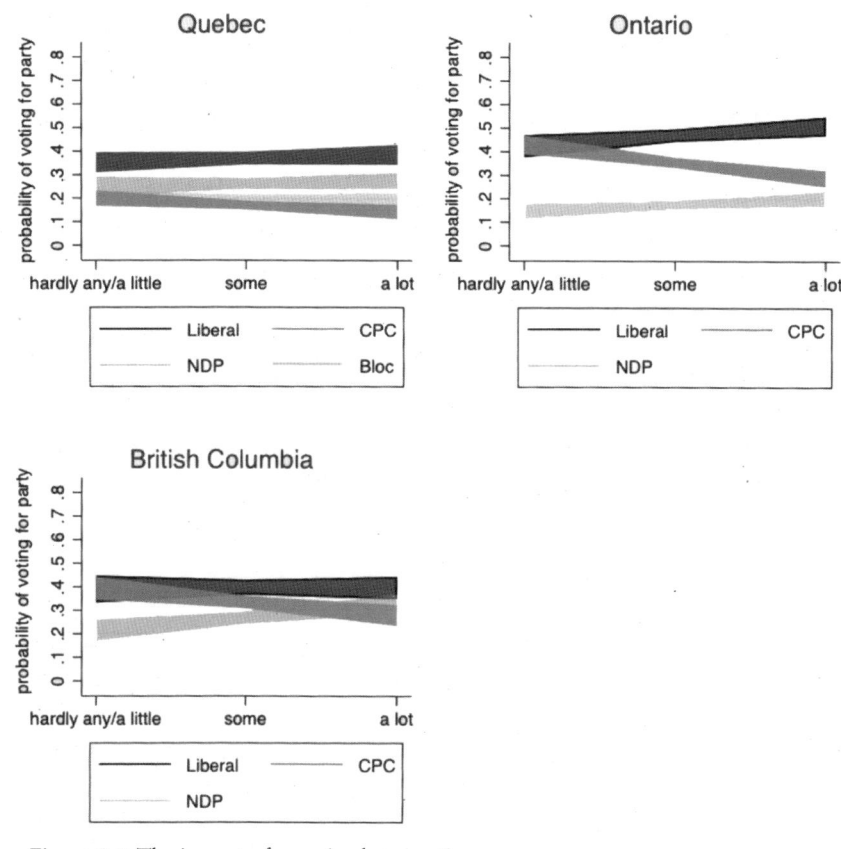

Figure 8.6 The impact of perceived corruption

liked of the leaders in all three provinces. When voters were asked to indicate how much they liked or disliked each leader on a scale from 0 to 10, the Conservative leader's average ratings pointed to his lack of popularity (see figure 8.8). The most popular leader in Quebec was the NDP's Mulcair, just ahead of the Liberal leader, Trudeau. Both leaders were more popular with Quebeckers than the Bloc's leader, Duceppe. In Ontario and British Columbia, Trudeau came out just ahead of his NDP rival.

Leader evaluations clearly mattered, but how much they mattered varied depending on both the province and the party (see figure 8.9). Harper's low ratings hurt his party the most in Quebec where voters who gave him a rating of less than five were extremely unlikely to

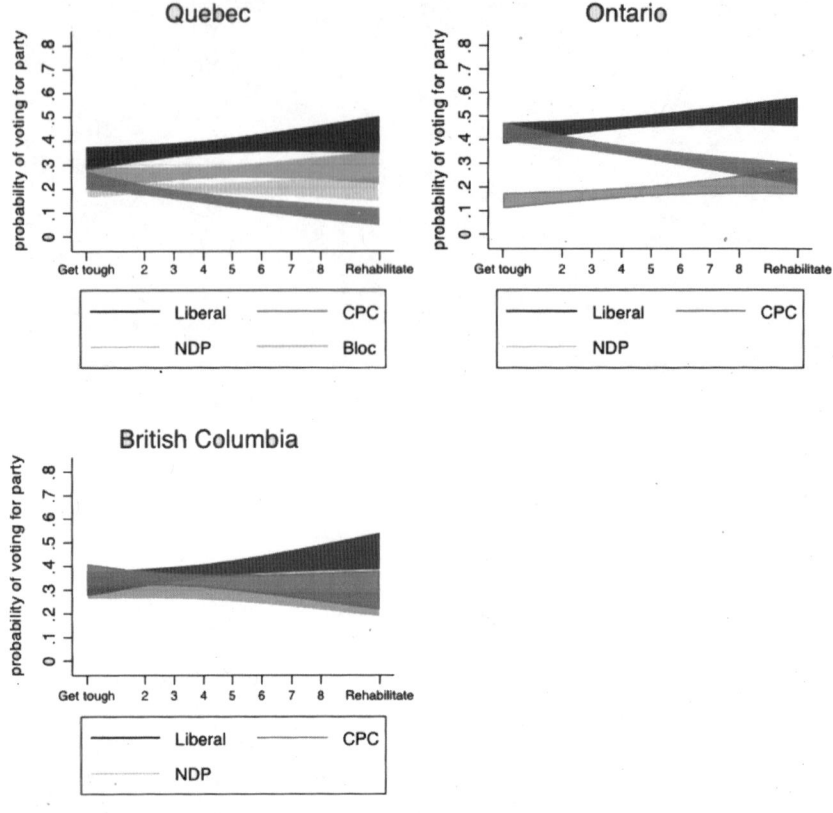

Figure 8.7 The impact of views about fighting crime

vote Conservative. Even voters who were more positively disposed were not very likely to vote for his party. The same was true of the impact of positive ratings of Mulcair and especially Duceppe. Even voters who gave Duceppe a ten had only a 34 per cent probability of voting for his party. In Quebec, it was clearly the Liberals who were the most likely to reap the benefits of having a popular leader. This was also the case in Ontario, where Mulcair's relative popularity was even less help to his party. Even voters who gave him the maximum score only had a 50 per cent chance of voting for his party. Harper's low ratings did not hurt his party quite as much in Ontario as they did in Quebec, and voters who liked him were more likely to vote Conservative than their Quebec counterparts. In British Columbia, meanwhile, leader evaluations had similarly strong effects on voting for both the Liberals and the Conservatives. Given that

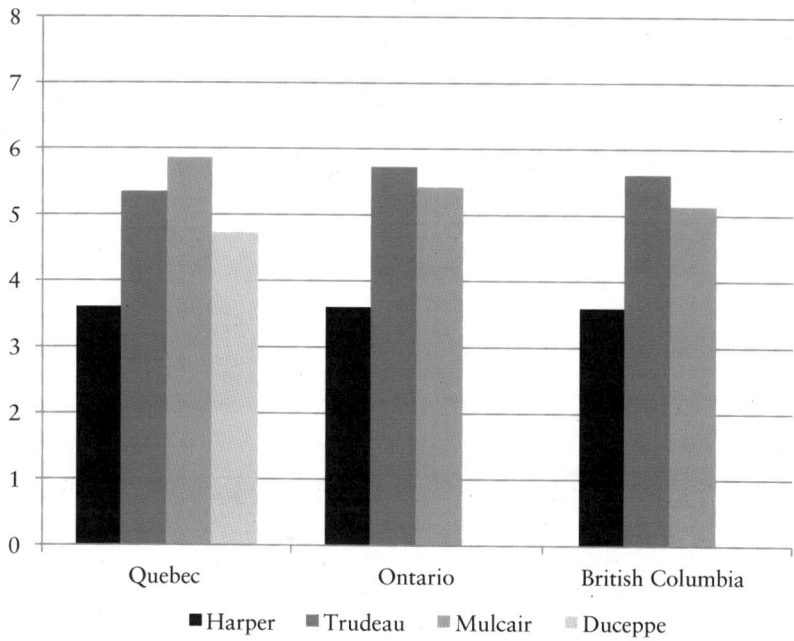

Figure 8.8 Leader evaluations

Trudeau was much more popular in the province than Harper, this clearly worked to his party's advantage. Mulcair was not far behind Trudeau in the popularity stakes, but low ratings were more damaging to his party's chances.

STRATEGIC DEFECTIONS

The high proportion of NDP partisans who voted Liberal, especially in Ontario, raises the question of whether these defections were strategic. Strategic voting involves voting for a party that is not the voter's first choice because the latter is perceived to have little or no chance of winning (Blais et al. 2001). A strategic voter votes instead for her second-choice party in hopes of defeating the party she likes least (Cox 1997). The literature on strategic voting in Canada suggests that it occurs less frequently than media coverage would suggest (Blais and Nadeau 1996; Blais et al. 2001; Gidengil et al. 2012; Merolla and Stephenson 2007). It will often be the case that a voter's preferred party has a chance of winning, and so there is no incentive

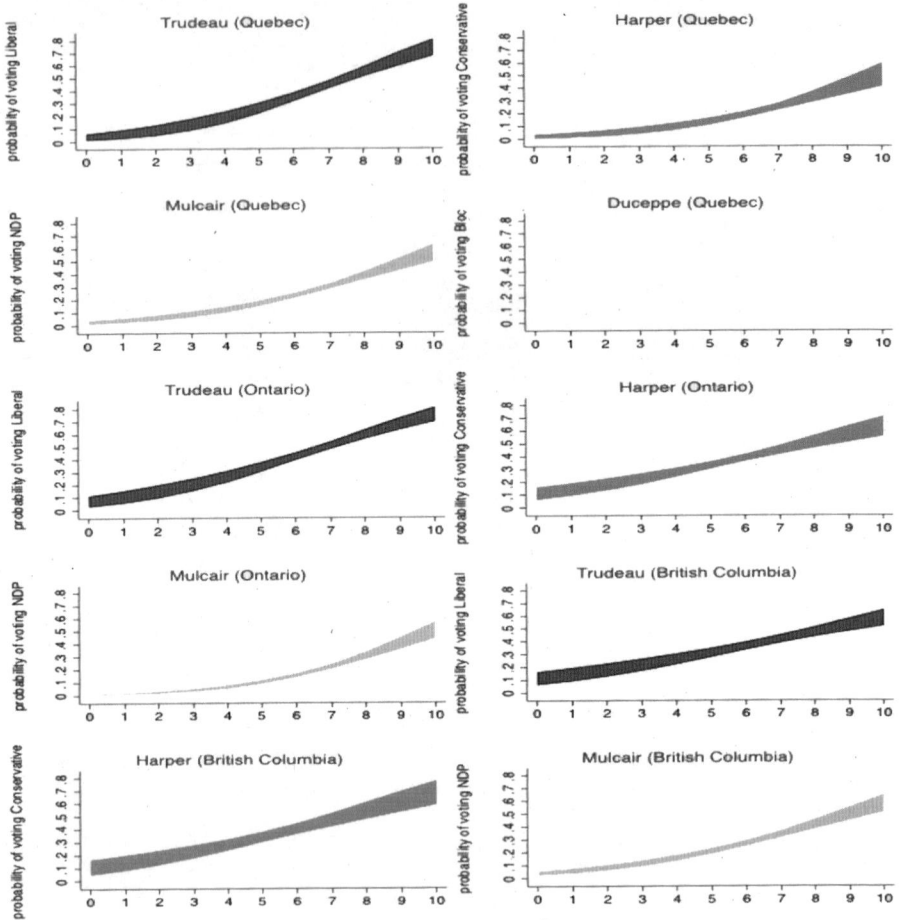

Figure 8.9 The impact of leader evaluations

to desert their first choice (Alvarez et al. 2006), but even among voters whose first choice is unlikely to win, only a minority cast a strategic vote (Blais et al. 2009). Most of these voters vote sincerely for their preferred party despite the strategic incentives to defect. There are at least two possible explanations for the low level of strategic voting, despite the incentives offered by our first-past-the-post electoral system (Blais 2002). First, many voters may opt to vote sincerely rather than strategically because they have a strong preference for their first-choice party and do not harbour a strong dislike of the likely winner. Second, voters are apt to overestimate their preferred party's chances of winning in their constituency and thus fail to realize that it is trailing in third or fourth place (Blais and Turgeon 2004; Blais and Bodet 2006).

To see how much of a role strategic voting played in our three provinces, we focus on voters who had an incentive to vote strategically because they perceived that their first-choice party had no chance of winning. These were voters who rated their party's chances of winning in their riding at four or less on a 0 to 10 scale. There was clearly an important element of wishful thinking when voters rated their preferred party's chances. For example, in Ontario, fully 81 per cent of those who preferred the NDP estimated its chances of winning their riding at 50 per cent or better, compared with only 59 per cent of those who preferred another party. A similar pattern held for all of the parties in all three provinces: voters who liked a party were more optimistic about its chances. This misplaced optimism necessarily limited the number of strategic votes that could be cast.

Even among those with a strategic incentive to defect, many opted to vote sincerely. In all three provinces, a majority of voters who liked the Liberals or the Conservatives best voted for their preferred party even when recognizing that it had little or no chance of winning in their riding. The same was true of voters who preferred the Bloc in Quebec. The story was very different for the NDP, especially in Ontario. Fully 58 per cent of Ontario voters who liked the NDP best chose to vote for another party if they realized that the NDP was very unlikely to win in their riding. The same was true of 48 per cent of their Quebec counterparts and 49 per cent of their British Columbia counterparts. In all three provinces, their votes went overwhelmingly to the Liberal candidate. This is strongly suggestive of strategic voting, but we should bear in mind that the numbers are small, given the tendency in all three provinces to overstate the party's chances.

CONCLUSION

The story of regional differences in the parties' electoral fortunes is very much about differences in the vote calculus across the provinces. The Quebec story is a simple one: as in previous elections, the key factors were language and sovereignty. Perhaps the most surprising finding involves the issue of the niqab. Opinion in the province was massively on the side of the Conservatives, but it was not a winning issue for the party, and there is no evidence that the N D P suffered on election day as a result of their opposition to the Conservatives' stance.

The story is more complicated in Ontario and British Columbia. In contrast to Quebec, the vote in both provinces was influenced by a variety of social background characteristics. However, the characteristics that mattered were not necessarily the same. Notably, lack of appeal to women and big-city residents cost the Conservatives votes in Ontario but were less of a factor in British Columbia. Conversely, there was more evidence of a class cleavage in British Columbia than Ontario. The most striking difference, though, related to the traditional left-right cleavage, which divided the Conservatives from the Liberals in Ontario but pitted the N D P against the Conservatives in British Columbia. Issue attitudes also played out differently in the two provinces. Notably, the economy had a greater impact in Ontario than British Columbia. The same was true of strategic considerations. To the extent that voters engaged in strategic voting, it was in Ontario that the N D P paid the highest price.

In light of what we have analyzed in other chapters, these results suggest that most of the provincial differences observed in the 2015 election are rooted in the voters themselves, rather than in any provincial-level strategic choices made by the parties or the media. The economy is a prime example. Despite the emphasis that the candidates, the parties, and the media all put on this issue, the economy did not play in British Columbia and was only a minor factor in Quebeckers' choice of party. In the following chapter, we take a closer look at what the results in this and our other chapters mean for the nature of federal elections in Canada.

9

A Distinctly National Prize

We began this book project with a clear goal: to better understand the sources of variation in party support across provinces in Canadian elections. The results of the 2015 election made clear that support for the eventual winner, the Liberal Party, was not equally distributed across the country. This regionalization of electoral support has implications for the quality of democratic governance and representation, and, given the history of regional unrest and the articulation of different policy preferences across regions in Canada, is of substantial interest.

As outlined in chapter 2, regionalism is a topic that has been entertained by scholars of Canadian politics for years. While there is no absolute consensus, several observers have characterized regionalism as rooted in variation in political cultures across the country (see, for example, Elkins and Simeon 1980). Others have argued that regionalized vote choice reflects substantial differences in the priorities held by voters in different provinces (see, for example, Gidengil et al. 1999). This has played out at both the provincial and federal levels in party politics and policy evolution. But the source of this variation remains difficult to capture. Gidengil et al. (1999) used a decomposition analysis, similar to the one performed in chapter 1, to show that, in the 1997 election, the gaps in support for the Liberal and Reform parties were not driven by socio-demographic variation. Support for the parties reflected political priorities that distinguished parts of the country. It is quite possible, and indeed likely, that such inherent variation in priorities was also relevant in 2015. Yet, what drives that variation in political priorities has remained unclear.

The goal of this project was to use the existing research as a starting point for a new direction for analysis – one that placed the focus squarely on the key elements of an election as experienced in the provinces. We took the idea of regional political priorities seriously and sought to disentangle organic voter preferences from those induced by the strategic choices of parties or the media. Instead of considering the election across the country, we narrowed our view to examine how the federal election unfolded in British Columbia, Ontario, and Quebec. Following the design of Cross et al. (2015) in their analysis of the 2011 election in Ontario, and in the spirit of the Making Electoral Democracy Work project (Blais 2010), we focused on three sets of actors – the parties, the media, and the voters – which allowed us to develop a more fulsome picture of how the election was experienced by voters. The chapters of this volume have thus been designed to provide a comprehensive analysis of the 2015 election in the three largest Canadian provinces. As noted in chapter 1, the social composition of the various provinces cannot really explain the election outcomes, nor can the unique provincial party systems. The usual (and obvious) suspects, so to speak, cannot be blamed. Something else is driving the variation in vote choice across the country. In this final chapter, we take stock of our findings across the diverse data sources and analyses that have been presented in order to consider what they contribute to our understanding of regionalization in Canadian elections.

TAKING STOCK

Chapters 2 and 3 are essential reading for understanding the subsequent analyses of the 2015 election campaign. Chapter 2 provides the background to the dimensions of regionalization in Canada and generates a framework for our analysis. From this review of the literature, we observe that, for voters, parties, and the media, regionalization is a central (and well-documented) feature of Canadian life. The existing literature, in Canada and elsewhere, demonstrates that elections in federal states cannot be understood as purely national contests. Indeed, Elias et al. (2015) have outlined four different strategies for parties in systems characterized by both left-right and territorial cleavages – ignoring one dimension of competition, blurring the lines between the two, defining one in terms of the other, or embracing the duality fully. In our estimation, Canadian parties in 2015 seemed to design their platforms to cover federal issues only, but the candidate-level delivery of those messages was often done through local lenses.

This is a sensible multi-level strategy if we think of parties as centre-periphery organizations with candidates as the agents on the ground. Our analysis shows the importance of regarding multiple levels of competition – federal/provincial, national/local, and anglophone/francophone – when considering an election contest.

Existing work on regionalism in Canada led us to develop three hypotheses that could explain why the 2015 election unfolded the way it did:

1 Parties differ: they present different information to voters in different regions.
2 The media differ: they present campaign messages from the parties differently across regions.
3 Voters differ across regions: they have different values, priorities, or preferences.

Each hypothesis proposes a plausible explanation for the differences in regional outcomes, and each hypothesis could complement another to form a richer explanation. Using this framework, differences in electoral outcomes were to be expected, and furthermore, would be explained by the active and strategic choices pursued by parties and the media, as well as regional differences among voters that go beyond basic socio-demographics.

Before turning to specific analyses, however, we needed to understand what was going on before and while the campaign was being waged. Chapter 3 provides that overview, with a discussion of expectations, events, and public opinion from the inter-election and election periods. The greatest point of interest, from an observer's point of view, is the dramatic rise in support for the Liberal Party since the 2011 election. Unsurprisingly, a big part of that rise came about with the election of Justin Trudeau as leader. The party received a 10-point boost that had remarkable staying power (about eighteen months), compared to the smaller (5-point) and less durable increase the NDP received with the election of Thomas Mulcair, or the 3-point boost the Conservatives received around their handling of the terrorist attacks in October 2014.

However, events in Alberta (for example, the electoral victory of Rachel Notley's NDP) created the most dramatic upset. Clearly voters were impressed by the NDP's success in Alberta, and it created momentum for their federal counterpart. Going into the 2015 campaign, the

NDP was the frontrunner at the federal level, followed by the Conservatives and the Liberals in third place. That the eventual outcome was so different speaks to the importance of the campaign itself and the importance of leadership to party success. During the campaign, the dramatic unfolding of key events – such as the leaders' debates, the fraud trial of Mike Duffy, the increased salience of the refugee crisis after the death of a young Syrian refugee, and the Conservative promises to appeal the Federal Court of Appeal decision about niqabs and to establish a "barbaric cultural practices" hotline – motivated shifts in vote intentions and reprioritized issues at the regional level.

Chapter 3 also provides some insight into how the campaign was expected to unfold, on the basis of constituencies that had been won by narrow margins in 2011 (27 per cent of constituencies across the country). Based on an analysis of which parties had come in second, Ontario seemed to be the most promising battleground for the Liberals, with Quebec being the most concerning. The opposite pattern held for the Conservatives. Yet, there was no pattern evident in British Columbia. It would have been logical, then, to see the two parties concentrate their efforts in specific constituencies in Ontario and Quebec. This set up a hypothesis that parties targeted critical ridings; we looked for evidence of this and other targeting in subsequent chapters.

Our overall goal was to understand whether and how parties, the media, and voters contributed to regionalization by triangulating multiple empirical sources. We began in chapters 4 and 5 at the party level. While we often speak of elections in terms of parties and leaders, the reality is that candidates are the ones conducting the majority of campaign activity. Our analysis of campaign personalization in chapter 4 showed that there is variation in how constituency campaigns are conducted across provinces. Campaign tailoring at the regional level took more than one form – primarily, variation in the issues highlighted, but also the degree of emphasis on the party brand. At the same time, our investigation revealed that some candidate-level specificity was encouraged by the parties at the federal level, as both regionally tailored advice and campaign training were provided to local candidates by the central parties. This supports our expectation that parties do, at least to some degree, tailor their efforts to appeal to specific audiences. However, while we had provincial-level expectations, our data suggest that riding-level targeting was more common.

Again, this is a sensible strategy if we think parties will be targeted by their opponents for overtly communicating multiple messages: it is far more difficult for an opposition party to identify 338 minor variations on the central strategy than it would be to simply catch the leader conveying contradictory messages in different regions of the country.

Moving away from specific candidates, the data in chapter 5 suggest less evidence of strategic campaigning by the parties, in terms of emphasizing specific issues in specific locations, than we might expect. The locations of leaders' visits provide evidence of some effort to build support in specific locations, and there is some indication that party leaders altered their messages to respect the local dynamics when it was possible to do so. However, at least in the latter case, this was most likely to occur in Quebec, which is hardly surprising given the linguistic and historical political differences that have traditionally played out in the province. For the most part, the leaders each emphasized similar issues everywhere, and the parties were consistent in the focus of their campaign platforms across regions. Looking at campaigns at the candidate level suggests some real variation in on-the-ground efforts, but when it comes to the federal story there is less evidence of regional campaigning. The impression one gets is that a national campaign was waged, but that key battles at the constituency level received particular attention from the central party office and leader. For our first hypothesis, then, we have only modest support: it holds to some extent at the local level, but not for the national parties and their leaders.

The next two chapters of the book addressed our second hypothesis and examined how the media presented the 2015 campaign to voters. Chapter 6 focused on print news, including papers with both national and regional audiences, and regionally televised nightly news broadcasts (in Montreal, Vancouver, and Toronto). In terms of coverage overall, our results suggest that the horserace took a back seat to issues and leaders, even though the media are often accused of focusing too much on who is ahead and who is behind. This is surprising given the conventional wisdom in the literature, but not an unwelcome finding. If the media focused on issues and leaders, then voters were given a better opportunity to gain substantive knowledge about the campaigns before they had to cast their ballots. While this is encouraging from a democratic quality point of view, we again found little to support our contention that the media tailored its coverage of party campaigns to match their regional salience. We did, however, find that the parties and leaders were not all treated equally. Leader coverage varied, disadvantaging the incumbent prime minister, Stephen Harper, while favouring challengers Justin Trudeau and Thomas Mulcair, with an emphasis on the former. While this suggests that the media play a role in how voters understand election campaigns, it does not point to any clear regional variation that could have had an impact on the outcome of the 2015 election. We found little support for the idea that the media contribute to regionalized vote outcomes by varying issue coverage.

Of course, simply looking at the inputs (party communications and media presentations) does not really help us to understand the main outcome we are interested in – how voters responded to the parties. To do that most effectively, we considered two items of interest in chapter 7. We first looked at which types of media coverage reached voters. This provided insight into what voters learned about the party platforms and leaders. Second, using survey data that provided indicators of media preferences, reader/viewership and evaluations, we examined whether a link exists between media consumption and factors that influence voting. Although we did not see significant regional variation in newspaper or televised coverage in chapter 6, we did find variation between the two types of coverage. In other words, voters who only read print news received a different impression of the campaign than those who only watched broadcast news. This finding led us to ask whether the differences in coverage influenced evaluations by voters. The short answer is no. We found very little evidence of specific media effects on evaluations or expectations that could account for the vote outcome differences. Our analysis suggests that voters were not swayed by the tone of the coverage they received. On the one hand, voters' information sources may be far richer and more varied than we have been able to consider here. If that is the case, then a lack of direct correspondence between media coverage and vote is not that surprising, as we have not been able to account for the full range of voters' information environments (including what social media they may have had exposure to). On the other hand, perhaps voters' evaluations are more sophisticated than they are typically given credit for. Voters may have received information from the media *and countered* information that was not balanced (Zaller 1992). Investigating this further is beyond the scope of this book, and certainly beyond the data that we have access to, but it is a very intriguing possibility.

Finally, our book culminates with an examination of the factors that directly affected vote choice in order to assess the final possible explanation for the observed vote outcome differences: that voters themselves differ across the provinces. In chapter 8, we investigated whether the decision calculus differed across the provinces. This enabled us to look beyond aggregate vote shares to see if the combination of factors that led to a decline in NDP votes, for example, varied by province. It also enabled us to look for evidence of party and media strategies affecting voters, as well as the success of party strategies in shaping the election. We employed a block recursive approach, looking at socio-economic factors, then adding ideological cleavages like views about redistribution, followed by party identification, short-term factors like the economy and issues, and finally leader evaluations. Here we found that the provincial differences in vote outcome observed in the 2015 election were rooted in the voters themselves, rather than the strategic choices made by parties or differentiated media coverage. The choices of Quebec voters, as in previous elections, were driven by the parties' responses to key issues that stoked controversy in the province. In Ontario and British Columbia, the mix of relevant vote factors was different, both from Quebec and from one another. Most notably, ideology, in the form of the left-right cleavage, divided the Liberals from the Conservatives in Ontario, but pitted the NDP against the Conservatives in British Columbia.

In summary, we have little evidence that regional strategies of the parties or the media affected voters' choices in a way that is consistent across voters in a specific geographic area. To the (limited) extent that campaigns varied across constituencies and provinces, we did not find that vote choice was affected. Even accounting for the most obvious aspects of voters' political information environments, there was simply no corresponding difference in vote choice.

So, what does this mean in light of our hypotheses? There was limited evidence of regional campaigns in the 2015 federal election. One cannot attribute the regional differences in party support across the country to anything systematic or strategic on the part of the parties or the media. They also have little to do with variations in the social background characteristics of provincial populations. Instead, our findings suggest that we need to recognize the great diversity of our country. Canadians are simply not the same from province to province. They care about different issues and evaluate candidates and parties according to different criteria. Of course, these differences may be influenced by long-term variations in party positions and campaign behaviour that are not as apparent in a single election. Nonetheless, it is these differences in provincial electorates, and not the proximate party campaigns or media reports, that lead to highly differentiated outcomes like the 2015 election and several before it. This type of regionalism is truly based on voters' long-term preferences. While our findings are largely null in terms of our hypotheses, they are in some sense rather encouraging. In fact, the absence of highly regionalized campaigns suggests a more nuanced understanding of parties, the media, and voters in Canadian elections.

THE UPSIDE

Our analysis of party behaviour contrasts with findings from earlier elections where parties could be (at least partially) blamed for similarly regionalized outcomes. For example, Cairns (1968) identified regionalized party attention as one consequence of Canada's first-past-the-post electoral system. In his view, parties fight for votes in the most efficient way possible, so when there is little chance of winning, the parties give up on the contest. The result would be clear differences in effort and attention across the country. Work by Carty, Cross, and Young (2000) also points to this type of regionalized campaign strategy. Prior to the introduction of television to campaigns, parties were able to target their appeals because media outlets had a more limited reach, yet even in 1997, when the media environment was far more sophisticated (and national), Cross (2002b) found that parties competed unevenly across the country. This probably reflected the nature of partisan competition in that election (the Reform Party concentrated in the West and the Bloc in Quebec), but nonetheless it is remarkable given the national audience of the other parties.

Now that there is less regionalization in the party system, our findings that the parties did little in the way of regionalizing their messages, but made some regionalized effort in terms of constituency campaigns and leader visits, may reflect a new reality and an important development in the study of regionalism. With the move to a constant media environment and the emergence of the "permanent campaign" (Marland et al. 2017), accusations of uneven campaigning can be much more damaging for parties that compete across the country. Consider, for example, Trudeau's much-reported accusation that Mulcair said different things in French than English (Walkom 2015). While any mixed-messaging by parties or leaders would be looked upon poorly by the electorate, the act of being caught by an opponent or the media delivering contradictory information might be more damaging to a party or leader when it was delivered in different languages, as that suggests that leaders may be trying to leverage the traditional linguistic fault line to their advantage.

Is the fact that national campaigns have become less regionalized simply a matter of the technological changes that have shaped today's media environment? Or, to put it another way, is this about the popularity of social media and the advent of the constant news cycle? We live in a time when news is continually updated and particularly salacious or salient news spreads virally. Social media sit at the intersection of media reporting, party strategy, and public engagement. Professional journalism has come under fire in this new model of information transmission as the rise of low- and no-cost digital technology platforms and social media outreach has greatly democratized the ability to spread information. Though the Canadian news environment has never been so corporately concentrated, we are seeing the entry of new players in the campaign media sphere. Attention drawn to campaign events by social media influencers has the power to shift attention away from the mainstream press and influence the agenda-setting process (Chacon, Giasson, and Lawlor 2018). Furthermore, voters are, in some cases, choosing to bypass the mainstream press altogether and have their news curated by sources of interest through social media.

While this is not the first election to highlight candidate scandals and embarrassing pictures or events, the ability to electronically deliver such information in real time with analysis and personal commentary has made social media a force to be reckoned with. Parties and leaders have quickly found that this is not a trend that can be avoided. They have to engage social media audiences, and, if possible, set the tone for social media commentary to prevent hostile forces from dominating the online narrative. This multimedia approach appears to have resulted in the need for highly centralized and highly controlled party communication. If a leader is perceived to offer one set of promises to one region and a different set to another, there is no doubt that it would quickly make the news. Differentiated campaigning and inconsistent messaging have simply become too risky.

If concentrated and consistent messaging is the new priority, then it should not surprise us that everything comes down to the way that the party (and party leader) is represented in the media. Our analysis of media coverage shows that issues and leaders dominated campaign coverage. As we noted earlier, this is contrary to some of the research on campaign coverage and is, therefore, a finding of particular import. Criticism of the media for concentrating on horserace coverage instead of substantive issues is not new (Wilson 1980/81, Wagenberg et al. 1988, Andersen 2000). Commentary by Mark Brister (2012) is particularly harsh:

> We cannot possibly place the entire burden of civic enlighten-
> ment and national coalescence at the feet of the fourth estate,
> but a small constellation of traditional media organizations
> nonetheless remains the critical conduit carrying complex politi-
> cal messages to nescient publics. Judged by its proficiency in
> executing this function, national media coverage of the 2011 fed-
> eral election was an utter failure. Instead of preparing Canadians,
> reporters bombarded us with commentary fantasizing about seat
> distribution permutations, scoring the exchanges of party leaders,
> and incessantly regurgitating a torrent of polls tracking the rela-
> tive standing of parties. Media obsession with evaluating events
> in terms of how they may impact the potential outcome of the
> election displaced other elements of national dialogue, impover-
> ishing our collective deliberation at a watershed moment in the
> country's history.

What our data suggest, however, is that any emphasis on the horserace character of elections comes toward the end of a campaign and is, in fact, overwhelmed by substantive reporting. Whether our findings reflect a change precipitated in part by reaction to the coverage of previous campaigns is not clear, but it is nonetheless remarkable.

Another point to consider is the type of impact that campaign and pre-campaign events have on voters. For the lay observer (and even us as authors, prior to analyzing the data), it seemed obvious that campaign events were a major part of the story of 2015. After all, going into the election, it appeared that the NDP had its first real chance at forming the government. In great part, that seemed due to the provincial NDP's success in Alberta, which surprised many, and seemed to suggest a trend when coupled with the NDP's Quebec suc-cess in the 2011 federal election. The polls seemed to reflect a new, more overtly progressive mood among voters, and it seemed as if voters were asking themselves, "If a traditionally conservative province could elect the NDP, why couldn't the country?" This optimism was short-lived once the election campaign began. Skepticism around Mulcair's hold on the leader's office created a feeling of uncertainty for undecided voters. This, coupled with the NDP's dramatic loss of popularity in Quebec owing to their handling of the niqab issue, resulted in a poor showing in areas where they were predicted to fare well. As ever, the Liberals were prepared to reap this gain, and their increase in vote support appears to be a direct consequence of the NDP's losses.

This presentation of the 2015 election probably rings true for many readers. It reflects the mainstream interpretation of events as they unfolded throughout the campaign. Yet, such a conventional analysis is challenged by the findings in chapter 8. When we move from the aggregate to the individual level, our conjectures about trends are not borne out. Our vote choice model shows that when it came time to vote, the niqab does not seem to have been the deciding factor for the NDP in Quebec. Even more surprising, it did little to advance the Bloc (the probable recipient of the NDP's support given its stance on the issue). How can we make sense of this? One possibility, which we cannot test with our data, is that the NDP's position on the niqab issue affected voters' broader perceptions of the party, and thus had an indirect effect on the vote outcome. That is, the unpopularity of their stance may have led voters to revisit their views about the party and to consider other options especially as it became clear that the NDP was unlikely to win the election.

This type of re-evaluation probably happened with other campaign events as well. The issue of refugees, for example, is not one that can be glossed over. The publication, on 4 September 2015, of Alan Kurdi's picture across the nation's newspapers was a heart-breaking and galvanizing turning point in the campaign, as it forced the parties to respond to the issue of Western intervention in Syria and Canada's commitment to settling refugees from the conflict. That the parties' responses were so varied gave voters a different piece of information to incorporate into their decisions. We suggest, then, that it would be useful to contextualize any analysis of voting behaviour in light of critical events that may have disrupted established vote decisions or swayed the undecided in one direction or another. Our results suggest that one need not have absolute or definitive preferences on issues to be affected by the atmosphere created by events that portray a party in a new (and possibly negative) way. In line with this, our findings are notable for the confirmation they provide about the complexity of Canadian vote choice. As is clear from the analysis in chapter 8, Canadians are not single-issue voters.

Our findings have important implications for our understanding of regionalism in Canada. The differences truly are at the individual level – they are not, at least in the short term, manufactured or engineered by the activities of political parties or the media. Despite the evidence from earlier elections, the 2015 contest was fought using similar methods across the country. Parties typically did not strategically manipulate and leverage regional differences, and, to the extent that they did, it did not resonate with voters or the media. Parties certainly recognized regional variation and some of the issues that overlap with cleavages, but our evidence demonstrates that regional targeting was not an overriding campaign strategy. The desire for national support was evident and parties recognized the importance of appealing to voters across the country. Further, our analysis of media coverage shows that outlets generally did not serve regional audiences. There were differences in terms of medium, but this was not exacerbated by specific targeting. Clearly, neither parties nor the media are dividing the Canadian public along regional lines to the extent some might suggest.

At the same time, our individual-level results reveal stark differences in the vote calculus employed by citizens in different provinces. Canadians do not differ much across regions in their values and opinions on the issues of the day. But they do differ when it comes to deciding how much weight to give to various considerations in their vote choice. Even something so basic as ideology, which should affect voters equally given that the same parties are being considered (with some exception in Quebec), has a differentiated impact. In British Columbia, left-right considerations divided support for the NDP and the Conservatives; in Ontario, it was the centrist Liberals who countered the Conservatives on the right. This follows the lines of party competition in each of these provinces and thus makes sense, but it also reinforces the idea that governance of heterogeneous polities can be difficult, particularly along ideological lines. While this is not a particularly rosy outlook, it is encouraging in that our research shows that the differences cannot be attributed to self-interested manipulation by the parties or media.

Governing a heterogeneous polity raises many representational issues that need to remain central as governments attempt to govern for the entire country. Voters are represented by their local representatives, not by provincial groups. Candidates and parties appear to understand this extremely well, as we observed some targeted behaviour among individual candidates but not among parties at the regional level. Yet, there remains clear provincial variation in voters' priorities and preferences. To what extent are these being communicated in parliament? In reality, it depends upon which party forms the government. If the winning national party is also the winning party in a province, then those individuals are more likely to have their interests heard in caucus and thus potentially translated into policy. If a province is represented mostly by opposition M P s, however, then it is interesting to think about the implications for the quality of democratic representation. How are those voices and priorities heard? In minority government situations, one can imagine that the need for compromise would elevate the government's willingness to address the priorities of non-government M P s. In a majority government, however, no such incentives exist. Coupled with strong party discipline, this could mean that the preferences of electoral losers are disregarded.

Finally, our results suggest that we should give voters more credit. Their vote decisions are complex and their preferences are nuanced. Voters in Canada are not so easily swayed by current events that they abandon long-held vote considerations. Further, considerations vary by province. This should not be surprising. After all, Canadian voters occupy two political worlds – federal and provincial – and navigate both simultaneously. Expecting that they should all view federal elections through the same lens is naïve. Although the election is fought as one coordinated federal war, it can play out as provincial battles, not because of regionalized appeals or how information is presented, but because of actual priorities held by citizens in heterogeneous contexts across the country.

Notes

CHAPTER ONE

1 More recently, social media has created new avenues for politicians to reach voters directly, which has led to an increase in individualized campaigns.

2 The voter surveys used in our analyses were gathered as part of the Making Electoral Democracy Work project (Blais 2010). Each study consisted of two survey waves – a pre-election wave (conducted between 9 and 18 October 2015) and a post-election wave (conducted between 20 October and 6 November 2015). The surveys were fielded by Nielsen using a quota-based sampling approach that took into account age, sex, region and education. Respondents who completed the pre-election wave were recontacted about completing the post-election wave. In British Columbia, 1,959 qualified respondents completed the first wave, and 1,426 completed the second. In Ontario, 1,974 completed the first wave, and 1,545 completed the second. In Quebec, 1,920 completed the first wave, and 1,381 completed the second.

3 The decomposition was executed using the Stata package mvdcmp.

4 We included measures of sex, age, education, income, language, religion, racial background, and type of community in the model. In order to conserve cases, the models also include a dummy variable for respondents who did not know or refused to disclose their income.

CHAPTER TWO

1 In a similar vein, Blake (1978, 293) concluded that, "much of what lies behind apparent regional variation in party support consists of relatively

more tractable environmental factors." These factors include the differential distribution of voters predisposed to support particular parties, the
competitiveness of the constituency, and the number and nature of the
alternatives presented to voters.

2 Their discussion equates the left-right dimension with an economic dimension, but they recognize that it could also encompass religious values,
sexual mores, and lifestyle questions.

3 It has been suggested that campaign spending is not an adequate surrogate
for campaign effort in Canada, given the lack of association between the
availability of volunteers and spending on the campaign (Eagles and
Hagley 2010).

4 Sayers argues that the competitiveness of the local party, the openness of the
party structure, and the nature of the nomination contest (where there is one)
combine to lead to the nomination of four different types of candidates.

5 However, when transfers from local and regional organizations were taken
into account as well, there was evidence of targeting winnable constituencies.

CHAPTER THREE

1 The analysis that follows is based on data provided on the Simon Fraser
University Elections website: https://www.sfu.ca/~aheard/elections/
marginal-seats.html.

2 Our assessment of the impact of the various events is based on a close
reading of figures 3.1 to 3.4 but is also consistent with ARIMA estima-
tions. See Blais and Guntermann (2015).

3 The data from May 2011 to May 2015 were kindly provided by Éric
Grenier, creator of the ThreeHundredEight website, and the data from
May 2015 to July 2015 were provided by Claire Durand, from the
Université de Montréal. Each data point indicates the mean level of support for a given party in all the polls that were conducted in a particular
month. The month of each poll was identified on the basis of the median
day of fieldwork. The percentages of support were computed on the basis
of vote intentions for the four main parties (the Conservatives, the NDP,
the Liberals, and the Bloc). We excluded the "other" category, which had
different meanings in different surveys. There was only one survey in the
month of July 2011. For that month we used that survey plus one that
took place in late June (23–24).

4 Some speculated that the early writ-drop was a product of the Harper
Government's desire to limit the ability of third parties to spend,

unencumbered by campaign spending limits, outside of the official campaign period.

5 The analysis in this section is a revision and extension of Blais and Lavoie (2016).

6 Daily estimates correspond to the mean of all the polls that were in the field that day. We thank Claire Durand for providing the data. The estimated vote shares on 18 October 2015 are close to the actual outcome of the election, except for the Liberal vote in Quebec, which is underestimated (31 per cent vs 36 per cent) and Conservative support in British Columbia, which is overestimated (35 per cent vs 30 per cent).

7 NDP support seems to have peaked at 46 per cent a week earlier, on 10 September 2015, which could suggest that NDP vote intentions had started to decline before the niqab issue emerged. But a more plausible reading is that NDP support had been quite stable at around 43–44 per cent for the whole month of September, with a very short blip on 10 and 11 September. That blip is due to an Environics poll conducted between 10 and 15 October that showed 52 per cent of vote intentions for the NDP in Quebec. This is the only poll that had the NDP over 50 per cent in September.

8 Most of the polls published between 20 and 23 September 2015, showed the Liberals slightly ahead of the NDP. See Wikipedia, Opinion polling in the Canadian federal election, 2015. https://en.wikipedia.org/wiki/Opinion_polling_for_the_2015_Canadian_federal_election.

CHAPTER FOUR

1 For a full discussion of this, see Cross (2016).

2 Consistent with the theme of this volume, the analysis here is focused on the regional dimensions of personalized/localized campaigns. There are, of course, other factors that influence the degree to which local candidates may run campaigns distinct from their national party. For a full discussion of these, see Cross and Young (2015) and Pruysers and Cross (2018).

3 While this chapter focuses on the three main parties (Conservatives, Liberals, and New Democrats), where appropriate, the Bloc is included in the analysis. Data are from an online survey of candidates conducted between November 2015 and January 2016. E-mail addresses were provided by the parties (note that valid addresses were not provided for 25 per cent of NDP candidates). The response rate by party is 41.2 per cent for the Conservatives (138), 23.1 per cent for the Liberals (78),

44.3 per cent for the New Democrats (113), and 14.1 per cent for the Bloc Québécois (11).

4 For a full discussion of the organizational relationship between parties at the provincial and federal levels see Blake (1985), Pruysers (2014), and Esselment (2010).

CHAPTER FIVE

1 For an earlier study of Canadian leaders' tours, see Mintz (1985).

2 See DiStaso (2012) for an overview of the role of the press release in public relations generally.

3 Not included are byline references at the top of releases, references to particular newspapers or reporters (e.g., *Toronto Star* or *Vancouver Sun*), and names of ridings used to identify candidates (e.g., University-Rosedale MP Chrystia Freeland) unless the release otherwise mentions a region or province.

4 A number of the press releases reported on the party's site also seem prime ministerial in nature. For example, in separate releases on 15 August 2015, Harper acknowledged the sixty-eighth anniversary of India's independence and the seventieth of South Korea.

5 For more on this type of campaigning in a provincial context, see Cross et al. (2015).

CHAPTER SIX

1 Gregg (2017) notes that seven out of ten online media users get their news from the websites of traditional news media organizations.

2 Ontario papers include *24 Hours Toronto* (a free commuter daily), *Kingston Whig Standard, North Bay Nugget, Ottawa Citizen, Sault Star, Hamilton Spectator, London Free Press, Toronto Star, Toronto Sun, Timmins Daily Press, Windsor Star*; Quebec papers include *Journal de Montréal, Journal de Québec, L'Express* (Drummondville), *La Presse* (Montreal/throughout Quebec), *La Tribune* (Sherbrooke), *Le Devoir* (Montreal/throughout Quebec), *Le Nouvelliste* (Trois-Rivières), *Le Soleil* (Québec City), *Montreal Gazette, L'Hebdo du Saint-Maurice*; British Columbia papers include *24 Hours Vancouver, Abbotsford News, Kelowna Capital News, Nanaimo Daily News, Prince George Citizen, Vancouver Province, Vancouver Sun*, and *Victoria Times-Colonist*. When regional data are presented, we have aggregated all French and English sources, unless otherwise indicated.

3 Mentions of tone were coded using Lexicoder's sentence proximity feature that calculates the tone of any sentence that also contains a reference to a party leader.

4 We chose to follow CTV because of its strong regional coverage and audience share. Two research assistants coded the video coverage for mentions of parties, issues, leaders, and local candidates. Note that while we were able to capture local Toronto coverage for each day of the campaign, our coding of coverage in Montreal began on 17 August and on 12 August for Vancouver.

CHAPTER SEVEN

1 The television sources included in the survey question were Global, Radio-Canada (Quebec only), Citytv, CTV, CBC, Omni (Ontario and BC only), and TVA (Quebec only). The print sources included in the survey question were the *Globe and Mail*, *National Post*, *Le Devoir* (Quebec only), *La Presse* (Quebec only), *Montreal Gazette* (Quebec only), *Toronto Star* (Ontario only), *Toronto Sun* (Ontario only), *Vancouver Sun* (British Columbia only), *Vancouver Province* (British Columbia only), commuter papers, and local papers. We do not differentiate between reading newspapers online or in print. Given the similarity in content, we consider both modes as equivalent use of the source.

2 Two popular publications in Quebec, *Journal de Montréal* and *Journal de Québec,* were not asked about in our survey. As a result, the regional print value for Quebec may be artificially deflated.

3 Separate models were run for each type of media attention. Information about variables and coding can be found in the appendix, available at http://www.chairelectoral.com/provincial-battles-national-prize-appendix. html.

4 We created indicators for the *Globe and Mail, National Post, Le Devoir* (Quebec only), *La Presse* (Quebec only), *Montreal Gazette* (Quebec only), *Toronto Star* (Ontario only), *Toronto Sun* (Ontario only), *Vancouver Sun* (British Columbia only), and *Vancouver Province* (British Columbia only).

CHAPTER EIGHT

1 The appendix can be accessed at http://www.chairelectoral.com/ provincial-battles-national-prize-appendix.html.

2 Similarly to what we did for the analysis in chapter 1, we included a
  dummy variable for respondents who did not know or refused to disclose
  their income in the models. This variable is insignificant in all models.
3 Less affluent voters were less likely to vote Conservative (8 points) and so
  were university graduates (6 points). Meanwhile, Catholics were less likely
  to vote NDP (8 points). Voters who were employed or self-employed were
  more likely to vote Liberal (6 points) and so were voters who lived in a
  big city (7 points). At the same time, residents of big cities were less likely
  to vote Bloc (5 points).
4 Suburban voters in British Columbia were also more likely to vote Liberal
  (6 points), and they were less likely to vote NDP (7 points).
5 This inference is reinforced by the fact that university graduates in the
  province were less likely to vote Conservative (8 points).
6 Catholic voters were 8 points less likely to vote Conservative in both
  provinces.
7 There was only a 12-point difference in the probability of voting Conservative for voters at opposite ends of the 11-point scale.
8 Even without any controls at all, the niqab issue did not have a significant
  effect on voting NDP in Quebec (p=.38). Twenty-five per cent of anti-
  niqab voters voted NDP, compared with 28 per cent of pro-niqab voters.
9 There was only an 11-point difference in the probability of voting
  Conservative for voters at opposite ends of the 11-point scale in Ontario
  and a 10-point difference in Quebec. The effect on Liberal voting was
  similarly modest in Ontario.

References

Alford, Robert. 1963. *Party and Society: The Anglo-American Democracies*. Chicago: Rand-McNally.

Alonso, Sonia. 2012. *Challenging the State: Devolution and the Battle for Partisan Credibility*. Oxford: Oxford University Press.

Alonso, Sonia, Laura Cabeza, and Braulio Gómez. 2015. "Parties' Electoral Strategies in a Two-Dimensional Political Space: Evidence from Spain and Great Britain." *Party Politics* 21(6): 851–65.

Alvarez, R. Michael, Frederick J. Boehmke, and Jonathan Nagler. 2006. "Strategic Voting in British Elections." *Electoral Studies* 25(1): 1–19.

Andersen, Robert. 2000. "Reporting Public Opinion Polls: The Media and the 1997 Canadian Election." *International Journal of Public Opinion Research* 12(3): 285–98.

Anderson, Cameron. 2010. "Regional Heterogeneity and Policy Preferences in Canada, 1979–2006." *Regional & Federal Studies* 20(4–5): 447–68.

Archer, Keith. 1985. "The Failure of the New Democratic Party: Unions, Unionists, and Politics in Canada." *Canadian Journal of Political Science* 18(2): 353–66.

Bartels, Larry M. 2002. "Beyond the Running Tally: Partisan Bias in Political Perceptions." *Political Behavior* 24(2): 117–50.

Basile, Linda. 2015. "A Dwarf among Giants? Party Competition between Ethno-Regionalist Parties on the Territorial Dimension: The Case of Italy (1963–2013)." *Party Politics* 21(6): 887–99.

Bélanger, Éric. 2003. "Issue Ownership by Canadian Political Parties 1953–2001." *Canadian Journal of Political Science* 36(3): 539–58.

Bélanger, Éric, and Bonnie M. Meguid. 2008. "Issue Salience, Issue Ownership, and Issue-Based Vote Choice." *Electoral Studies* 27(3): 477–91.

Belanger, P., R.K. Carty, and M. Eagles. 2003. "The Geography of
  Canadian Parties' Electoral Campaigns: Leaders' Tours and
  Constituency Election Results." *Political Geography* 22(4): 439–55.
Bittner, Amanda. 2011. *Platform or Personality? The Role of Party
  Leaders in Elections*. Oxford: Oxford University Press.
Blais, André. 2002. "Why is There So Little Strategic Voting in Canadian
  Plurality Rule Elections?" *Political Studies* 50: 445–54.
– 2005. "Accounting for the Success of the Liberal Party of Canada."
  Canadian Journal of Political Science 38(4): 821–40.
– 2010. "Making Electoral Democracy Work." *Electoral Studies* 29(1):
  169–70.
Blais, André, and Marc André Bodet. 2006. "How Do Voters Form
  Expectations about the Parties' Chances of Winning the Election?"
  Social Science Quarterly 87(3): 477–93.
Blais, André, Eugénie Dostie-Goulet, and Marc André Bodet. 2009.
  "Voting Strategically in Canada and Britain." In *Duverger's Law of
  Plurality Voting: The Logic of Party Competition in Canada, India, the
  United Kingdom and the United States*, edited by Shaun Bowler, André
  Blais, and Bernard Grofman, 13–25. New York: Springer.
Blais, André, Elisabeth Gidengil, Richard Nadeau, and Neil Nevitte. 2002.
  *Anatomy of a Liberal Victory: Making Sense of the 2000 Canadian
  Election*. Peterborough: Broadview Press.
Blais, André, and Eric Guntermann. 2015. "The Ups and Downs of Party
  Support in Canada, 2011–2015." *Making Electoral Democracy Work*.
  17 August 2015. http://electoraldemocracy.com/ups-downs-party-
  support-canada-20112015-1969.
Blais, André, Jiyoon Kim, Elisabeth Gidengil, Joanna Everitt, Patrick
  Fournier, and Neil Nevitte. 2010. "Political Judgments, Perceptions of
  Facts, and Partisan Effects." *Electoral Studies* 29(1): 1–12.
Blais, André, and Jean-Michel Lavoie. 2016. "The Evolution of Vote
  Intentions during the 2015 Canadian Election Campaign." *Making
  Electoral Democracy Work*. 25 January 2016. http://electoraldemocracy.
  com/evolution-vote-intentions-2015-canadian-election-campaign-2077.
Blais, André, and Richard Nadeau. 1996. "Measuring Strategic Voting:
  A Two-Step Procedure." *Electoral Studies* 15: 39–52.
Blais, André, Richard Nadeau, Elisabeth Gidengil, and Neil Nevitte. 2001.
  "Measuring Strategic Voting in Multiparty Plurality Elections."
  Electoral Studies 20: 343–52.
Blais, André, and Mathieu Turgeon. 2004. "How Good Are Voters at
  Sorting Out the Weakest Candidate in Their Constituency?" *Electoral
  Studies* 23(3): 455–61.

Blake, Donald. 1985. *Two Political Worlds: Parties and Voting in British Columbia*. Vancouver: University of British Columbia Press.

Blake, Donald E. 1972. "The Measurement of Regionalism in Canadian Voting Patterns." *Canadian Journal of Political Science* 5(1): 55–81.

– 1978. "Constituency contexts and Canadian elections: An exploratory study." *Canadian Journal of Political Science* 11(2): 279–305.

– 1982. "The Consistency of Inconsistency: Party Identification in Federal and Provincial Politics." *Canadian Journal of Political Science* 15(4): 691–710.

Blevis, Mark, and David Coletto. 2017. "Matters of Opinion 2017: 8 Things We Learned about Politics, the News, and the Internet." *Abacus Data*. 7 February 2017. http://abacusdata.ca/matters-of-opinion-2017–8-things-we-learned-about-politics-the-news-and-the-internet/.

Blinder, Alan S. 1973. "Wage Discrimination: Reduced Form and Structural Estimates." *Journal of Human Resources* 8(4): 436–455.

Brister, Mark. 2012. "National Media Coverage of the 2011 Federal Election Was a Failure." *Toronto Star*, 31 May 2012. https://www.thestar.com/opinion/editorialopinion/2012/05/31/national_media_coverage_of_the_2011_federal_election_was_a_failure.html.

Cairns, Alan C. 1968. "The Electoral System and the Party System in Canada, 1921–1965." *Canadian Journal of Political Science* 1(1): 55–80.

Campbell, Angus, Philip E. Converse, Warren E. Miller, and Donald E. Stokes. 1960. *The American Voter*. Chicago: Chicago University Press.

Capella, Joseph N., and Kathleen Hall Jamieson. 1997. *Spiral of Cynicism: The Press and the Public Good*. Oxford: Oxford University Press.

Carty, R. Kenneth. 1991. *Canadian Political Parties in the Constituencies*. Toronto: Dundurn Press.

– 1992. "Three Canadian Party Systems," In *Canadian Political Party Systems: a Reader*, edited by R. Kenneth Carty. Peterborough: Broadview Press.

– 2002. "The Politics of Tecumseh Corners: Canadian Political Parties as Franchise Organizations." *Canadian Journal of Political Science* 35(4): 723–45.

– 2004. "Parties as Franchise Systems: The Stratarchical Organizational Imperative." *Party Politics* 10(1): 5–24.

– 2015. *Big Tent Politics: The Liberal Party's Long Mastery of Canada's Public Life*. Vancouver: University of British Columbia Press.

Carty, R. Kenneth, and William Cross. 2006. "Can Stratarchically Organized Parties Be Democratic? The Canadian Case." *Journal of Elections, Public Opinion and Parties* 16(2): 93–114.

– 2010. "Political Parties and the Practice of Brokerage Politics." In *The Oxford Handbook of Canadian Politics,* edited by John C. Courtney and David E. Smith, 191–207. Oxford: Oxford University Press.

Carty, R. Kenneth, William Cross, and Lisa Young. 2000. *Rebuilding Canadian Party Politics.* Vancouver: University of British Columbia Press.

Carty, R. Kenneth, and Munroe Eagles. 2005. *Politics is Local: National Politics at the Grassroots.* Oxford: Oxford University Press.

Chacon, Geneviève, Thierry Giasson, and Andrea Lawlor. 2018. "Hybridity and Mobility: Media Elite Status on Political Twitter Hashtags." In *Political Elites: Power in Instantaneous Times,* edited by Alex Marland, Thierry Giasson, and Andrea Lawlor. Vancouver: University of British Columbia Press.

Charlton, Sébastien and Colette Brin. 2017. "Traditional Media Still Most Trusted." *Policy Options.* 22 June 2017. http://policyoptions.irpp.org/magazines/june-2017/traditional-media-still-most-trusted/.

Cheal, David. 1978. "Models of mass politics in Canada." *Canadian Review of Sociology and Anthropology* 15(3): 325–38.

Clarke, Harold D., Jane Jenson, Lawrence LeDuc, and Jon Pammett. 1974. *Canadian National Election Study, 1974.* Ann Arbor, MI: Inter-university Consortium for Political and Social Research [distributor], 1992-02-16. https://doi.org/10.3886/ICPSR07379.v1.

Clarke, Harold D., Jane Jenson, Lawrence LeDuc, and Jon H. Pammett. 1979. *Political Choice in Canada.* Toronto: McGraw-Hill Ryerson.

Clarke, Harold D. and Marianne C. Stewart. 1987. "Partisan Inconsistency and Partisan Change in Federal States: The Case of Canada." *American Journal of Political Science* 31(2): 383–407.

Clough, Emily. 2007. "Two Political Worlds? The Influence of Provincial Party Loyalty Federal Voting in Canada." *Electoral Studies* 26(4): 787–96

Cochrane, Christopher, and Andrea Perrella. 2012. "Regions, Regionalism and Regional Differences in Canada." *Canadian Journal of Political Science* 45(4): 829–53.

Cohen, Bernard C. 1963. *The Press and Foreign Policy.* New Jersey: Princeton University Press.

Coletto, David, and Munroe Eagles. 2011. "The Impact of Election Finance Reforms on Local Party Organization." In *Money, Politics & Democracy: Canada's Party Finance Reforms,* edited by Lisa Young and Harold J. Jensen. Vancouver: University of British Columbia Press.

Coletto, David, Harold Jensen, and Lisa Young. 2011. "Stratarchical Party Organization and Party Finance in Canada." *Canadian Journal of Political Science* 44(1): 111–36.

Cox, Gary W. 1997. *Making Votes Count: Strategic Coordination in the World's Electoral Systems*. New York: Cambridge University Press.

Cross, William P. 2002a. "Grassroots Participation in Candidate Nominations." In *Citizen Politics: Research and Theory in Canadian Political Behaviour*, edited by Joanna Everitt and Brenda O'Neill. Toronto: Oxford University Press.

– 2002b. "The Increasing Importance of Region to Canadian Election Campaigns." In *Regionalism and Party Politics in Canada*, edited by Lisa Young and Keith Archer, 116–28. Toronto: Oxford University Press.

– 2004. *Political Parties*. Vancouver: University of British Columbia Press.

– 2016a. "The Importance of Local Party Activity in Understanding Canadian Politics: Winning from the Ground Up in the 2015 Federal Election," *Canadian Journal of Political Science* 49(4): 601–20.

– 2016b. "Understanding Power Sharing within Political Parties: Stratarchy as Mutual Interdependence between the Party in the Centre and the Party On the Ground." *Government and Opposition* 53(2): 205–30.

Cross, William P, Jonathan Malloy, Tamara A. Small, and Laura B. Stephenson. 2015. *Fighting for Votes*. Vancouver: University of British Columbia Press.

Cross, William P., and Lisa Young. 2002. "Policy Attitudes of Party Members in Canada: Evidence of Ideological Politics." *Canadian Journal of Political Science* 35(4): 859–80.

– 2015. "Personalization of Campaigns in an SMP System: The Canadian Case." *Electoral Studies* 39(3): 306–15.

Cutler, Fred, and Richard Jenkins. 2000. "Where One Lives and What One Thinks: Implications for Rural/Urban Opinion Cleavages for Canadian Federalism." Paper presented at the Transformation of Canadian Political Culture and the State of the Federation Conference, Institute of Intergovernmental Affairs, Queen's University, Kingston, ON, 13–14 October 2000.

Deacon, David, Dominic Wring, and Peter Golding. 2006. "Same Campaign, Differing Agendas: Analyzing News Media Coverage of the 2005 General Election." *British Politics* 1(2): 222–56.

Denver, David, Gordon Hands, Justin Fisher, and Iain MacAllister. 2003. "Constituency Campaigning in Britain 1992–2001." *Party Politics* 9(5): 541–59.

Detterbeck, Klaus, and Eve Hepburn. 2010. "Party Politics in Multi-Level Systems." In *New Directions in Federalism Studies*, edited by Jan Erk and Wilfried Swenden, 106–25. London/New York: Routledge.

DiStaso, Marcia W. 2012. "The Annual Earnings Press Release's Dual Role: An Examination of Relationships with Local and National Media Coverage and Reputation." *Journal of Public Relations Research* 24(2): 123–43.

Dobrzynska, Agnieszka, André Blais, and Richard Nadeau. 2003. "Do the Media Have a Direct Impact on the Vote? The Case of the 1997 Canadian Election." *International Journal of Public Opinion Research* 15(1): 27–43.

Doyle, Gillian. 2002. *Media Ownership: The Economics and Politics of Convergence and Concentration in the UK and European Media.* Thousand Oaks, CA: Sage Publications Inc.

Eagles, Munroe, and Annika Hagley. 2010. "Constituency Campaigning in Canada." In *Elections*, edited by Heather MacIvor, 109–34. Toronto: Emond Montgomery Publications.

Elias, Anwen, Edina Szöcsik, and Christina Isabel Zuber. 2015. "Position, Selective Emphasis and Framing: How Parties Deal with a Second Dimension in Competition." *Party Politics* 21(6): 839–50.

Elkin, Frederick. 1975. "Communications Media and Identity Formation in Canada." In *Communications in Canadian Society,* rev. ed., edited by Benjamin D. Singer 229–43. Toronto: Copp Clark.

Elkins, David J., and Richard Simeon, eds. 1980. *Small Worlds: Provinces and Parties in Canadian Political Life.* Toronto: Methuen.

Ellis, Faron. 2016. "Stephen Harper and the 2015 Conservative Campaign: Defeated but Not Devastated." In *The Canadian Federal Election of 2015*, edited by Jon Pammett and Christopher Dornan, 23–56. Toronto: Dundurn.

Esselment, Anna Lennox. 2010. "Fighting Elections: Cross-Level Political Party Integration in Ontario." *Canadian Journal of Political Science* 43(4): 71–92.

Fieldhouse, Edward, and David Cutts. 2009. "The Effectiveness of Local Party Campaigns in 2005: Combining Evidence from Campaign Spending and Agent Survey Data." *British Journal of Political Science* 39(2): 367–88.

Fisher, Stephen D. 2000. "Class Contextual Effects on the Conservative Vote in 1983." *British Journal of Political Science* 30(2): 347–60.

Flanagan, Thomas 2010. "Campaign Strategy: Triage and the Concentration of Resources." In *Election*, edited by Heather McIvor, 155–72. Peterborough: Emond Montgomery.

Forum Research. 2015a. "NDP Leads in First Post-Writ Poll." 2 August 2015. http://poll.forumresearch.com/post/334/new-democrats-headed-for-solid-minority/.

– 2015b. "NDP Maintains Strong Lead." 10 September 2015. http://poll.
  forumresearch.com/post/1374/liberals-tied-with-conservatives-in-
  second.http://poll.forumresearch.com/post/1374/liberals-tied-with-
  conservatives-in-second.
Fournier, Patrick, Fred Cutler, Stuart Soroka, Dietlind Stolle, and Éric
  Bélanger. 2013. "Riding the Orange Wave: Leadership, Values, Issues
  and the 2011 Canadian Election." *Canadian Journal of Political Science*
  46(4): 863–97.
Frizzell, Alan, and Anthony Westell. 1989. "The Media and the Campaign."
  In *The Canadian General Election of 1988*, edited by Alan Frizzell, Jon
  H. Pammett, and Anthony Westell, 75–90. Ottawa: Carleton University
  Press.
Garzia, Diego. 2011. "The Personalization of Politics in Western Democracies:
  Causes and Consequences of Leader-Follower Relationship." *Leadership
  Quarterly* 22(4): 697–709.
Gidengil, Elisabeth. 1989a. "Class and Region in Canadian Voting: A Depen-
  dency Interpretation." *Canadian Journal of Political Science* 22(3): 563–87.
– 1989b. "Diversity within Unity: On Analyzing Regional Dependency."
  Studies in Political Economy 29(1): 91–122.
– 2002. "The Class Voting Conundrum." In *Political Sociology: Canadian
  Perspectives*, edited by Douglas Baer, 307–24. Don Mills: Oxford
  University Press.
– 2008. "Media Matters: Election Coverage in Canada." In *Handbook of
  Election Coverage around the World*, edited by Jesper Strömbäck and
  Lynda Lee Kaid, 58–72. New York: Routledge.
– 2014. "Setting the Agenda? A Case Study of Newspaper Coverage of the
  2006 Canadian Election Campaign." In *Political Communication in
  Canada*, edited by Alex Marland, Thierry Giasson, and Tamara Small,
  127–43. Vancouver: University of British Columbia Press.
Gidengil, Elisabeth, André Blais, Joanna Everitt, Patrick Fournier and Neil
  Nevitte. 2012. *Dominance and Decline: Making Sense of Recent
  Canadian Elections*. Toronto: University of Toronto Press.
Gidengil, Elisabeth, André Blais, Neil Nevitte, and Richard Nadeau. 1999.
  "Making Sense of Regional Voting in the 1997 Federal Election: Liberal
  and Reform Support Outside Quebec." *Canadian Journal of Political
  Science* 32(2): 247–72.
– 2004. *Citizens*. Vancouver: University of British Columbia Press.
Gidengil, Elisabeth, Joanna Everitt, André Blais, Patrick Fournier, and Neil
  Nevitte. 2013. "Explaining the Modern Gender Gap." In *Mind the Gap:
  Canadian Perspectives on Gender and Politics*, edited by Roberta Lexier
  and Tamara Small, 48–63. Toronto: Fernwood Press.

Goodyear-Grant, Elizabeth. 2013. *Gendered News: Media Coverage and Electoral Politics in Canada*. Vancouver: University of British Columbia Press.

Gordon, Donald. 1966. *National News in Canadian Newspapers*. Report presented to the Royal Commission on Bilingualism and Biculturalism.

Graber, Doris A. 2009. *Mass Media and American Politics*, 8th ed. Washington, DC: CQ Press.

Gregg, Allan R. 2017. "What Canadians Think of the News Media." *Policy Options*. 10 February 2017. http://policyoptions.irpp.org/magazines/february-2017/what-canadians-think-of-the-news-media/. http://policyoptions.irpp.org/magazines/february-2017/what-canadians-think-of-the-news-media/.

Harell, Allison. 2013. "Revisiting the 'Ethnic' Vote: Liberal Allegiance and Vote Choice among Racialized Minorities." In *Parties, Elections and the Future of Canadian Politics*, edited by Amanda Bittner and Royce Koop, 140–60. Vancouver: University of British Columbia Press.

Henderson, Ailsa. 2004. "Regional Political Cultures in Canada." *Canadian Journal of Political Science* 29(3): 595–615.

– 2010. "Why Regions Matter: Sub-State Polities in Comparative Perspective." *Regional and Federal Studies* 20(4–5): 439–45.

Hepburn, Eve, and Klaus Detterbeck. 2013. "Federalism, Regionalism and the Dynamics of Party Politics." In *The Routledge Handbook of Federalism and Regionalism*, edited by John Loughlin, John Kincaid and Wilfried Swenden, 76–92. London and New York: Routledge.

Héroux-Legault, Maxime. 2016. "Substate Variations in Political Values in Canada." *Regional and Federal Studies* 26(2): 171–97.

Inglehart, Ronald, and Pippa Norris. 2003. *Rising Tide: Gender Equality and Cultural Change Around the World*. New York: Cambridge University Press.

Irvine, William. P. 1974. "Explaining the Religious Basis of the Canadian Partisan Identity: Success on the Third Try." *Canadian Journal of Political Science* 7(3): 560–563.

Jeffrey, Brooke. 2016. "Back to the Future: The Resurgent Liberals." In *The Canadian Federal Election of 2015*, edited by Jon Pammett and Christopher Dornan, 57–84. Toronto: Dundurn.

Jenson, Jane. 1976. "Party Systems." In *The Provincial Political Systems: Comparative Essays* edited by David J. Bellamy, Jon H. Pammett, and Donald C. Rowat, 118–31. Toronto: Methuen.

Johnston, R. J. 1987. "The Geography of the Working Class and the Geography of the Labour Vote in England, 1983: A Prefatory Note to a Research Agenda." *Political Geography Quarterly* 6(1): 7–16.

Johnston, Richard. 2017. *The Canadian Party System: An Analytic History*. Vancouver: University of British Columbia Press.

Johnston, Richard G., André Blais, Henry E. Brady, and Jean Crête. 1992. *Letting the People Decide*. Montreal and Kingston: McGill-Queen's University Press.

Johnston, Ron, Kelvyn Jones, Carol Propper, and Simon Burgess. 2007. "Region, Local Context, and Voting at the 1997 General Election in England." *American Journal of Political Science* 51(3): 640–54.

Johnston, Ron, and Charles Pattie. 1998. "Composition and Context: Region and Voting in Britain Revisited during Labour's 1990s' Revival." *Geoforum* 29(3): 309–29.

– 2006. *Putting Voters in their Place: Geography and Elections in Great Britain*. Oxford: Oxford University Press.

Johnston, Ron, Carol Propper, Simon Burgess, Rebecca Sarker, Anne Bolster, and Kelvyn Jones. 2005. "Spatial Scale and the Neighbourhood Effect: Multinomial Models of Voting at Two Recent British General Elections." *British Journal of Political Science* 35(3): 487–514.

Kay, Barry, and Andrea Perrella. 2012. "Eclipse of Class: A Review of Demographic Variables, 1974–2006." In *The Canadian Election Studies: Assessing Four Decades of Influence*, edited by Mebs Kanji, Antoine Bilodeau, and Thomas J. Scotto, 121–35. Vancouver: University of British Columbia Press.

Koop, Royce. 2011. *Grassroots Liberals: Organizing for Local and National Politics*. Vancouver: University of British Columbia Press.

Lambert, Ronald D., James E. Curtis, Steven D. Brown, and Barry J. Kay. 1986. "In Search of Left/Right Beliefs in the Canadian Electorate." *Canadian Journal of Political Science* 19: 541–6.

Lazarsfeld, Paul F., Bernard Berelson and Hazel Gaudet. 1948. *The People's Choice: How the Voter Makes Up His Mind in a Presidential Campaign*. 2nd ed. New York: Columbia University Press.

Lippmann, Walter. 1922. *Public Opinion*. New York: Harcourt, Brace and Co.

Lipset, Seymour Martin, and Stein Rokkan. 1967. "Cleavage Structures, Party Systems, and Voter Alignments: An Introduction." In *Party Systems and Voter Alignments*, edited by Seymour Martin Lipset and Stein Rokkan, 1–64. New York: Free Press.

MacCharles, Tonda. 2008. "Newfoundland Premier Says: 'Anyone But Harper.'" *Toronto Star*, 10 September 2008.

Marland, Alex, Thierry Giasson, and Anna Lennox Esselment, eds. 2017. *Permanent Campaigning in Canada*. Vancouver: University of British Columbia Press.

Marzolini, Michael. 2001. "The Politics of Values: Designing the 2000 Liberal Campaign." In *The Canadian General Election of 2000*, edited by Jon H. Pammett and Christopher Dornan. Toronto: Dundurn Press.

Massetti, Emanuele, and Arjan H. Schakel. 2015. "From Class to Region: How Regionalist Parties Link (and Subsume) Left-Right into Centre-Periphery Politics." *Party Politics* 21(6): 866–86.

Matthews, Ralph, and J. Campbell Davis. 1986. "The Comparative Influence of Region, Status, Class and Ethnicity on Canadian Attitudes and Values." In *Regionalism in Canada*, edited by Robert J. Brym, 89–122. Toronto: Irwin.

McAllister, Ian. 1987. "Comment on Johnston and Pattie." *Political Geography Quarterly* 6(4): 351–4.

McAllister, Ian, and Donley T. Studlar. 1992. "Region and Voting in Britain, 1979–87: Territorial Polarization or Artifact?" *American Journal of Political Science* 36(1): 168–99.

McCombs, Maxwell, and Donald L. Shaw. 1972. "The Agenda-Setting Function of Mass Media." *Public Opinion Quarterly* 36(2): 176–187.

McGrane, David. 2016. "From Third to First and Back to Third: The 2015 NDP Campaign." In *The Canadian Federal Election of 2015*, edited by Jon Pammett and Christopher Dornan, 85–116. Toronto: Dundurn.

McGrane, David, and Loleen Berdahl. 2013. "'Small Worlds' No More: Reconsidering Provincial Political Cultures in Canada." *Regional and Federal Studies* 23(4): 479–93.

Mendelsohn, Matthew. 1998. "The Construction of Electoral Mandates: Media Coverage of Election Results in Canada." *Political Communication* 15(2): 239–53.

Mendelsohn, Matthew, and Richard Nadeau. 1999. "The Rise and Fall of Candidates in Canadian Election Campaigns." *Harvard International Journal of Press/Politics* 4(2): 63–76.

Merolla, Jennifer L., and Laura B. Stephenson. 2007. "Strategic Voting in Canada: A Cross Time Analysis." *Electoral Studies* 26: 235–46.

Middleton, Alia. 2015. "The Effectiveness of Leader Visits during the 2010 British General Election Campaign." *British Journal of Politics and International Relations* 17(2): 244–59.

Montpetit, Eric, Erick Lachapelle, and Simon Kiss. 2017. "Does Canadian Federalism Amplify Policy Disagreements?" IRPP Study 65, Institute for Research on Public Policy, September 2017.

Mintz, Eric. 1985. "Election campaign tours in Canada." *Political Geography Quarterly* 4(1): 47–54.

Mughan, Anthony 2000. *Media and the Presidentialization of Parliamentary Elections*. London: Palgrave.

Nadeau, Richard, Neil Nevitte, André Blais, and Elisabeth Gidengil. 2008. "Election Campaigns as Information Campaigns: Who Learns What and Does It Matter." *Political Communication* 25(3): 229–48.

Newswire. 2017. "2016/2017 Canadian Television Report Card: CTV is Canada's Most-Watched Network for the 16th Year in a Row." 5 June 2017. https://www.newswire.ca/news-releases/20162017-canadian-television-report-card-ctv-is-canadas-most-watched-network-for-the-16th-year-in-a-row-626460411.html.

Oaxaca, Ronald. 1973. "Male-Female Wage Differentials in Urban Labor Markets." *International Economic Review* 14(3): 693–709.

Ornstein, Michael D., H. Michael Stevenson, and A. Paul Williams. 1980. "Region, Class and Political Culture in Canada." *Canadian Journal of Political Science* 13(2): 227–71.

Ornstein, Michael, and Michael Stevenson. 1999. *Politics and Ideology in Canada: Elite and Public Opinion in the Transformation of a Welfare State*. Montreal and Kingston: McGill-Queen's University Press.

Pattie, C.J., R.J. Johnston, Mariken Schipper, and Laura Potts. 2015. "Are Regions Important in British Elections? Valence Politics and Local Economic Contexts at the 2010 General Election." *Regional Studies* 49(9): 1561–74.

Pattie, Charles J., and Ronald J. Johnston. 2003. "Local Battles in a National Landslide: Constituency Campaigning at the 2001 British General Election." *Political Geography* 22(4): 381–414.

Pattie, Charles J., Ronald J. Johnston, and Edward A. Fieldhouse. 1994. "Winning the Local Vote: The Effectiveness of Constituency Campaign Spending in Great Britain, 1983–1992." *American Political Science Review* 89(4): 969–83.

Poguntke, Thomas, and Paul Webb. 2005. *The Presidentialization of Politics*. Oxford: Oxford University Press.

Powers, Daniel, Hirotoshi Yoshioka, and Myeong-Su Yun. 2011. "mvdcmp: Multivariate decomposition for nonlinear response models." *Stata Journal* 11(4): 556–576.

Pruysers, Scott. 2014. "Reconsidering Vertical Integration: An Examination of National Political Parties and their Counterparts in Ontario." *Canadian Journal of Political Science* 47(2): 237–58.

– 2015. "Two Political Worlds? Reconsidering Vertical Party Integration in Canada: Evidence from Ontario." Unpublished PhD thesis, Carleton University.

Pruysers, Scott, and William P. Cross. 2016. "Candidate Selection in Canada: Local Autonomy, Centralization and Competing Democratic Norms." *American Behavioral Scientist* 60(7): 781–98.

– 2018. "Personalism and Election Campaigning: National and Local Dynamics." In *The Personalization of Democratic Politics and the Challenge for Political Parties*, edited by William P. Cross, Richard S. Katz, and Scott Pruysers. London: Rowman and Littlefield Press.

Reevely, David. 2015. "Trudeau's Victory: the Wynne Effect." *Ottawa Citizen*. 25 October 2015.

Robinson, Michael J., and Margaret A. Shehan. 1980. *Over the Wire and On TV*. New York: Russell Sage Foundation.

Rovny, Jan. 2013. "Where Do Radical Right Parties Stand? Position Blurring in Multidimensional Competition." *European Political Science Review* 5(1): 1–26.

– 2015. "Riker and Rokkan: Remarks on the Strategy and Structure of Party Competition." *Party Politics* 21(6): 912–18.

Sayers, Anthony. 1999. *Parties, Candidates, and Constituency Campaigns in Canadian Elections*. Vancouver: University of British Columbia Press.

Schwartz, Mildred A. 1974. *Politics and Territory: The Sociology of Regional Persistence in Canada*. Montreal: McGill-Queen's University Press.

Shin, Michael. 2001. "The Politicization of Place in Italy." *Political Geography* 20(3): 331–52.

Siegel, Arthur. 1979. "French and English Broadcasting in Canada: A Political Evaluation." *Canadian Journal of Communication* 5(3): 1–17.

Silver, Daniel, and Diana Miller. 2014. "Cultural Scenes and Voting Patterns in Canada." *Canadian Journal of Political Science* 47(3): 425–50.

Simeon, Richard, and David J. Elkins. 1980. "Provincial Political Cultures in Canada." In *Small Worlds: Provinces and Parties in Canadian Political Life*, edited by David J. Elkins and Richard Simeon, 31–76. Toronto: Methuen.

Small, Tamara A. 2008. "The Facebook Effect? On-Line Campaigning in the 2008 Canadian and US Elections." *Policy Options*, 14(1).

– 2012. "e-Government in the Age of Social Media: An Analysis of the Canadian Government's Use of Twitter." *Policy and Internet* 4(3–4): 91–111.

Soderlund, Walter C., Colette Brin, Lydia Miljan, and Kai Hildebrandt. 2012. *Cross-Media Ownership and Democratic Practice in Canada. Content-Sharing and the Impact of New Media*. Edmonton: University of Alberta Press.

Soderlund, Walter C., Ronald H. Wagenberg, E. Donald Briggs, and Ralph C. Nelson. 1980. "Regional and Linguistic Agenda-Setting in Canada:

A Study of Newspaper Coverage of Issues Affecting Political Integration
  in 1976." *Canadian Journal of Political Science* 13(2): 347–56.

Soroka, Stuart N. 2002. *Agenda-Setting Dynamics in Canada.* Vancouver:
  University of British Columbia Press.

Soroka, Stuart, and Blake Andrew. 2009. "Media Coverage of Canadian
  Elections: Horse-Race Coverage and Negativity in Election Campaigns."
  In *Mediating Canadian Politics,* edited by Linda Trimble and Shannon
  Sampert, 113–228. Toronto: Pearson Education.

Soroka, Stuart, Marc André Bodet, Lori Young, and Blake Andrew. 2009.
  "Campaign News and Vote Intentions." *Journal of Elections, Public
  Opinion and Parties* 19(4): 359–76.

Stephenson, Laura B. 2010. "The Catholic-Liberal Connection: A Test
  of Strength." In *Voting Behaviour in Canada,* edited by Cameron D.
  Anderson and Laura B. Stephenson, 86–106. Vancouver: University
  of British Columbia Press.

Stewart, David K., Anthony Sayers, and R. Kenneth Carty. 2015.
  "Partisan Competition in the Canadian Provinces." In *Provinces,*
  edited by Christopher Dunn, 135–57. Toronto: University of Toronto
  Press.

Stewart, Marianne C., and Harold D. Clarke. 1998. "The Dynamics of
  Party Identification in Federal Systems: The Canadian Case." *American
  Journal of Political Science* 42(1): 97–116.

Taber, Charles S., and Milton Lodge. 2006. "Motivated Skepticism in the
  Evaluation of Political Beliefs." *American Journal of Political Science*
  50(3): 755–69.

Trussler, Marc, and Stuart Soroka. 2014. "Consumer Demand for Cynical
  and Negative News Frames." *International Journal of Press and Politics*
  19(3): 360–79.

Turcotte, Martin. 2001. "L'opposition rural/urbain a-t-elle fait son temps?
  Le cas du traditionalisme moral." *Canadian Journal of Sociology* 26(1):
  1–29.

Wagenberg, R.H., W.C. Soderlund, W.I. Romanow, and E.D. Briggs. 1988.
  "Campaigns, Images and Polls: Mass Media Coverage of the 1984
  Canadian Election." *Canadian Journal of Political Science* 21(1):
  117–30.

Walkom, Thomas. 2015. "Justin Trudeau and Tom Mulcair Battle Each
  Other as Stephen Harper Pulls Ahead." *Toronto Star,* 1 October 2015.
  https://www.thestar.com/news/federal-election/2015/10/01/justin-
  trudeau-and-tom-mulcair-battle-each-other-as-stephen-harper-pulls-
  ahead-walkom.html.

Walks, R. Alan. 2004. "Place of Residence, Party Preferences, and Political Attitudes in Canadian Cities and Suburbs." *Journal of Urban Affairs* 26(3): 269–95.

– 2005. "The City-Suburban Cleavage in Canadian Federal Politics." *Canadian Journal of Political Science* 38(2): 383–413.

– 2006. "The Causes of City-Suburban Polarization? A Canadian Case Study." *Annals of the Association of American Geographers* 96(2): 390–414.

Wesley, Jared. 2011. *Code Politics: Campaigns and Cultures on the Canadian Prairies*. Vancouver: University of British Columbia Press.

Wilson, John. 1974. "The Canadian Political Cultures: Towards a Redefinition of the Nature of the Canadian Political System." *Canadian Journal of Political Science* 7(3): 438–83.

Wilson, R. Jeremy. 1980/81. "Media Coverage of Canadian Election Campaigns: Horserace Journalism and the Meta-Campaign." *Journal of Canadian Studies* 15(4): 56–68.

Wiseman, Nelson. 2007. *In Search of Canadian Political Culture*. Vancouver: Cambridge University Press.

Young, Lisa, and Keith Archer, eds. 2002. *Regionalism and Party Politics in Canada*. Toronto: Oxford University Press.

Young, Lori, and Stuart Soroka. 2012. "Affective News: The Automated Coding of Sentiment in Political Texts." *Political Communication* 29(2): 205–231.

Zaller, John R. 1992. *The Nature and Origins of Mass Opinion*. Cambridge: Cambridge University Press.

Index

Note: Page numbers in italics indicate illustrated material